WITHDRAWN

HENRY KISSINGER
and the American Approach
to Foreign Policy

HENRY KISSINGER
and the American Approach to Foreign Policy

Gregory D. Cleva

Lewisburg
Bucknell University Press
London and Toronto: Associated University Presses

Associated University Presses
440 Forsgate Drive
Cranbury, NJ 08512

Associated University Presses
25 Sicilian Avenue
London WC1A 2QH, England

Associated University Presses
P.O. Box 488, Port Credit
Mississauga, Ontario
Canada L5G 4M2

The paper used in this publication meets the requirements of the American National Standard for Permanence of Paper for Printed Library Materials Z39.48-1984.   ∙

Library of Congress Cataloging-in-Publication Data

Cleva, Gregory D., 1947–
  Henry Kissinger and the American approach to foreign policy.

  Bibliography: p.
  Includes index.
  1. Kissinger, Henry, 1923– . 2. United States
—Foreign relations—Philosophy.   3. United States
—Foreign relations—1945– .   I. Title.
E840.8.K58C56   1989   327.73′0092′4   87-46431
ISBN 0-8387-5147-4 (alk. paper)

PRINTED IN THE UNITED STATES OF AMERICA

FOR SANDRA

In the years ahead, the most profound challenge to American policy will be philosophical: to develop some concept of order in a world which is bipolar militarily but multipolar politically. But a philosophical deepening will not come easily to those brought up in the American tradition of foreign policy.

—Henry Kissinger, 1968

Contents

Acknowledgments

Muсн of the inspiration for this book came from Henry Kissinger himself. Kissinger's stewardship of American foreign policy as well as his own scholarly background in history and philosophy attracted me to the study of international politics. Recalling the turbulent years of the Nixon presidency and America's changing role in the world, I found that the policies that Kissinger fostered both defined an era of transition and gave general direction for the future. It seemed to me then that Kissinger's historical perspective, which allowed him to explain the issues of the moment in a broader context, acted to curb our native impulsiveness and quest for total solutions during a difficult period in the nation's life.

I wish to express my gratitude to Dr. Claes Ryn of The Catholic University of America for key suggestions—particularly in the area of historicism—which helped to shape my understanding of Kissinger's thought. Dr. James O'Leary provided me with great insight and assistance over several years both as teacher and friend. I wish also to acknowledge the memory of Dr. James Dornan of Catholic University. Dr. Dornan's enthusiasm for the subject of American foreign policy and his vibrant conservative philosophy influenced many who studied under him.

Much appreciation is keenly felt for my wife Sandra who helped to edit and review this text and who offered many valuable suggestions for improvement. I also wish to thank Gwen McNamee who carefully typed the initial manuscript.

Finally, I have dedicated this book to my wife Sandra. Throughout the years in which it was being researched and written she had to make innumerable sacrifices—not the least of which was enduring more discussions of Henry Kissinger's thought than any literature major could possibly have wished. She offered great encouragement to me throughout the entire project while giving birth to our daughter Elise in the process.

For all of the shortcomings of this work and for any failings of interpretation, I acknowledge full responsibility.

I wish to thank the following for having given me permission to quote from published and unpublished works:

Henry Kissinger and Harvard University Archives, for permission to quote from Henry Kissinger, "The Meaning of History: Reflections on Spengler, Toynbee and Kant," unpublished undergraduate honors thesis, 1950. Reprinted by permission of Harvard University Archives.

The Council on Foreign Relations for permission to quote from the following works of Henry Kissinger: *Nuclear Weapons and Foreign Policy*, published by Harper & Row for the Council on Foreign Relations, 1957; *The Troubled Partnership: A Re-appraisal of the Atlantic Alliance*, 1965; "Reflections on American Diplomacy," *Foreign Affairs* 34 (October 1956): 37–56; and "Military Policy and Defense of the 'Grey Areas'," *Foreign Affairs* 33 (April 1955): 416–28.

Houghton Mifflin Company, for permission to quote from *A World Restored: Metternich, Castlereagh, and the Problems of Peace, 1812–1822* by Henry Kissinger. Published in 1957 by Houghton Mifflin Company.

Harper & Row, Publishers, Inc., and Chatto & Windus, Ltd., for permission to excerpt from Henry Kissinger, *The Necessity for Choice: Prospects of American Foreign Policy*, 1960, 1961. Reprinted by permission of Harper & Row, Publishers, Inc., and Chatto & Windus, Ltd.

McGraw-Hill Book Company, for permission to quote from Henry Kissinger, *The Troubled Partnership: A Re-appraisal of the Atlantic Alliance*. Published in 1965 for the Council on Foreign Relations and used with the permission of McGraw-Hill Book Company.

W. W. Norton & Company, Inc., for permission to quote from Henry Kissinger, *American Foreign Policy*, 3d ed., 1977; and Stephen R. Graubard, *Kissinger: Portrait of a Mind*, 1973.

The New York Times, for permission to quote from "Partial Transcript of an Interview with Kissinger on the State of the Western World," (interview by James Reston), October 13, 1974. Copyright © 1974 by The New York Times Company. Reprinted by permission.

Henry Kissinger, for permission to quote from *For The Record: Selected Statements, 1977–1980* by Henry Kissinger. Published in 1981 by Little, Brown and Company.

Introduction

HENRY Kissinger continues to enjoy a certain prominence in American public life, even though more than a decade has passed since he served as secretary of state. His views are sought by congressional committees and foreign policy groups; his articles on international issues appear in distinguished journals and newspapers. Kissinger is consulted by foreign statesmen when they visit the United States, and he travels frequently to foreign capitals. His chairmanship of the 1983 National Bipartisan Commission on Central America was viewed by the Reagan administration as enhancing the stature of the commission and its work.

Kissinger's stewardship of American foreign policy, however, is not treated as favorably as his prominence would suggest. Large sections of the American public continue to see his "European" mode of thought and approach to international politics as an aberration. His legacy to contemporary American foreign policy is questionable. The Nixon-Kissinger approach of *Realpolitik* has not been claimed by either the political right or the left. The Carter and Reagan administrations, reacting in part to different aspects of this *Realpolitik*, have sought a return to more traditional patterns of American foreign policy.

Kissinger's role in American foreign policy remains an anomaly. Many consider his efforts, such as the 1972 SALT agreements and the 1973–74 Middle East shuttle diplomacy, to have been genuinely creative accomplishments. Yet his statecraft is also seen as having destroyed American values; for example, critics point to the lack of moral content in his détente policies toward the Soviet Union. The anomaly of Kissinger's position is not that Americans have praised his successes as a statesman while rejecting his thought about foreign policy. The anomaly is that his thought remains little known to most Americans despite his successes. Americans have found it easier to assimilate his diplomatic exploits into the folklore of popular culture than to integrate his thinking into the nation's outlook on foreign policy.

Stephen Graubard pointed out that American journalists would consider the discovery of a confidential document written by Kissinger a sensational story.[1] Yet these same journalists were unfamiliar with his scholarly writings—writings that have spanned almost three decades and then numbered six books and over forty articles.

Kissinger's works and ideas present considerable difficulties for American readers. Scholars who acknowledge the continuity of his thought complain of the "elusiveness" of his basic principles.[2] Kissinger's subject matter accounts for some of this difficulty. His works are also heavily influenced by German philosophical idealism and historiography. Americans have not been receptive to this mode of thought. They have demonstrated a deep commitment to empirical and pragmatic views that are in some respects diametrically opposed to those of philosophical idealism. Finally, there appears to be a seemingly unresolved conflict in Kissinger's own thinking—a conflict between the tragic and fatalistic aspects of his thought and his belief that men can shape history. As a result, even prominent American scholars have not penetrated the deeper meaning of Kissinger's thought. This work is in large part an attempt to overcome these shortcomings of American scholarship.

Kissinger and the American Approach to Foreign Policy

This book is about the thought of Henry Kissinger. Specifically, it deals with the historical and philosophical foundations of Kissinger's outlook on international relations, and the critique of American foreign policy that this outlook inspires. I wish to point out from the beginning that this work does not deal primarily with Kissinger's own statecraft. Its major focus is on his years as a scholar, the period between 1947 and 1968. The parallels between his early ideas and his later policies as a statesman are the subject of the final chapter.

Despite the preparations he made for playing a larger and more public role in American foreign policy, Kissinger remained, rather self-consciously, an intellectual. His years as a student at Harvard were characterized by a singleminded determination to master the rudiments of the life of the mind. For him, this meant principally history and philosophy, although his undergraduate essays were also filled with references to literature and psychology. Kissinger formulated his own intellectual orientation, which, although it was not completely original, contains many unique elements. This orientation has been largely implicit in his criticism of the American approach to foreign policy.

There has been one explicit theme in Kissinger's writings, however, which I believe serves as a guide to the deeper meaning of his thought and criticism. I offer it as the central theme of this work. From the time of his doctoral dissertation, a work published under the title *A World Restored: Metternich, Castlereagh and the Problems of Peace, 1812–1822*, Kissinger has distinguished between what he termed the island nation and the continental nation. In his description of post-Napoleonic Europe, England represented the island power and Austria the continental one. These nations held significantly different views regarding their defense and national interest. Their statecraft and foreign policy traditions stood far apart. These differences were not a matter of geography; they grew out of important aspects of their national life. The leaders who epitomized these national traditions—the English statesman, Castlereagh, and the Austrian, Metternich—possessed different historical and political beliefs.

Kissinger continues to use the term "island power" in writing about contemporary America and its foreign policy three decades after writing his dissertation. He associates American "insularity" with specific patterns of historical and philosophical thought; insularity involves a complex of attitudes and values that characterize a nation's outlook and shape its foreign policy. Kissinger specifically identifies insular statecraft with the Anglo-American political tradition, but he finds examples of "inward-looking" nations even in Europe. His works contain a pervasive criticism of the insular patterns of American foreign policy.

I will highlight the principal aspects of Kissinger's philosophy by contrasting his own continental views with his idea of American insularity. Kissinger never formally identifies his own views as such. Yet in criticizing the insularity of the Anglo-American political tradition and the American approach to foreign policy, Kissinger employs a distinctly continental or European perspective.

The Impact of Kissinger's Thought

There are several reasons why an understanding of Kissinger's thought is important to American political scholarship. Foremost among these is the influence that Kissinger's thought has had on U.S. foreign policy in the contemporary era. This influence should be understood in two ways.

First, Kissinger's prominence as a statesman overshadows the effect that his writings had on American foreign policy prior to his entry into government in 1969. In at least one area—U.S. military doctrine—his influence has been as significant as a writer-polemicist as it has been as a public official. Throughout the 1950s, Kissinger was regarded as a leading critic of the American military strategy of massive nuclear retaliation. Although his criticism extended to the policy of containment and to the American leadership style, his name and scholarly reputation were linked to the doctrine of limited war. Kissinger's book *Nuclear Weapons and Foreign Policy* contributed greatly to the intellectual climate that made the notion of limited war acceptable. Many of the arguments that the

Kennedy administration used in renouncing Eisenhower's defense policies paralleled those Kissinger had advanced.

The second area of Kissinger's influence involves his public statements
and speeches, and the four "State of the World"[3] messages that were
published between 1970 and 1973. Like his writings as a scholar, these
texts have not received the same attention as has his peripatetic mode of
statecraft. No less an observer of American politics than the late Robert
Osgood notes that these works were unusually articulate and substantive. They provide the conceptual basis for U.S. foreign policy in a
pivotal era.[4] I maintain that long after the details of Kissinger's Middle
East shuttle diplomacy or his secret mission to China are forgotten, these
works and his memoirs will be appreciated for what they represent—a
critical examination of the American approach to foreign policy, as well
as a justification for specific policies that departed from the traditional
American approach. Because Kissinger's thought has changed little over
the years with respect to underlying patterns of American foreign policy,
I will occasionally use these more recent writings to illustrate key points,
even though a detailed description of his statecraft lies outside the scope
of this work.

Beyond the impact of Kissinger's thought on specific policies, the
nature of his criticism commands attention. Kissinger's criticism of the
American approach to foreign policy is decidedly European or continental and it addresses fundamental national attitudes. Part of the value of
his work is that it makes us question American presuppositions about
foreign policy by elevating to a conscious level traditional patterns of
action and thought that we express spontaneously.

It should be stressed that Kissinger's thought stands outside the real-
ist-idealist dichotomy that is used to distinguish American theorists.
This assertion may well be unsettling to some readers, because Kissinger
is usually described as the political realist par excellence. But, as I will
show, his philosophical orientation is clearly distinguishable from American realism. In the entire body of Kissinger's work, his criticism of
realism far outweighs any criticism of American idealism. Actually, both
realism and idealism are, for Kissinger, aspects of American insularity.

Kissinger in American Scholarship

Numerous books and articles about Kissinger have appeared in recent
years. For the most part, American scholars and journalists have treated
him favorably. In particular, members of the academic community have
taken a vicarious pleasure in recounting his diplomatic triumphs. For

many theorists of international politics, he exemplifies the intellectual-activist.

It is significant that only a handful of these works deals in any substantive way with Kissinger's thought. Stephen Graubard's study *Kissinger: Portrait of a Mind* offered the first extended treatment of Kissinger's scholarship. It is a tribute to Graubard's own erudition that his work remains the best presentation of Kissinger's writings.

Peter Dickson's work *Kissinger and the Meaning of History*[5] provides the best treatment of Kissinger's earliest scholarship. Dickson examines Kissinger's undergraduate honors thesis in which he formed his own philosophy of history through reflection on the works of Spengler, Toynbee, and Kant. Although I am indebted to Dickson's scholarship for the compelling insights it provides in the area of Kissinger's intellectual development, I deal critically with aspects of his work in chapter 1. I believe that he too closely identifies Kissinger's thought with that of Kant. The cogency of Dickson's argument overshadows the full influence that Toynbee and Spengler, as well as other thinkers such as the German historicists, have had on Kissinger's philosophy.

John Stoessinger's *Henry Kissinger: The Anguish of Power*[6] should also be read by those seeking to understand the relationship between Kissinger's thought and his diplomacy. In chapter 1, I cite two articles on Kissinger's historical philosophy by Thomas J. Noer and William T. Weber.[7] These articles alone discuss Kissinger as a historian—a characterization he has used to refer to himself.

A Word on Methodology

This work relies largely on Kissinger's writings and statements. It does so because his texts and articles represent a painstaking effort to formulate ideas on the problems confronting American foreign policy. They reflect the evolution of his thought over two decades. There was no scholarly pursuit that Kissinger took more seriously. Graubard suggests that Kissinger's writings will prove immensely rich and invaluable to anyone who explores them patiently. Emphasizing this point, he writes:

> Kissinger, as an adult, gave himself unstintingly to his writing. It was the activity that occupied him most completely, consuming the greatest part of his always abundant energies and providing him with many satisfactions. Anyone who has observed Kissinger pore over successive drafts of one of his manuscripts, starting with a badly handwritten foolscap version, and ending with last-minute revisions of a typed text which has generally circulated among friends and

passed through three or four revisions, is aware that writing was never a chore he took lightly.[8]

Two points regarding my treatment of Kissinger's works need to be mentioned. First, the interpretation that I offer of his criticism of American policy—particularly its relationship to his historical philosophy—should not be sought explicitly in Kissinger's writings on foreign policy. The approach he adopted in criticizing American foreign policy was part of an overall intellectual orientation. He expressed this orientation with a subtlety that only the student of his earliest scholarship can appreciate. I have tried to interpret Kissinger's works in a way that renders their meaning faithfully and yet also clarifies their intellectual sources.

Second, I have deliberately avoided any psychological interpretation of Kissinger's thought. This approach has been used in biographical works about Kissinger, of which Bruce Mazlish's *Kissinger: The European Mind in American Policy* is the most encompassing.[9] These works relate the main patterns of Kissinger's thought to underlying psychological traits or needs. Kissinger's emphasis on order and stability, for example, is seen as an unconscious reaction to the turmoil of his own life as a Jewish émigré from Nazi Germany. I maintain, to the contrary, that Kissinger was so self-consciously an intellectual that it is unlikely that he would advance his most important arguments on the basis of unexamined psychological traits. Even if he were inclined to hold certain views for psychological reasons, these views would be subject to the scrutiny of a dedicated scholar.

Similarly, scholarly works using empirical approaches such as the "operational code" or "value analysis" offer many keen insights into Kissinger's thought. Although I have benefited from these methodologies,[10] I have not employed them in this work because of my preference for a more traditional approach.

Organization

This book is organized into three parts. In part 1, I discuss Kissinger's outlook on world politics. In part 2, I deal with Kissinger's criticism of the American approach to foreign policy and show how it is related to his distinctive intellectual orientation. Part 3 deals with the elements of continuity in Kissinger's thought and statecraft, as well as his legacy to American foreign policy.

Part 1 includes two chapters. My purpose in chapter 1 is to discuss Kissinger's earliest scholarship—primarily the historical philosophy that he derived from that effort. The individual thinkers who influenced his thought are treated in detail. In chapter 2, I discuss Kissinger's political ideas. My major purpose is to show the relationship between Kissinger's historical philosophy and his political concepts. This relationship is apparent in his writings on great statesmen and on statecraft itself. I have termed Kissinger's political beliefs continental because of the link between his historical philosophy and the European form of statecraft that occupied his attention.

Part 2 consists of chapters 3 through 6. Kissinger's views on America's approach to foreign policy are discussed in chapter 3. Kissinger's critique centers on America's insularity. America's attempt to be immune from the actions of other nations, its quest for total solutions, and its corresponding reactive approach to foreign policy are as much a result of its historical experience as of its geographical position. In chapter 4, I deal with Kissinger's criticism of American leadership—particularly during the Eisenhower and Kennedy years. Of all America's shortcomings in foreign policy, Kissinger regards the inability of its leaders to define the purposes of its policies as the most significant. Chapters 5 and 6 are concerned with the specific failures of American defense policy and foreign policy, respectively. Kissinger viewed the doctrine of containment that governed America's actions in the cold war era as the clearest manifestation of the nation's insular approach. The criticism of this doctrine with reference to America's military strategy and diplomacy was the subject of much of his professional writing.

Finally, part 3 consists of chapter 7. Here, I consider the relationship between Kissinger's thought and the policies that he fostered during the Nixon years. My purpose in this concluding chapter is also to evaluate Kissinger's influence on America's approach to foreign policy in the future.

The scholarly literature on the policies of the Nixon years will continue to grow. Henry Kissinger's role will be assessed from different political viewpoints and in the light of events that have occurred since he left office. But no assessment will fully grasp the significance of what Stanley Hoffmann refers to as the "Kissinger cycle"[11] in American foreign policy until we first understand the philosophy from which his policies evolved.

HENRY KISSINGER
and the American Approach
to Foreign Policy

PART 1

Kissinger's Historical Philosophy

1
The Historicism of Henry Kissinger

The Footsteps of History

Few American leaders have viewed international relations from such a deliberately historical perspective as Henry Kissinger. As secretary of state, he explained contemporary events by relating them to the historical context in which they occurred. He dealt with issues of the moment concerning U.S.–Soviet relations or American involvement in Vietnam in terms of the larger historical patterns of which he said they were a part. He justified major foreign policy initiatives such as détente or the reversal of U.S. relations with China not in terms of immediate and tangible goals, but as a means of influencing the direction of history.

Kissinger sees a fundamental connection between statecraft and the "historical process."[1] Paraphrasing the German leader Bismarck, he indicates that the art of statesmanship develops from a deep historical sensitivity—a sensitivity through which "one can perhaps discern the footsteps of history."[2]

Kissinger refers to himself as a historian. He suggests that his outlook as such sheds more light on his views than his acts as America's foreign minister.[3] In his memoirs, he states that when he entered office in 1969 he brought with him "a philosophy formed by two decades of the study of history."[4] It is a central thesis of this work that Kissinger's approach to international relations and his criticism of American foreign policy cannot be understood apart from his historical philosophy. Kissinger's historical beliefs build on the tradition of nineteenth-century European historiography (particularly that of the German school), which is referred to by scholars as "historicism." For this reason, I use the term "historicism" to describe his historical philosophy.

Kissinger makes the clearest statement of his historicism in the closing section of his doctoral dissertation on the diplomacy of post-Napoleonic Europe, a work published in 1957 as *A World Restored: Metternich, Castlereagh and the Problems of Peace, 1812–1822*. In this passage, he affirms the value of his conclusions regarding the role of statecraft and the nature of world order precisely because his study of politics is linked to a study of history. Moreover, he asserts that historical knowledge is as fundamental to the study of international relations as sensory data is to the study of the physical laws of nature:

> No profound conclusions were drawn in the natural sciences before the significance of sensory experience was admitted by what was essentially a moral act. No significant conclusions are possible in the study of foreign affairs—the study of states acting as units—without an awareness of the historical context.[5]

How are we to regard the central role that Kissinger gives to history? On one level, it signifies a rejection of the "behaviorist" and "quantitative" approaches that have influenced the study of politics in America for the past three decades. It represents a conscious choice by Kissinger as a young Harvard undergraduate to associate himself with an older, more European intellectual tradition. Kissinger's intellectual and cultural influences were decidedly European. One searches his works in vain for the influence of American political theorists. Instead, his philosophy was formed by his readings of European historians and by such thinkers as Croce, Dostoevski, Nietzsche, and Ortega y Gasset.

Kissinger's rejection of the empirical approaches to politics should not lead us to conclude that these approaches are of little value in our understanding of his outlook on international relations. With the exception of a few works,[6] many American scholars have dealt with Kissinger using empirical approaches. Some scholars attempt to relate his worldview to an underlying "cognitive map" or "operational code";[7] others try to understand his beliefs in terms of "value analysis"[8] and psychological factors.[9] Each has enhanced our understanding of Kissinger's thought and provided insight into his actions as a statesman.

The fact that Kissinger as scholar and statesman emphasizes the study of history is neither novel nor, in itself, a definitive statement about his thought. An understanding of foreign relations has been linked to history at least since Thucydides. Other American theorists of the traditionalist school such as Hans Morgenthau, George Kennan, and Arnold Wolfers—writing in the first period of America's sustained involvement in global politics—affirm the value of historical inquiry. How then is Kissinger's approach different?

First, Kissinger's purpose in studying the past, i.e., the value he attaches to history, distinguishes him from the traditionalists. Stanley Hoffmann emphasizes this difference in a thoughtful essay on Kissinger's ideas. Hoffmann acknowledges that Kissinger belongs to "the same universe of discourse" as Morgenthau and Kennan, because, like them, he emphasizes the requirements of power politics and the Clausewitzian integration of force and diplomacy.[10] However, Kissinger's approach to the past sets him apart: "Among his contemporaries, Kissinger was unique in attempting to use the past as a normative model of world politics instead of treating it merely as history or as a prelude to the present."[11] History, for Kissinger, has a contemporaneous quality—both in the sense that the past is embodied in and influences the present, and that it offers parallels and similarities to the present. Thomas Noer writes that Kissinger approaches the past with a "present-mindedness,"[12] drawing comparisons and contrasts between the problems of previous historical eras and those of the present day.

Kissinger derives from history a coherent set of beliefs regarding the normative basis of international order and the role of statecraft. We should understand these beliefs as historical generalizations and concepts, rather than as a rigorous theory of international politics. Kissinger's ideas are not those of a theorist of international politics or even of a pragmatic statesman. They are those of a historian.[13]

A second point regarding the primacy that Kissinger attaches to history is the meaning that he believes it reveals. If we return to his statement at the conclusion of *A World Restored*, we read that the key to international politics is "an awareness of the historical context." I would like to underscore the word "awareness," because it is not history as past occurrences that matters to Kissinger, but the manner in which the past is understood. How Kissinger understands the meaning of history provides the heart of his historicist philosophy.

Kissinger's historical studies contain a unique outlook regarding the course of world history—an outlook I will explore at length. In this respect, his historicism is both a political philosophy as well as a philosophy of history. Elements of his thought may be compared to the thought of Hegel, Spengler, and Toynbee—whose works he studied in depth. His readings as an undergraduate reveal an attraction to this genre of historical writing. His undergraduate honors thesis, "The Meaning of History: Reflections on Spengler, Toynbee and Kant," describes these scholars' philosophies of history.

Kissinger's study of and reflection on world history influence his later style as both scholar and diplomat. I maintain that Kissinger's historicism provides him the same high ground from which to view political reality as the Marxist philosophy of historical materialism gives its adherents. It accounts for the assuredness, and even arrogance, with which he argues his views. More importantly, it explains why he exhorts American statesmen to value historical understanding as the basis for political leadership—a point that I will discuss in chapter 4.

Kissinger's historicism can only be appreciated against the background of his earliest scholarly experiences and writings. It is to the influences of this period and to his first scholarly works that I now turn.

The Foundation of Kissinger's Historical Beliefs

Among the factors that have contributed to Kissinger's historical beliefs, two stand out as most important. The first is the nature of his intellectual formation at Harvard from 1947 to 1954—particularly the influence of two thinkers who gave direction to his scholarly interests. The second is the historical works he wrote as an undergraduate and graduate student; their major themes are still found in his current writings and statements.

Kissinger's mentors at Harvard included two of the most distinguished professors in the Department of Government: Carl Friedrich and William Elliott. Both were advocates of the classical approach to education; they believed that the most profound understanding of man and his life in society could be found in the ageless works of history, literature, and philosophy. Each exposed Kissinger to the recurring themes of the humanistic tradition. Acknowledging the influence of his Harvard years, Kissinger praises Elliott by recalling the close and personal manner in which they shared ideas:

> We met every week for years. . . . Elliott made me discover Dostoevski and Hegel, Kant, Spinoza, and Homer. On many Sundays we took long walks in Concord. . . . He discussed greatness and excellence. And while I did not always follow his words, I knew that I was in the presence of a remarkable man.[14]

Both Friedrich and Elliott had been educated in Europe in the 1920s. As Peter Dickson points out, they acted as a bridge between Kissinger's intellectual development and his own European background.[15] Friedrich had studied at the University of Heidelberg, and Elliott, after graduating from Vanderbilt University, had been a Rhodes Scholar at Balliol College, Oxford. Although in later years Kissinger's ties to Elliott grew stronger than his ties to Friedrich, both men evoked in him a "feeling for political philosophy" and for the "epic nature of history."[16] More importantly, both emphasized the connection between philosophy and history. This connection was a prominent theme in their own writings. While a student, Kissinger served as a reader for Elliott's book on political theory, *Western Political Heritage* (a book written with Neil McDonald), and for Friedrich's anthology, *The Philosophy of Hegel*. Describing the writing of *A World Restored*, Kissinger acknowledges that it was Friedrich who encouraged him in his effort "to combine a study of history with that of politics."[17]

There are other ways in which Friedrich and Elliott contributed to Kissinger's philosophy. They are significant both for what they directed Kissinger toward and for what they guarded him against. Harvard in the late 1940s and early 1950s was expanding the reach of the quasi-scientific disciplines of economics and sociology. The methods of science were being applied to the study of history and politics with the promise that the lack of precise knowledge in these fields would give way to verifiable and predictive laws. The Kalbs point out that at that time Harvard's recently established Russian Research Institute had as many sociologists on its staff as historians. Projects sponsored by the institute included psychological portraits of Soviet leaders that were thought to shed light on postwar Soviet actions, and interviews with East European refugees in order to better understand the nature of totalitarian societies.[18]

There was no reason why Kissinger, like his peers, would not have been attracted to these new approaches. The world seemed to be entering a new period for which there were no historical parallels. An emphasis on the future diminished the influence of history and enhanced the status of scientific approaches for the study of politics.

The fact that Kissinger was not influenced by these new methodologies is due largely to Friedrich and Elliott. By directing his interest to the world of European scholarship—emphasizing philosophy and history—they set his intellectual development apart from the philosophical empiricism and pragmatism that are dominant in America. Dickson affirms this view of the influence of Friedrich and Elliott, writing that "each in his own unique way helped to insulate the young German from the prevailing intellectual traditions of America . . . and in the process predisposed him toward metaphysics."[19]

Dickson's point regarding Kissinger's inclination toward metaphysics is of major importance. In addition to stressing the study and interrelationship of philosophy and history, Friedrich and Elliott were influenced by German idealist thought and they conveyed this metaphysical approach in their own writings. As a philosophy, German idealism holds that the primary nature of reality is spiritual or "idea-ist." As an approach to history, historical idealism emphasizes the spiritual nature of historical development—i.e., the ideas that shape and inform reality and the purposeful acts that create and change it. Hence, history is essentially the record of the ideas, beliefs, and choices of men and nations.

Dickson points out that Friedrich had been exposed to this school of thought at Heidelberg where he studied under the prominent neo-Kantian philosophers Paul Natorp and Heinrich Rickert.[20] Natorp was a leader of the Marburg School; he assumed an even more radically idealistic position than Kant, affirming that all reality exists only within consciousness. Elliott's association with German idealism can be traced to Oxford where he came into contact with Hegelian thought through the writings of such English idealists as Bernard Bosanquet, T. H. Green, and A. D. Lindsay.[21]

Dickson concludes that these influences led Kissinger to the study of Kant and a lifelong attraction to Kantian thought. Although Kant's philosophy does play a prominent part in the formation of Kissinger's historicism, I believe the identification of Kissinger's thought with Kant-ianism obscures the other important influences on his historical beliefs. The proper relationship of Kant to Kissinger's thought will be discussed later. For the present, it is important to note that Kissinger is heavily influenced by idealism—both as a philosophy that is primarily meta-physical and as an approach to history—but that his historicism de-velops from a more complex foundation than only idealism.

The second factor important to Kissinger's intellectual formation is the two major historical works he wrote during this period. Kissinger com-pleted "The Meaning of History: Reflections on Spengler, Toynbee and Kant" in 1950, earning his undergraduate degree *summa cum laude*. He deleted sections on the philosophies of history of Hegel and Albert Schweitzer from the final manuscript because of its already-imposing length. *A World Restored*, his Ph.D. dissertation completed in 1954, was a historical study of the diplomacy of the Congress of Vienna period. In it, Kissinger focuses primarily on the statecraft of Metternich, the Austrian foreign minister, and Castlereagh, his English counterpart, and their efforts to recreate the political and social order of Europe in the after-math of Napoleon's defeat.

Several points are significant regarding these works. The first is their relationship. Scholars have been satisfied to point out that these works are connected and that they contain Kissinger's principal beliefs. They have not, however, explored this connection. The relationship between the two texts can be stated succinctly. In "The Meaning of History," Kissinger formulates his philosophy of history; in *A World Restored*, he develops his outlook on statecraft by applying his historicist beliefs to a major episode in international relations. I will show how the principal elements in these works are related by discussing "The Meaning of History" in this chapter, and tracing the parallel ideas on statecraft that Kissinger explores in *A World Restored* in the next chapter.

A second important point about these works is Kissinger's purpose in writing them. As Stephen Graubard observes, Kissinger approaches both works in a deliberate effort to educate himself—first, to the broad themes of philosophy and history that he uses to form his philosophical approach; and second, to the diplomacy of two major leaders during a pivotal period in European history, which he uses to shape his own views on statecraft.[22]

The educative purpose of these works refutes two misconceptions about Kissinger's early scholarship. Some critics have argued that his undergraduate attraction to the philosophy of history indicates that he experienced a crisis of values as both a Jew and an intellectual in the aftermath of the Holocaust and World War II.[23] I find no support for this view. Kissinger's writings find meaning in history. His undergraduate thesis is not retrospective, or even introspective; the theme of the text is purely scholarly—a conscious preparation for the works to follow. To say that Kissinger did not experience a crisis of values as a young man, however, is not to suggest that he was morally insensitive or not deeply affected by the Holocaust. The war and its aftermath may not have caused him to question his values and beliefs because those values and beliefs were not yet sufficiently formed.

Scholars also use Kissinger's early works to argue that he is a disciple of Metternich (or later of Bismarck).[24] Although Kissinger praises Metternich's diplomatic skills, he faults the Austrian statesman for having lacked conceptual ability and tragic stature. The problems that confronted Metternich—problems that provide insight into the basis of international order—are Kissinger's true interest. As several scholars have observed, his concern is not with historical figures per se, but with the challenges that individual statesmen faced and the nature of their responses.[25]

A third significant point about Kissinger's early works is their scholarly import. Even as an elder statesman, Kissinger has yet to achieve again the originality and insight that characterize these writings. Both texts are reflective and questioning. Kissinger moves from one view to another, openly weighing arguments and factors, until he arrives at his own position. His "reflections" on Spengler, Toynbee, and Kant are precisely that—reflections that provide the basis for his philosophy of history. Similarly, both Metternich and Castlereagh are important to an understanding of Kissinger's thought insofar as their experiences help him to derive his views on statecraft. So instrumental are these early works to Kissinger's beliefs and so important was the creative act involved in preparing them that entire passages recur verbatim in the speeches and policy statements he made as secretary of state.

Finally, both works present a contrast that deserves mention because of its importance to the contents of later chapters. This contrast sets the Anglo-American tradition of foreign policy against the European or continental tradition. In "The Meaning of History," Kissinger contrasts the empiricism of Toynbee with the epistemological views of Kant and, to some extent, Spengler. In *A World Restored*, he compares the Anglo-

American political mentality epitomized by Castlereagh—particularly its insularity regarding international politics—with the European mind and continental diplomacy of Metternich.

The Meaning of History

Because of its importance to my analysis, I will consider "The Meaning of History" before discussing the nature of Kissinger's historicism. Kissinger's honors thesis is divided into five sections:

Section 1: "The Argument," in which he introduces the central thesis he will discuss against the background of each scholar's philosophy;

Section 2: "History-as-Intuition (Spengler)";

Section 3: "History-as-an-Empirical-Science (Toynbee)";

Section 4: "History and Man's Experience of Morality (Kant)"; and

Section 5: "The Sense of Responsibility," in which he offers his own answers to the questions he poses and outlines his own philosophy of history.

The titles of Sections 2, 3, and 4 provide the key to Kissinger's view of these scholars and suggest how he intends to analyze their thought. Kissinger adopts a novel methodology by trying to convey the essence of each author's work in that individual's own style. (This is especially significant in the section on Spengler because of the latter's poetic and metaphysical passages.) Kissinger argues that purely analytical criticism of Spengler and, to some extent of Toynbee, "falsifies the real essence of [their] philosophy."[26] Kissinger's pairing of Spengler and Toynbee, contemporaries who share a cyclical view of history, with the seventeenth-century German philosopher Kant is central to his thesis. His historicism develops from this union.

How does Kissinger define his search for meaning in history? From the beginning, he focuses on the problem of necessity and freedom. Do events occur in predetermined patterns? Is there a fatedness to history? Or is man free to shape history by imparting his own uniqueness to events? Kissinger regards the answers to these questions as essential to an understanding of history.

Kissinger begins "The Meaning of History" by posing its central question as a paradox—i.e., actions in retrospect appear inevitable, yet we act with the conviction of choice. Kissinger asks how we can reconcile our knowledge that events seem to occur irrevocably with our inward experience of freedom. He uses a metaphorical description of life to demonstrate this historical paradox. Every man journeys across a broad plain. At the start of that journey, all paths are open; man confronts "the seemingly limitless possibilities of his youth."[27] Every step he takes is taken freely, with an inward sense of choice. Yet with each step, man commits himself to a definite course. The path chosen determines how he will cross the plain. Each step forward preconditions the next, closing off other courses. "No longer is life a broad plain with forests and mountains beckoning all around, but it becomes apparent that one's journey across the meadows has indeed followed a regular path, that one can no longer go this way or that, but that the direction is set, the limits defined."[28] But which is the true reality? Our knowledge of the inevitability of the path—necessity? Or our sense of each willed step—freedom?

Kissinger confronts a second question in his introductory chapter—the question of historical understanding. If we resolve the paradox of meaning in history, how are we to understand this meaning? Kissinger poses this epistemological question:

> Is history an open book, a set of theorems that contains in itself all the aspirations of mankind as well as the key to the world's purpose? Or does history reveal a series of meaningless incidents, a challenge to our normative concepts, only through conformity to which it can obtain significance? Is meaning, in short, an attribute of reality or a metaphysical construction attendant on our recognition of significance?[29]

How Kissinger answers this question of historical understanding is significant. He concludes that the meaning of history cannot be derived empirically from the facts themselves. He rejects the principle of verifiability proposed by the logical positivists; the latter maintain that facts are true if they correspond to reality. Kissinger argues that anthropological research shows that different cultures create their own views of reality—facts are by no means absolute. Similarly, he argues that a rigorous adherence to the principle of verifiability makes all value judgments meaningless. Kissinger writes that "an inward experience cannot be proved by empirical data. A philosophy of history without a profound metaphysics will forever juxtapose surface data and can never satisfy the totality of man's desire for meaning."[30] Instead, we must approach history philosophically, because the questions we ask of it will determine the answers it yields.

> Thus meaning represents the emanation of a metaphysical context. Just as every man in a certain sense creates his picture of the world, just as the scientist can find in nature only what he puts in it in the

formulation of his hypothesis, just as every question determines at least the range of answers, so history does not exhibit the same portent to everybody but yields only the meanings inherent in the nature of our query. Therefore, too, the philosophy of history is inseparable from metaphysics, and involves a deep awareness of the mysteries and possibilities not only of nature but of human nature.[31]

In this manner, Kissinger introduces his central theme and the way in which he will develop his topic. Meaning in history lies in the philosophical approach we take toward it. Kissinger equates the philosophy of history with metaphysics, describing it as "metaphysics of a very high order."[32] The question he then confronts is: how did Spengler, Toynbee, and Kant address the problem of necessity and freedom in history? How did their metaphysical beliefs resolve this paradox? "In the reaction of the various thinkers to the problem of human necessity and human freedom, in their capacity to experience depths inaccessible to reason alone, lies the answer to the meaning of history."[33]

Kissinger next presents an extended commentary on the philosophy and works of each thinker. His analysis runs to over three hundred pages. He discusses Spengler's *Decline of the West*, Toynbee's *A Study of History*, and Kant's *Idea for a Universal History, Essay on Eternal Peace, Critique of Practical Reason,* and *Critique of Pure Reason* in detail. The contrast between the views of Spengler and Toynbee and those of Kant provides the key to Kissinger's thesis.

Both Spengler and Toynbee see history as a process involving the growth and decline of great civilizations. They stand outside of the historiographical approaches that developed from the thought of the French Enlightenment and that greatly influenced historical thinking in America. They reject this tradition's linear representation of history—a representation that credits man and his institutions with progressive development over time. Similarly, they regard the delineation of history into separate periods of man's evolution (such as ancient, medieval, and modern) as a fatuous kind of distinction. Instead, they describe history as a circular process in which great civilizations experience similar phases of development and decline.[34] The character of social life in civilizations as diverse as Sumeria and Western society exhibit similar patterns during stages of expansion and contraction. Spengler actually calls his method "morphological," using this biological term to indicate that the structural stages of birth, youth, maturity, and decline recur in the organic development of every culture, just as they do in the life of every biological organism.

In addition to the circular movement of history, Spengler and Toynbee both emphasize the cultural unity of great civilizations as both the unit of historical study and the key to its meaning. History is not economic or social history, but the history of these civilizations. Spengler identifies nine original civilizations and Toynbee twenty-one. Within each culture, unique attitudes permeate all life and thought. These attitudes shape the culture's art and philosophy, as well as its legal and political institutions. All cultures manifest a soul or spiritual element that is unique to that civilization and that transcends the people and lands which comprise the civilization. Paraphrasing Spengler, Kissinger explains that "the history of each culture [consists of] a ripening and deepening of its soul-picture."[35]

In arriving at a final evaluation of the thought of Spengler and Toynbee, Kissinger confronts the determinism of their work. Returning to the central paradox of necessity and freedom, he finds that both Spengler and Toynbee emphasize the necessity of historical occurrence—i.e., the cyclical recurrence of historical patterns. Their metaphysical approaches diminish the unique—the element of human freedom in history. It is on this basis that Kissinger ultimately judges their philosophies of history as inadequate explanations of history's meaning.

Kissinger is attracted to the poetical lyricism of Spengler's work and to his tragic vision. He takes from Spengler a feeling for history's "becoming"—a feeling that Spengler attributes in his philosophy to the influence of Goethe. History is life and development, movement and destiny. Unlike the objects studied by the physical sciences, which are categorized as general phenomena and observed to follow regular laws, the subjects of history are things-becoming and not the thing-become.[36] Kissinger observes that:

> Purely analytical criticism of Spengler will, however, never discover the profounder levels of his philosophy. These reside in his evocation of those elements of life that will ever be the subject of an inner experience, in his intuition of a mystic relationship to the infinite that expresses personality. Spengler's vision encompassed an approach to history which—whatever our opinion of his conclusions—transcended the mere causal analysis of data and the shallow dogmatism of many progress theories. . . . After all has been said, the conviction remains that Spengler has found a poetry in life which rises above the barren systematization of its manifestations.[37]

Yet Kissinger faults Spengler's philosophy for its naturalistic element, i.e., for the view that great cultures develop organically in a determined pattern. Spengler sees a fatedness in historical occurrences that attracts Kissinger because of its neoromantic and tragic character. This fatedness, however, leaves out the inner dimension of freedom and the role of choice in history.

Similarly, Kissinger finds elements to admire in Toynbee's scholarship. His own writings are heavily influenced by Toynbee's analysis of civilizations—particularly the factors involved in their breakdown. He refers to the "nemesis of creativity" in which success becomes the very condition of later tragedy. Toynbee had observed in his study of civilizations a tendency for societies to rest on their accomplishments. Because of this, they either did not perceive new challenges or attempted to deal with them by applying past solutions. This often led to disaster. Kissinger also refers to such Toynbee expressions as "the suicidalness of militarism." Here, military expansion and conquest cause a society to lose its inner balance or sense of limits. The society overreaches itself. This loss of equilibrium has also led to disaster.[38] But overall, Kissinger finds Toynbee's philosophy lacking, because it does not address the element of freedom in history either.

Ironically, Toynbee deliberately tries to transcend Spengler's naturalism by emphasizing the purposive content of history. The central concept of his work is the process of "challenge-and-response." This process explains the various phases in the development of civilizations. Toynbee identifies origin and growth with successful responses to challenges, and breakdown with a failure of response. Although Toynbee intends this concept to express the purposiveness of history, Kissinger judges it to have the opposite result. According to Kissinger, Toynbee's challenge-and-response pattern becomes a deterministic mechanism that offers empirical knowledge about history but little understanding of its inner dimensions which are shaped by countless choices of men. The empiricism Toynbee reveals in his quest for immutable laws of history diminishes the sense of history as willed occurrence. A sense of the unique is also lost, Kissinger explains, because Toynbee addresses the meaning of history by establishing the generalities of challenges rather than examining the uniqueness of responses. Further, "Toynbee's empiricism allows him to distinguish challenges only by their origin and magnitude, not by their inner meaning."[39] Kissinger views this as a major shortcoming in Toynbee's thought since it is the manner in which civilizations respond to crises that they develop their identity. This is the "inner meaning" of the challenges that civilizations face.

Against this background, Kissinger turns to Kant. He sees Kant's thought as counterbalancing the determinism of Spengler and Toynbee. Kant's metaphysical and epistemological idealism provides Kissinger with an understanding of the element of freedom in history. The contrast between the determinism of Spengler and Toynbee and the indeterminism of Kant is central to Kissinger's argument.

Kissinger is drawn to two elements of Kantian idealism. First, Kantian philosophy reverses the mind-reality relationship that the seventeenth-century empiricists propagated. According to Kant, reality cannot be known as it is in itself. Instead, man, the active and thinking subject, imparts meaning to reality through innate categories of thought such as time, space, and causality. Empiricism holds that uniform patterns exist in reality, which man detects through his senses. In contrast, Kant insists that these sensations are merely disconnected images until the mind's innate forms of thought shape them and give them meaning. This philosophical outlook provides the foundation of Kissinger's belief that meaning in history emanates from a metaphysical construct and not from an empirical appreciation of the facts of history.

A second element of Kant's thought is even more important to Kissinger, because it gives him insight into the paradox of freedom and necessity. Kantian idealism emphasizes man's subjective perception of external reality. It also suggests that there is a level of reality that is not subject to perception—a spiritual realm made up of acts of will and ideas whose influences can be felt, but that cannot be seen as "real" objects in an empirical sense. Kant distinguishes between the "phenomenal" world—the world of objects that can be understood through the categories of time, space, and causality—and this "noumenal" realm. Because the noumenal or spiritual level of reality is connected with man's free will, the mental categories that structure man's thought about the physical world cannot be applied to it. It is in this concept of a noumenal realm that transcends the physical level of history that Kissinger finds a basis for freedom in history. Kant's metaphysical approach offers a more comprehensive answer to the paradox of necessity and freedom, and greater insight into the meaning of history, than the ideas of Spengler and Toynbee.

Are we to conclude, as Dickson does, that Kissinger accepts Kantian philosophy as his own? No one familiar with Kissinger's writings would deny the influence of philosophical idealism on his thought. Kissinger asserts that mind and ideas constitute the primary nature of reality; he emphasizes the thinking subject who shapes reality; and he rejects positivist and empirical patterns of thought. He is attracted to Kant's concern with the inner dimension of man's personality—what Dickson refers to as "the Protestant notion of spiritual inwardness."[40] Kissinger's historical and political beliefs are shaped by a similar concern about the element of choice in the acts of men both past and present. But it is also true that, although Kissinger accepts the major tenets of philosophical idealism, he finds Kant's own philosophy of history untenable. In fact, he sees Kant's deterministic philosophy of history as contradicting his earlier insights regarding man's transcendence. This contradiction stems from the fact that Kant derives his view of history from his moral philosophy rather than from his metaphysical principles.

Kant believes that mankind is evolving according to an *a priori* natural process toward a state of eternal peace.[41] Kant universalizes the categorical imperative—extending the injunction to treat every human being as an end in itself to the relationship between sovereign nations. Kant believes that this teleological purpose in history reveals a divine plan. Kissinger argues that Kant errs seriously on this point. Just as Toynbee's failure lay in his attempt to join freedom and necessity in history under the guise of empirical laws, so Kant's failure lay in his attempt to unite the two by means of a divine teleology.

> Kant's attempt to expand the philosophy of history into a guarantee for the attainability of the moral law failed for the same reason as Toynbee's. The realm of freedom and necessity cannot be reconciled except by an inward experience. The mechanism of nature offers no obvious assurance for the implementation of freedom. The identification of the ethical with the natural makes the meaning of history the emanation of the disposition of the will only in so far as this volition is conceived as the tool of an organic necessity.[42]

The lines of Kissinger's own historicism begin to emerge in his reflections on these philosophies. He gives them form in the final chapter of his thesis. It is significant that he calls this chapter "The Sense of Responsibility." This title gives us a clue to the attitude he believes man should assume when faced with the inexorability of historical events and the burden of his own freedom. It is to the essence of Kissinger's own historical philosophy that we now turn.

Kissinger's Historicism Defined

I have indicated that Kissinger's historicism is evident in his statement that insight regarding foreign affairs depends upon an awareness of the historical context. Further, I stressed that the emphasis in this statement should be placed on the notion of awareness. Kissinger believes that it is the manner in which we approach history, i.e., our metaphysical presuppositions, that reveals its deepest meaning. These two considerations define the essence of Kissinger's historicism.

The first of these elements involves the historical foundation of political understanding—particularly that involved in understanding interstate relations. It is worthwhile pausing to consider this primary relationship between history and international politics in Kissinger's thought.

Kissinger argues that the very nature of international politics means that it must be studied historically. Behind this contention is the assumption that because nature and man are fundamentally different, they must be approached differently. Science is suited for studying the recurring patterns and laws that govern nature. The relations between states, however, reflect man's changing conceptions and will, and, therefore, these relations require historical understanding.

This primacy of history is among the elements that link Kissinger's thought to nineteenth-century European historiography—particularly that of the German school. Carlo Antoni suggests that there exists no one form of historicism but rather a variety of European historicisms "all profoundly different in accordance with the national traditions to which they belonged."[43] Common to each was the belief that history is the proper approach for the study of society and culture. In Germany, historicism received its widest definition. Friedrich Engel-Janosi describes its role as the "magistra" of all learning.[44] Similarly, Friedrich Meinecke, Ernst Troeltsch, and other German historians regard historicism as "Germany's greatest contribution to Western thought since the Reformation."[45] Georg Iggers calls attention to the connection between European historicism and political thought—a connection we find in Kissinger's work. Iggers writes:

> The relation between history and political science was reversed generally in Europe. The historian no longer looked to political philosophy for the principles of rational politics, as in the Enlightenment, rather, the political theorist turned to history. Not only conservative writers, such as Burke and Carlyle, but liberal theorists as well (Constant, Thierry, Michelet, Macaulay, and Acton) sought the roots of French or English liberty in the remote national past rather than in the rights of man. Even the positivistic sociology of Auguste Comte or Herbert Spencer, which later German critics regarded as the antithesis of German historicism, viewed society in terms of historical growth.[46]

Kissinger's belief in the historical foundation of political understanding is based on the analogous nature of the knowledge derived from history. Because historical circumstances constantly change, and because they involve unique persons who once lived, the lessons of history can never be applied automatically to new political situations. As Kissinger writes, "history teaches by analogy, not identity."[47] The statesman must take into account not only the changing nature of history but also the historicity of his own understanding. His understanding of the past and the analogies he draws are themselves timebound, and thus influenced by his present circumstances. Describing the historical foundation of political understanding, Kissinger writes:

> History is not a cookbook which gives recipes; it teaches by analogy and forces us to decide what, if anything, is analogous. History gives us a feel for the significance of events, but it does not teach which

individual events are significant. It is impossible to write down a
conceptual scheme and apply it mechanically to evolving situations.
Certain principles can be developed, certain understandings can be
elaborated, but it is impossible to predict in advance how they apply
to concrete situations.[48]

The second element of Kissinger's historicism involves the metaphysical presuppositions that shape his study of history—his own philosophy regarding history's meaning. This philosophy involves the
reconciliation of necessity and freedom—elements that he regards as
history's central paradox. What is the nature of this reconciliation?

Kissinger's metaphysical position may be explained as follows: History is known to us, in retrospect, in its patterns of recurrence and in its
seeming inevitability. "The inevitability results from a contemplation of
the completed actions, from an apprehension of the facts of occurrence,
from the unfolding of a chain of events which the mind orders into a
causal sequence."[49] Yet while history is known in this fashion, it is
understood by means of its essential uniqueness—what Kissinger describes as the inward spirituality of choice and conviction or "the unique
which each man imparts to the inevitable."[50] To borrow terms from the
English historian, R. G. Collingwood, Kissinger implies that historical
knowledge of recurring patterns is knowledge of the "outside" of events.
History's meaning, however, lies in a grasp of the "inside" of events—
the acts of choice and volition by which man imparts meaning to
events.[51] For Kissinger, the understanding of both history and life involve a reconciliation of their inexorable "outside" and their self-willed
"inside."

> Life is suffering, birth involves death. Transitoriness is the fate of
> existence. No civilization has yet been permanent, no longing com-
> pletely fulfilled. This is necessity, the fatedness of history, the di-
> lemma of mortality. But Spengler's assertion that the appearance of life
> exhausts its meaning denies the transcendental fact of existence. We
> know we must die and yet live with a mode of permanence. However
> determined our actions appear in retrospect we perform them with an
> inward conviction of choice.[52]

I have used the term "reconciliation" repeatedly in describing
Kissinger's views. Kissinger himself describes his philosophy in this
manner.[53] This term, however, does not imply that Kissinger tries to
solve the paradox of necessity and freedom. Nor does his acceptance of
this paradox amount to a synthesis of necessity and freedom. Instead, I
use "reconciliation" to denote the coexistence of two apparently opposite
positions whose very opposition evokes the living reality of history.
Kissinger moves beyond the paradox to a plane of understanding where

he accepts both necessity and freedom as integral parts of the meaning of history. Bruce Mazlish traces the influence of Hegel in Kissinger's resolution of this paradox:

> The effect of Elliott's Hegel on Kissinger was profound, and some observers profess to see the mark of the dialectic in Kissinger's later thinking; one observer, in fact, sees Hegel's notion of *aufgeheben*—literally not solving problems as such, but outgrowing them, i.e., solving them on another level—as a clue to Henry Kissinger's general approach.[54]

Kissinger's reconciliation embodies a form of what German historiography refers to as *"anti-begrifflichkeit"*—the rejection of purely conceptualized thinking. Instead, historical understanding requires a "feel" for the inside of events, an element of intuition *(Ahnung)* or poetical recreation. In arriving at his reconciliation of necessity and freedom, Kissinger draws on the poetry of Homer, Virgil, Dante, and Milton, all of whom he quotes in the last chapter of his thesis. "Poetry testifies to humanity's longing in the face of the fatedness of existence, to the unique which each man imparts to his determined surroundings."[55] This rejection of purely conceptual thinking explains Kissinger's attraction to Spengler's poetical lyricism and use of *"erfuhlen"* or intuitive perception. "The ultimate mysteries of life," Kissinger writes, "are perhaps not approachable by dissection, but require the poet's view who grasps the unity of life, which is greater than any, however painstaking, analysis of its manifestations."[56] Intuitional forms of historical understanding figure prominently in Kissinger's ideas concerning the wisdom of the statesman.

Kissinger's metaphysical beliefs involve reconciliation on several levels. Beyond necessity and freedom, history entails the reconciliation of recurrence and uniqueness. We can discern patterns in history, but within those patterns we can also detect the unique choices made by men faced with conflicting options. Kissinger bridges the deterministic thought of Spengler and Toynbee with the indeterminism embodied in the Kantian noumena. To an extent, we can say that Kissinger "spiritualizes" Spengler and Toynbee. In this context, he sees Toynbee's challenge-and-response mechanism as the outward manifestation of man's inner capacity to experience challenge and to respond creatively. Similarly, he infuses a spirituality into Spengler's concept of the organic decline of civilizations:

> Life seems to involve death in history as in individuals. Though aging in a culture is not analogous to physical decay, it does bear a similarity to another problem of existence, the process of disenchantment. Just

as the life of every person exhibits a gradual loss of the wonder at the world, so history reveals an increase of familiarity with the environment, a tired grasping for a certainty which will obviate all struggles, a quest for a guarantee of man's hopes in nature's mechanism.[57]

Kissinger's metaphysical assumptions involve one final reconciliation—that between man's historical knowledge and his need to act and thus shape events. This is the most poignant of all Kissinger's reconciliations and it accounts for the title of the last chapter of his thesis, "The Sense of Responsibility." Despite man's knowledge of history (of its seemingly recurring patterns, of the fatedness of decline), he still has an obligation to act. He must impart his uniqueness to events that his historical knowledge tells him are inevitable. "Matter," Kissinger writes, "can defeat only those who have no spirituality to impart to it."[58] Hence, man's freedom entails a responsibility to act in the face of history's fatedness.

Many scholars identify this element of neoromanticism in Kissinger's writings without recognizing its origin. Significantly, Kissinger evokes the same romantic quality that characterizes his undergraduate writings in the most important interview he gave during his tenure as America's chief statesman. In response to a question by James Reston of *The New York Times* concerning his celebrated pessimism or tragic sense, Kissinger replies:

> I think of myself as a historian more than as a statesman. As a historian, you have to be conscious of the fact that every civilization that has ever existed has ultimately collapsed. History is a tale of efforts that failed, of aspirations that weren't realized, of wishes that were fulfilled and then turned out to be different from what one expected. So, as a historian, one has to live with the inevitability of tragedy. As a statesman, one has to act on the assumption that problems must be solved. Each generation lives in time, and even though ultimately perhaps societies have all suffered a decline, that is of no help to any one generation, and the decline is usually traceable to a loss of creativity and inspiration and therefore avoidable. It is probably true that insofar as I think historically I must look at the tragedies which have occurred. Insofar as I act, my motive force, of which I am conscious, is to try and avoid them.[59]

It is important to consider the parallels that exist between Kissinger's historicism and that of the German school. Kissinger's intellectual development mirrors the evolution of historicism in nineteenth-century Germany. As we have seen, Kissinger's basic approach to the study of history was heavily influenced by Kantian idealism. Similarly, the early German historicist thinkers, such as Wilhelm von Humboldt, Johann

Gottfried Herder, and Leopold von Ranke, were educated in the German philosophical tradition—a tradition that emphasized Kantianism. Their ideas on the individuality and spiritual basis of the state find their origin in idealist thought. In this respect, Kissinger was a historicist before he was familiar with the historicist thinkers. By the time he wrote *A World Restored,* he had read widely among their works. His bibliography shows a distinct preference for German historians; he contrasts their historiography with what he describes as the inferior works of French and particularly English historians.

The German historicist concepts of national individuality and the spiritual basis of the state resemble Spengler and Toynbee's emphasis on unique civilizations—an emphasis that influenced Kissinger. Although the historicists take states rather than cultures as their unit of study, they too focus on patterns of growth and decline. Additionally, both Kissinger and the German historicists emphasize the nonconceptual or intuitive aspects of historical understanding.

Scholars overlook the fact that although German historicism distinguishes between natural and human phenomena, German historians do not reject the facts of history, only the scientific laws of history that these facts supposedly demonstrate. American historians interpret Ranke as a positivist because of his oft-quoted maxim that the historian must "establish what actually happened" *(wie es eigentlich gewesen).* Yet Ranke's positivism—if we choose to call it that—was for him the basis for insight concerning the spiritual content of history. We can discern a parallel in Kissinger's historicism. He accepts the empirical facts of history, particularly as Toynbee presents them, but he does not accept the latter's philosophy of empiricism.

There are other, perhaps more striking, parallels to German historicism in Kissinger's reflections on world history. Kissinger's historicism develops against the background of his thought on the historical process and the manner in which others have considered that process. In the final section of this chapter, I will examine the major elements of Kissinger's outlook on world history.

Kissinger's Outlook on World History

In describing historical events, Kissinger evokes a sense of ceaseless movement. History for Kissinger, as for the German historicists, is an organic stream—a current of flux and development. It cannot be explained as a succession of discrete events, but must be approached as a fluid process of change. Kissinger sees the primary elements of world history—the great states and their relations—as constantly changing elements rather than as static entities within a permanent framework.

The key to this aspect of Kissinger's historical thought lies in his interchangeable uses of the terms "history" and "historical process." As Dickson observes, Kissinger regards the conduct of foreign policy and his own significant initiatives (such as détente) as parts of a historical process. Foreign policy, Kissinger states, "knows no plateaus. What does not become a point of departure for a new advance soon turns into stagnation and then into retreat."[60]

Kissinger encounters this feel for the historical process, or history-as-process, in the writings of Spengler. He was captivated by the poetical and metaphysical passages that Spengler uses to evoke the sense of history's "becoming." Spengler's descriptions of the soul of a culture as "immanent impulse" and "waking consciousness" provide a sense of history as a process of change and development. In contrast, the more empirical approaches to the study of the past seemed lacking in a feel for history's underlying movement. Spengler's distinction between the "world-as-history" (which emphasizes the study of history as a living and developing reality) and the "world-as-nature" (which emphasizes laws and classifications—what Spengler termed the "stiff-forms" of causality) deeply influenced Kissinger.[61]

Kissinger translates Spengler's views into his own belief in history as an organic process. He believes that the past—no less than the present and future—must be seen as a process of becoming. He refers to an "ethical" level of historical analysis (as distinct from the empirical level) which views history as more than mere surface data or phenomenal appearance—which sees it in effect "as a key to action."[62] For Kissinger, history is alive with choices and must be regarded as the expression of willed-occurrences rather than as merely the past of completed acts. What it is essential to realize about the past is that it results from the moral choices of men (principally the leaders of the great states, such as Metternich and Bismarck) who, at the time of their decisions, faced "a multiplicity of available policies, counselling contradictory courses of action."[63]

An important distinction emerges in Kissinger's analysis of the historical process. Spengler regards the historical process as an organic development; great cultures or original forms unfold out of the formless timestream. The process itself transcends civilizations and peoples, and, in fact, sweeps them along in its movement. This same transcendence characterizes the historical idealism of Hegel and the historical materialism of Marx. For Kissinger, however, the driving force of the historical process is not a transcendent unfolding, but rather the choices made by individuals in different historical epochs. The acts of will and conceptions of great leaders constantly transform history.

Kissinger does not regard history as moving away from or toward an end extrinsic to itself. He rejects this teleological element in both Toynbee and Kant. Both see the hand of divine providence as the guiding force in history and the source of its ultimate purpose. For Kissinger, no ultimate end or external force explains history. Its purpose is realized in man's attempts to impart his uniqueness to the inexorable flow of events.

Dickson associates the absence of transcendence in Kissinger's outlook with his agnosticism and his tendency to equate the historical process with morality.[64] I believe that Dickson is correct on this point. Furthermore, I believe that Kissinger's equation of the historical process and morality accounts in part for the moral relativism that he has displayed on so many occasions as both scholar and statesman. Kissinger frequently justified the acts of statesmen (including his own) in terms of their effects on the flow of history rather than in moral terms of right or wrong. For example, he suggested that the Nixon administration's policies in Southeast Asia would be later judged by their contribution to world order rather than by specific episodes such as the bombing of Cambodia, which was widely criticized in moral terms. As Dickson suggests, juxtaposing history and morality ultimately separates politics from ethics.[65] I shall return to this point in chapter 2.

Kissinger's outlook on world history focuses on the "Great States."[66] These states emerge as islands of stability against the background of the endless historical process. The pivotal events and heroic conflicts of history, its great religious and class movements—all arise or culminate in the powerful nations that dominate history in different epochs. For Kissinger, world history is essentially the interaction of these great states.

This attitude reveals the influence of Spengler and Toynbee as well as that of the German historicists, particularly Ranke. While Spengler and Toynbee emphasize unique cultures, the historicists, beginning with Herder, stress the concept of the "individuality" of states. States represent entirely original and distinct entities; each has an individual "spirit" or "idea" that permeates its social life. Ranke, who emphasizes this spiritual basis of the state, gives the concept of individuality its most far-reaching definition. In his famous essay, "The Great Powers," he underscores the importance of the dominant nations in Europe. He describes the balance of power among them as the central instrument of the European order throughout history. Yet he differs markedly from most theorists of the balance of power, particularly those of the Anglo-American tradition, because he defines power in spiritual terms, emphasizing morale and will instead of purely physical power.[67] I shall explore a similar emphasis in Kissinger's thought in the next chapter.

Kissinger's own treatment of the great states straddles these influences. At times, he focuses on civilizations that transcend individual states as the proper unit of historical study as did Toynbee and Spengler. Thus, his works include references to Inca or Egyptian civilization, or to the cultural values of the industrialized West. For the most part, however, his historical and political writings emphasize the individual great states. His treatment of them stresses their uniqueness. But unlike the historicists who regard cultural values and institutions as untransferable, Kissinger suggests by his use of such terms as "industrial democracies" and the "Arab world" that nations are also parts of larger cultural groups.

Significantly, the emphasis Kissinger placed on the great states has meant that he gave little importance to the smaller, less powerful nations. These states had little significance in his thinking until relatively late in his career when he became increasingly involved in events in the Third World. They did not contribute to the dynamic of the historical process, nor did they play more than a marginal role in different historical epochs. In this sense, Kissinger viewed the smaller states as "unhistorical." His own historical knowledge of areas outside Europe—even of the United States—was negligible. Just as in his writings on the nineteenth century, he equated world order with the great states of Europe, so too in his actions as a statesman, he emphasized a global order in which the less powerful and developing nations were conspicuous by their absence. These views changed somewhat in the final years in which he was secretary of state as events in the Middle East and Africa threatened global stability.

In discussing the thought of the scholars who influenced Kissinger, I called attention to the notion of the state as a spiritual entity. The historicists espouse a metaphysical or "organismic" theory of the state.[68] They see the nation as an idea or spiritual principle that bears the same relationship to its physical manifestation in national values and institutions as the soul does to the body. Heavily influenced by the Neoplatonic thought of the German Enlightenment (Aufklaren), the historicists regard states as "real-geistig"—as both real and spiritual in their existence.[69] Iggers describes this spiritual view of the nation:

> The state is not merely an empirical concentration of power; it possesses a "positive spiritual content," an idea which cannot be expressed in general, abstract terms because it relates specifically to the particular state. This "idea that inspires and dominates the whole"

shapes the state into an organic unit, completely different from all other states. . . . In the states themselves, Ranke wrote, "instead of the passing conglomerations which the contractual theory of the states create like cloud formations, I perceive spiritual substances."[70]

Kissinger never elaborates a metaphysical theory of the state in his own writings; however, he clearly regards nations as something more than their physical existence. He rejects the positivist view of the state predominant among American theorists. Although I am reluctant to call his views metaphysical, he does attribute spiritual character to the state. He finds the basis for this character in the nation's historical consciousness or identity:

> Societies exist in time more than in space. At any given moment a state is but a collection of individuals, as positivist scholars have never wearied of pointing out. But it achieves identity through the consciousness of a common history. This is the only "experience" nations have.[71]

Beyond racial and linguistic differences, the radical distinctiveness of individual nations lies in what Kissinger alternately refers to as "historical identity" or "national substance."[72] Noer observes that "national experience" and "historical development" are central to Kissinger's idea of nations as unique entities. For Kissinger, "each nation has a unique history. . . . Nations, like individuals, have inherited characteristics and styles. History has shaped each state."[73] Nations' historical experiences account for their dominant traditions—including their historical and philosophical outlooks. Most importantly for Kissinger's political philosophy, the historical experiences of nations account for the fundamentally different perceptions of global politics held by their leaders. These perceptions, in turn, explain the different styles of foreign policy and different ways in which nations define their national interests and security. This is what Kissinger means by his somewhat paradoxical observation that "history is the memory of states."[74]

In considering individual nations, Kissinger stresses the importance of their domestic social structures. He defines such structures primarily in terms of the nations' leadership groups and governmental or administrative institutions. Kissinger emphasizes that a nation's leaders and government embody the dominant values of the society. The nation's cultural traditions—its philosophical and historical heritage—shape its leaders. Kissinger describes such statesmen as Metternich and de Gaulle as epitomizing the values of their countries.

Two factors regarding Kissinger's historical thought need to enter into our consideration at this point. First, Kissinger emphasizes the role of the heroic leader in history. The great states are central to history's pageantry, but their leaders actually make history. The great leader, in fact, can shape the historical process, directing it in a way that embodies his vision. History in this regard is not explained by impersonal economic and social forces but by the clash of wills and personalities of the leaders who create it.

Kissinger's description of the demonic force of character possessed by such leaders as Bismarck, de Gaulle, and Mao Tse-tung reveals a romantic strain that is similar to Hegel's belief in the "world-historical" figure. Noer observed that "to Kissinger the only spark of hope is the giant, the statesman, the leader."[75] All of Kissinger's intellectual influences (with the exception of Kant) stress the role of the great leader or of leadership groups as critical to a nation's fortunes. Toynbee writes of the "creative minorities" as the lifeblood of any civilization.[76]

Similarly, Spengler regards the genuine statesman as "incarnate history."[77] In keeping with the romantic element in his thinking, Kissinger sees the great leader as a rare phenomenon that occurs only once in several generations. Moreover, he depicts the genuine leader as a lonely and creative figure with artistic sensitivities. It is significant to Kissinger's views and later actions that the great leader is seen as acting alone—because his conception and creativity put him beyond the understanding of lesser men.

Second, Kissinger depicts the institutions that make up a nation's domestic social structures as experiencing the aging process that Spengler describes. Kissinger views this process not in physiological terms, but as a loss of creativity. He writes of the "conflict between inspiration and organization" as the "inextricable element of history."[78] Kissinger believes that the early creative acts of societies and the values and ideals that inspire creativity become hardened into institutions. He attributes the decline of nations to a decline of creativity represented by a reliance on institutional solutions. He describes Metternich's Austria, for example, as an antiquated remnant of a past era because of its seeming inability to reform or change social institutions that no longer were capable of responding to the problems that confronted the Hapsburg government in Vienna. A nation's historical experience and institutions limit "the range of its possible future adaptations";[79] the statesman must consider these factors in formulating foreign policy.

One final element in Kissinger's historical thought should be delineated—an element that I choose to call the structure of the age. The structure of the age is essentially the inner form of a particular historical epoch that results mainly from the relations of the great states. The alignment of power relations and the historical aspirations of the dominant nations give the age its particular shape and distinguish it from other historical periods. Kissinger, for example, frequently alludes to the present period as a "revolutionary age"—primarily because of the changing nature of interstate relations.

Kissinger acknowledges that many different forces help to shape historical periods. He indicates that changes in communication, transportation, military technology, economic arrangements, and ideologies have all played roles in the revolutionary temper of the modern period. However, he does not regard these changes as transnational elements, but instead sees them as occurring either in or through the great states.

Because history is a process, the structure of the age is always in flux. Kissinger emphasizes the "momentousness" of history, i.e., the turning points in the historical process. Great events can usually be traced to prior—often at first imperceptible—transformations in the relations between the great states. The historian must be extremely sensitive to the structure of each age in order to detect the elements that might signal important changes. This sensitivity includes an emphasis on the dialectical nature of change in history—the view that the structure of each age contains elements that lead to its own transformation. Structural changes provide a prelude to historical changes. This notion of history's turning points plays a prominent part in Kissinger's ideas on statecraft.

What can we say in conclusion about Kissinger's outlook on world history? I want to characterize it as a profoundly nonaffirmative historicism. Kissinger does not regard history as a benign process in which all that occurs is beneficial and progressive. He maintains that only a "shallow historicism"[80] would view history in so fatuous a manner. History is tragic in its very essence. Kissinger's writings contain frequent allusions to Greek and Roman tragedy. He associates tragedy with man's failure to achieve his goals and aspirations. Even more profoundly, tragedy signifies the ironic element in history. All too often man achieves his goals only to find them empty of meaning. However, Kissinger's pessimism does not mean that his historical philosophy is defeatist. Because of its importance, I will discuss this point in detail in chapter 7.

Kissinger's historicism emphasizes the pervasiveness of conflict. Because of the radical distinctiveness of the great states that are central to the historical process, strife is inevitable. History for Kissinger, as Hoffmann points out, "is not primarily the product of deep, irresistible forces; it is a clash of wills and a stage for leaders who are either the carriers of new principles or the creative defenders of past experience."[81] Since the issues that nations contest involve their own historical identities, conflict must be expected.

Kissinger's political ideas emerge from his historical philosophy. As I stated at the beginning of this chapter, Kissinger's ideas on statecraft and world order are primarily the ideas of a historian. It is to Kissinger's philosophy of international relations that we now turn our attention.

2

The Outlook of the Continental Statesman

A World Restored

EVEN if Henry Kissinger had not achieved prominence as a statesman, his dissertation on nineteenth-century European diplomacy, *A World Restored*, would still deserve to be read for the original insights that it offers on the subject of international politics. Among the so-called "action-intellectuals"[1] of recent years, Kissinger is unique. In contrast to the more pragmatic scholarship of other advisers, he possesses a worldview—a theoretical outlook on international politics and statecraft.

In *A World Restored*, Kissinger analyzes the diplomacy of the period from 1812 to 1822, the years of the Napoleonic wars and their aftermath. He focuses on the efforts of the Austrian Foreign Minister Metternich to transform the wartime coalition of Austria, England, Prussia, and Russia into a stable political and social order.

For Metternich, this stable order (or world restored) rested in part on the peace of conciliation—a peace that would allow France to assume its traditional role as one of the great powers of Europe. More importantly, the key to European stability involved England's "entering" the continent—both politically and philosophically—there to play a more permanent and integral part in European politics than its historical role as "balancer" had allowed.[2] Metternich saw in his wartime ally Czar Alexander of Russia a revolutionary challenge to the European order, potentially as destructive to the general equilibrium as was Napoleon's challenge. Prussia also posed a threat to the balance in central Europe, where it contested Austria's supremacy among the German principalities. Metternich turned to his English counterpart, Castlereagh, for the support of another power—the support needed to balance these threats and to stabilize European politics.

Kissinger highlights the Congress of Vienna of 1815. The agreements reached there represented the successful culmination of Metternich's diplomatic efforts; these agreements established the foundation of the European political and social order that lasted until World War I.

The narrative content of *A World Restored* is genuinely interesting. It is not my purpose, however, to deal with the historical events documented in Kissinger's work except insofar as they illustrate his ideas on international politics. Throughout the work, Kissinger interjects long, reflective passages in which he uses concrete events as a background against which he formulates his philosophy of statecraft. These ideas, offered as historical generalizations and concepts, provide the principal subject of this chapter.

Before treating Kissinger's substantive ideas on statecraft, I wish to consider two points about *A World Restored*. The first concerns its analogous content. Kissinger's choice of topic is guided by the similarities that he discerned between the post-Napoleonic era and the modern period of American foreign policy. He stresses this connection in his introduction:

The success of physical science depends on the selection of the "crucial" experiment: that of political science in the field of international affairs, on the selection of the "crucial" period. I have chosen for my topic the period between 1812 and 1822, partly, I am frank to say, because its problems seem to me analogous to those of our day. But I do not insist on this analogy.[3]

What were these analogous problems? Both periods were revolutionary. At the time of the Congress of Vienna, the state system was in turmoil. Kissinger writes that "hundreds of feudal states were being consolidated into larger national units, which meant that all the traditional power relationships had to be adjusted both physically and conceptually. As always in revolutionary periods, the emerging new forms existed alongside the old ones."[4] He compares this transformation to the break-up of the European colonies in Africa and Asia after World War II, and the emergence of over one hundred new states.

Both eras were marked by major changes in the nature of warfare. Napoleon's mass armies relied on average citizens rather than the professional soldiers of the ancien regime. As a result, entire societies became engulfed in war. In the modern period, the advent of nuclear weapons completed the transformation to total war.

Both periods also witnessed increased demands for social and economic reforms. In the earlier period, these demands were voiced principally within the dynastic regimes of Europe; in the later era, the postcolonial nations of the Third World issued the call for reform.

In both eras, the state system survived a revolutionary challenge from a conqueror bent on world domination only to face a new revolutionary challenge from a wartime ally. In the nineteenth century, a coalition that included Russia successfully defeated Napoleon's attempt to establish a world hegemony. In the aftermath of the Napoleonic wars, Russia itself posed a new threat to European stability. Czar Alexander tried to control Eastern Europe (particularly Poland) and to influence political life in Western Europe by naming the new French leader. Similarly, the allied powers in World War II, including the Soviet Union, defeated Hitler's revolutionary threat to world order. After 1945, however, this wartime coalition ended abruptly. The Soviet Union dominated Eastern Europe and adopted expansionist policies that threatened the rest of the European continent. Against this background, Kissinger sees the need for order as the central problem facing the statesmen of both eras.

I call attention to these similarities to prepare the way for what I believe to be the central analogy of Kissinger's work. The reader who encounters these parallels for the first time is intrigued by their apparent symmetry. In fact, part of the interest (and difficulty) in reading *A World Restored* is that in certain passages one can never be sure whether Kissinger is offering a retrospective analysis of English diplomacy or a prospective analysis of American statecraft. Stanley Hoffmann notes that "*A World Restored* gives a sense of multiple exposures, for it is at the same time a study of the Congress of Vienna, a critique of Versailles (and particularly Wilsonian diplomacy), and a series of shots at American diplomacy in World War II (and at the diplomacies of the democracies in the thirties)."[5]

It is clear from statements in *A World Restored* and later works that, beyond these "structural" similarities, Kissinger is aware that major changes had occurred in the content of international politics. The impact of nuclear weapons on the balance of power, the extreme heterogeneity of the contemporary state system, and the role of ideology are among the changes that occupy his attention. Kissinger himself stresses that historical analogies can never be applied directly, because their lessons are contingent upon the circumstances of the present.

I would, however, offer an exception to the above statement. *A World Restored* contains one analogy—which I choose to call the central analogy—which I believe can be directly applied. This is the analogy between the insular foreign policy of England in the post-Napoleonic era and America's insular foreign policy in the years following World War II. I pointed out earlier that it was an essential element of Metternich's strategy to convert the English statesman Castlereagh to a more "European" or "continental" outlook regarding the peace to be decided in Vienna in 1815. Similarly, a key to Kissinger's own thinking and the basis for much of his criticism of postwar American foreign policy is his belief that America needed to break away from its insular tradition and adopt a more continental approach.

I will deal with the nature and consequences of insularity as an approach to foreign policy in later chapters. I do not propose to offer more than a general distinction between it and the continental approach at this time. Essentially, insularity represents a country's attempt to escape the very practice of foreign policy. Kissinger equates it with a belief "that historical experience can be transcended, that problems can be solved permanently, that harmony can be the natural state of mankind."[6] The insular nation focuses on domestic politics. To the extent that it is forced to deal with foreign affairs, its political and military approach is reactive and discontinuous.

In contrast, continentalism is synonymous with immersion in the state system. The continental nation gives primacy to foreign policy, both as a matter of physical and psychological necessity as well as a matter of philosophical inclination. Its foreign policy is distinguished by its vigilance and what Kissinger terms its "precautionary" style.[7]

This leads to a second point that I wish to make before considering Kissinger's political philosophy. In the very title of this chapter, I refer to Kissinger's outlook on international relations as that of a continental statesman. This characterization suggests itself by reason of his sustained critique of American insularity. More significantly, however, it draws on the historicism that provides the basis of his political philosophy. It is thus important to clarify the specific relationship between his historical views and his continental outlook.

The "insular-continental typology" arises from Kissinger's study of history. He begins *A World Restored* by contrasting these two basic kinds of foreign policies.[8] Although Kissinger did not create this typology,[9] his discussion of these "mentalities"[10] and their impact on the practice of foreign policy represents one of his most significant theoretical contributions. Hence, "insular" and "continental" are historical concepts—concepts that illustrate Kissinger's view that political understanding arises from a proper awareness of history.

Kissinger expresses admiration for continental statesmen and their mode of statecraft throughout his scholarly writings. Metternich, Bismarck, de Gaulle, and Adenauer stand out in this regard. Beyond their technical virtuosity as diplomats, Kissinger admires these men for their desire to leave their mark on events. Each tried to shape the historical process through his ideas and actions. We must recall the connection between Kissinger's historicism and his philosophical idealism to appreciate his admiration for the continental mode of statecraft. He equates its precautionary style with a keen sensitivity to the movement of history and to the attempt to channel it in a direction that supports the national interest.

In the next section, I will discuss Kissinger's views on the nature of international politics. I will consider his understanding of the relations that states have with each other, and particularly, the manner in which conflict and moral norms enter into these relations. Subsequent sections will examine Kissinger's ideas of world order and the role of statecraft.

The Nature of International Politics

Kissinger is associated with the approach to international politics known as realism. His writings on statecraft and the requirements of international stability are cited along with those of such theorists as George Kennan, Reinhold Niebuhr, and Hans Morgenthau as representing the realist school in America.[11] Similarly, his stewardship of American foreign policy during the Nixon administration is alternately described as "power realism" or "conservative realpolitik."[12]

Most realists share several major tenets in their approach to international politics. The realists regard conflict as an inherent feature of the state system. The enmity of international life arises from the fact that nations are egotistical—they place greater importance on their national interests than on international cooperation. For this reason, nations should plan for conflict as part of a prudent foreign policy. Because international politics is synonymous with conflict, the realists emphasize the integration of force and diplomacy, and they interpret the balance of power as the fundamental mechanism of world order. Nations act with restraint only as long as physical safeguards ensure that acting without it may result in severe punishment. This emphasis on the balance of power implies that individual nations are the primary units of organized social life, and that schemes of collective security and world government are ineffective. The realists see any political act as morally ambiguous. The moral categories of good and evil that apply to the individual lose their clarity when they are applied to the statesman since he is often confronted with sanctioning acts such as killing and deceit in order to safeguard his own nation. Because the statesman faces choices that involve the entire nation and its existence, the realists believe that he cannot be judged by the norms of an individualistic morality. In practice, realists tend to separate ethics from politics, and to judge the actions of national leaders with reference to national interests or history itself.

Although it is true that Kissinger's outlook parallels that of the realists, he consistently seeks to distinguish himself from the realist doctrines articulated by American theorists. A fundamentally different epistemological perspective separates him from the American realists.[13] As a philosophical idealist, Kissinger emphasizes a more subjective perception of reality. Man does not merely accept political reality, he can transform it. In contrast, the American realists stress the objective nature of facts and the need to adjust one's actions to objective reality—a view Kissinger emphatically rejects.

> The issue may therefore turn on a philosophical problem. . . . The overemphasis on "realism" and the definition of "reality" as being entirely outside the observer may produce a certain passivity and a tendency to adapt to circumstance rather than to master it. It may also produce a gross underestimation of the ability to change, indeed to create, reality. To recapture the ability and the willingness to build our own reality is perhaps our ultimate challenge.[14]

This difference in epistemology is of strongest effect in the area of diplomacy. Kissinger stresses the capacity of creative diplomacy to resolve conflicts and to subordinate the military balance to political purposes. He decries American thinkers for their "excessive realism," which he regards as "the chief obstacle to realizing the opportunities before the West."[15] He speaks of the need for American realists to develop "a more embracing concept of reality"[16] than that encompassed by their empiricist philosophy. He summarizes this view in a comment that epitomizes his opposition to the static nature of American realism: "there are two kinds of realists: those who use facts and those who create them. The West requires nothing so much as men able to create their own reality."[17]

Because of this key difference, I maintain that the term "continental" provides a more apt description of Kissinger's political outlook than "realism" does. Although Kissinger reaches many of the same conclusions as the realists do, he does so for significantly different reasons. The background of realism therefore provides a valuable means for discussing his political philosophy.

THE INTERNATIONAL SYSTEM

Kissinger and the realists both see domestic life and international society as distinctly different. As Hoffmann points out, domestic politics involves an integrated society—a community of shared values and purpose in which power is centralized in the state. In contrast, international politics presents a "decentralized milieu divided into separate units." Because there is no central power in the state system, each nation must rely on its own power to safeguard its values and interests, in fact, its very existence.[18]

Both Kissinger and the realists reject the schemes for world government offered by utopian theorists. Instead, they see states continuing to act as separate units, protecting their sovereignty within an international society characterized by the absence of a central authority.

The realists, however, associate the international system with a Hobbesian state of nature. As Hedley Bull explains, they see international society as a state of war, for there is "a disposition on the part of every state to war with every other state. Sovereign states, even while they are at peace, nevertheless display a disposition to go to war with one another, inasmuch as they prepare for war and treat war as one of the options open to them."[19] The quest for power in such a setting becomes an end in itself, obscuring the interests that it is intended to safeguard. Seyom Brown suggests that in a Hobbesian world, power becomes the state's central nervous system without which it cannot function. "Even survival itself," Brown writes, "is meaningless without power, for without it one is a mere vegetable for others to manipulate."[20] Morgenthau sums up the realist view when he notes that in international relations, "power is pitted against power for survival and supremacy."[21]

Kissinger's views on the nature of international society are more sanguine than those of his realist counterparts. They parallel those of the German historian Leopold von Ranke to such an extent that I believe they can correctly be termed "Rankean." Neither Kissinger nor Ranke subscribes to the "state of nature" theory that the realists draw upon from Hobbes, Locke, and Rousseau. Both Kissinger and Ranke see international politics as more than a meaningless clash of power—more than what Hobbes describes as an uninterrupted and purely destructive "war of all against all."

History provides the key to Ranke's and Kissinger's more positive views on the nature of international society. Although they agree with the realists that conflict characterizes the relations of states, they associate the very meaning of history with these relations. Nations are unique entities that shape and are shaped by the historical process. Although conflict is inherent in this process, it provides opportunities for creativity as well as tragedy. We find in Ranke's analysis of the historical process an accurate description of Kissinger's views:

> World history does not present such a chaotic tumult, warring, and planless succession of states and peoples as appears at first sight. . . . There are forces and indeed spiritual, life-giving, creative forces . . . and there are moral energies, whose development we see. . . . They unfold, capture the world, appear in manifold expressions, dispute with and check and overpower one another. In their interaction and succession, in their life, in their decline or rejuvenation, which then encompasses an ever greater fullness, higher importance, and wider extent, lies the secret of world history.[22]

Kissinger and Ranke interpret conflict in positive terms; Spengler, Toynbee, and the other German historicists also see international strife as a positive force. The very origin and development of nations are said to result from strife. Like Toynbee, Kissinger regards this kind of struggle as a response to challenges posed by the physical environment or other national groups. A nation develops and solidifies its sense of identity through conflict; the wars it fights provide a basis for its historical consciousness.

Ranke equates life with adversity. Adversity provides the proper environment for human achievement. The purpose of life is not to live well or live happily, but to live with dignity. Georg Iggers explains that "the rejection of 'happiness' as an end of life was common to the whole tradition of historicist thought from Humboldt and Ranke to Meinecke. 'Eudaemonism' became a pejorative term by which the German historians tried to dissociate their own idealistic position from most of English and French historical thought."[23]

Kissinger also rejects happiness as a national goal. He faults American theorists for not acknowledging that "most major historical changes have been brought about to a greater or lesser degree by the threat of force"[24]—or by force itself. He regards conflict (albeit not the total war that has marked the twentieth century) as a means of articulating a physical equilibrium or balance of power. To the extent that international order rests on this physical balance, limited war actually contributes to a more stable structure, for it clarifies the power relations among nations during different historical periods.[25]

THE ORIGIN OF CONFLICT

Both Kissinger and the realists see conflict as an integral part of international society, but they describe international society and the role of conflict in very different terms. Their explanations of the origin of conflict are also fundamentally different.

For the most part, the realists explain the origin of conflict among nations through what Kenneth Waltz calls "first image" reasoning.[26] Such reasoning takes man as the key for understanding the state system; since men make up nations, nations behave toward each other the way men do. The realists, almost without exception, regard human nature as being radically flawed by egotism and sinfulness. Man is as much inclined toward selfish acts and wrongdoing as toward good. The realists thus see the conflict that characterizes international life as an extension of the brutish behavior that characterizes individual men.

Kissinger, however, does not view politics through the prism of human nature. He rarely refers to human behavior either in accounting for conflict in international life or in explaining the moral norms of statecraft. Instead, nations themselves provide the source of international conflict.

Waltz characterizes such views as an explanation of the "second image."[27] In this approach, the internal characteristics of nations—their political systems or economic and social structures—account for their behavior. Issues of war or peace are largely determined by the relative homogeneity or heterogeneity of the domestic social structures of the nations in the international system.

Kissinger's "second image," however, differs in emphasis from Waltz's. Although he stresses that states provide the source of international conflict, he sees the nation primarily as a "historical expression" rather than as an empirical or sociological entity. A nation's social and economic institutions reflect a unique national character, formed by its historical experience. Positivist historians mistakenly equate its institutions with the nation itself and describe international conflict as the product of institutional differences. For Kissinger, it is the fact that nations are different entities—or more precisely, that they are conscious of their historical distinctiveness—that accounts for conflict among them. Why is this so?

According to Kissinger, international relations "present every nation with a fundamental dilemma: how to reconcile its vision of itself with the vision of it as seen by others."[28] A nation views its domestic values and institutions as the embodiment of all that is just. In international society, however, its values and customs cease to be absolutes. To other states, this same nation represents "an expression of will"—the personification of an ethos that may endanger their own societies.[29] International politics thus confronts every nation with a condition of profound insecurity—a condition nations instinctively abhor. Kissinger observes that "could a power achieve all it wishes, it would strive for absolute security, a world-order free from the consciousness of foreign danger and where all problems have the manageability of domestic issues."[30]

Nations, however, cannot attain this goal within the international system. Instead, a nation in international society must undergo a fundamental reconciliation. It must confront the limits of its physical power with respect to other states. More profoundly, it confronts the inherent limits of its cultural and social values in relation to those of other nations. For these reasons, Kissinger emphasizes that:

> The whole domestic effort of a people exhibits an effort to transform force into obligation by means of a consensus on the nature of justice. The more spontaneous the pattern of obligation, the more "natural"

and "universal" will social values appear. But the international experience of a people is a challenge to the universality of its notion of justice, for the stability of an international order depends on self-limitation, on the reconciliation of different versions of legitimacy. . . . Not for nothing do so many nations exhibit a powerful if subconscious rebellion against foreign policy, which leaves the travail of the soul inherent in arriving at decisions unrewarded, against this double standard which considers what is defined as "justice" domestically, merely an object for negotiation internationally.[31]

Kissinger thus regards the differences of historical character among nations as the primary source of international conflict. Even in a relatively stable and homogeneous international order, these differences make conflict inevitable—although such conflicts ideally will be limited in scope. Nations struggle to impose their values on the international order, or, at a minimum, to ensure that the international order is not inimical to those values. Metternich, for example, tried to ensure that the social and political order of nineteenth-century Europe did nothing to diminish the legitimacy of the polyglot Austrian state.

Conflicts, however, are not always limited in scope. At times, nations cannot reconcile their historical identities with the international order, but instead try to universalize their values. Conflict in such situations becomes total. Nations no longer contest values within an established order; they struggle over the nature of the order itself. This last point anticipates the distinction between what Kissinger terms "legitimate" and "revolutionary" states[32]—a distinction that I will explore later in this chapter.

MORALITY AND INTERNATIONAL POLITICS

Kissinger believes that no universal moral code can govern the relations among nations. He maintains that the very nature of international life—a milieu of disparate and ethically self-sufficient states—prevents the elaboration of such a code. Instead, the state system is characterized by contrasting ethical norms and definitions of justice that represent the different value systems of individual states.

What leads Kissinger to these conclusions? I believe that here too he draws on the German historicist tradition—a tradition whose ethical precepts are fundamentally different from those of Anglo-American political thought.

For Kissinger, as for the historicists, values such as "justice" and "truthfulness" arise within the state and reflect a specific national context. A nation's moral values reflect its unique character and historical development. In this respect, the state itself is "ethical," for it expresses not only physical power, but also a particular spirit or "ethos."

This outlook leads to the belief that moral norms are not transcendent. Since such norms do not originate in an element common to all nations (such as human nature), they represent national rather than universal standards. In fact, the historicists reject the Stoic-Christian doctrine of natural moral law, i.e., the doctrine of "a fairly uniform set of transcendental moral standards" that apply to all men.[33] I believe that Kissinger too rejects this idea.

Kissinger's historicist philosophy leads him to a moral relativism regarding the practice of international politics. He sums up this relativism when he notes that what any nation considers just domestically is "merely an object for negotiation internationally."[34] Nations cannot formulate their foreign policy in moral terms, because these terms have no universal reference or relevance.

Kissinger believes that the introduction of moral appeals into international relations often results in turmoil. "When one or more states claim universal applicability for their particular structure, schisms grow deep."[35] Similarly, he believes it is beyond the province of foreign policy to attempt to alter the domestic structures of another nation because its moral system is different or even reprehensible. A nation with such a moral system may be contested only to the extent that it poses a threat to international society. This outlook has significance for the manner in which Kissinger has consistently viewed U. S. policies toward the Soviet Union. I address this subject in chapters 6 and 7. Kissinger also maintains that nations may at times find it in their interest to ally themselves with nations that profess fundamentally different values. Peter Dickson points to such a practice in Kissinger's own diplomacy:

> a certain moral ambiguity was inherent in Kissinger's clever argument that the need to avoid total war justified his specific policies. He tolerated and even indulged adversaries and other nondemocratic regimes in the name of international stability.[36]

As Dickson notes, the moral relativism of Kissinger's diplomacy created considerable concern in America. The "apparent disjunction between ethics and politics in Kissinger's thought clashed sharply with American cultural traditions, which have long preserved . . . the notion that moral considerations can and should govern the relations among nations."[37]

Although much of Kissinger's thought in this area parallels that of the realists, there is one important difference. For the most part, the realists accept the relevance of natural moral law. They do so despite their emphasis on the evil behavior of man and their profession of *raison d'etat*. Hence, there is a conflict in realist thought between the interests of the state (which are the primary end of foreign policy) and the norms established by natural moral law. Scholars such as Reinhold Niebuhr and Arnold Wolfers must thus explain what Wolfers terms the "fundamental discrepancy . . . between the morality of state and private behavior."[38]

Kissinger rarely deals with this discrepancy. What Morgenthau describes as the "ethical paradoxes" of politics is missing from Kissinger's work, for his historicist beliefs never lead him to confront the gap between the morality of state and private behavior. In less able hands than Kissinger's own, such relativism may have disastrous consequences. In the absence of an accepted moral code, the moral behavior of the state may become merely the subjective interpretation of the statesman.

Are there no elements of transcendence that restrain the statesman? Does the international system present solely an anarchy of national values? As I discussed in chapter 1, Dickson believes that the key to Kissinger's philosophy lies in his juxtaposition of the terms "history" and "morality." This juxtaposition suggests that, for Kissinger, the ultimate determination of the morality of the statesman must be left to the judgment of history. It is history that provides transcendence in Kissinger's outlook—history that fills the void created by the rejection of natural moral law.

Although I believe Dickson is correct in alerting us to Kissinger's close association of the terms "history" and "morality," it is important that their connection be made explicit. History, for Kissinger, is not a transcendent force divorced from the actual facts of history and their interpretation. Dickson rightly observes that an appeal to the judgment of history is essentially an appeal to the moral judgment of later historians.[39] On what is this judgment to be based?

I believe that in Kissinger's view, the connection between history and morality lies in what the German scholar Max Weber defines as the "ethic of responsibility." This ethic signifies a nonperfectionist morality that maintains that although a political act may involve evil, as for example sanctioning killing in certain circumstances, the statesman must accept responsibility for his actions by attempting to limit the harmful or destructive consequences that can result from his decisions.[40] The judgment of history (or of future historians) is, for Kissinger, a judgment regarding the efforts of the statesman to minimize the destructive consequences of a political act.

For this reason, as Dickson points out, Kissinger places great importance on stability and survival, suggesting that these goals set limits on political activity. He characterizes the preservation of the interstate system and of human life as moral values.[41] Describing the moral responsibility of leaders, Kissinger states that "we should never give up our principles nor ask other nations to surrender theirs. But we must also realize that neither we nor our allies nor the uncommitted can realize any principles unless we survive."[42]

Stability and survival depend on the statesman's ability to establish and maintain world order. I have described the elements of international politics out of which such order must be shaped. In the next section, I will discuss Kissinger's understanding of the requirements of world order.

The Conditions of World Order

The question of world order concerned Kissinger from the beginning of his historical studies. That it continued to preoccupy him as a scholar and statesman is evident from his writings. Although his subjects range from Bismarckian statecraft to nuclear deterrence, his works contain recurring allusions to the need for "order," "stability," "structure," and "framework." In his own philosophy, marked by historical and moral relativism, Kissinger gives order an absolute value. It is for him the central value of international politics. "The greatest need of the . . . international system is an agreed concept of order. In its absence, . . . stability will prove elusive."[43]

The following story illustrates the importance that Kissinger attaches to order—so much importance that order clearly overrides moral norms when the two conflict. John Stoessinger, himself a theorist of international relations, pressed Kissinger on one occasion when both were students at Harvard to relate the requirements of global stability to moral and humanitarian concerns. Which has primary claim on the statesman's attention? Kissinger chose order without hesitation, indicating that a statesman must make this same choice. He supported his view by quoting Goethe: "If I had to choose between justice and disorder, on the one hand, and injustice and order, on the other, I would always choose the latter."[44]

Kissinger believes that order is the essential requirement for international politics. Without order, diplomacy cannot function, for there would be no basis for reconciling the "particular aspirations" of different nations.[45] Kissinger maintains that because diplomacy involves the use of persuasion rather than force, it presupposes order, or what he terms "a determinate framework."[46] When this framework is absent, it becomes impossible to persuade nations of the "reasonableness" of a diplomatic claim. In such circumstances, it is as if diplomats "have ceased to speak the same language."[47] Without an agreed upon concept of order, nations lose the ability to define a "reasonable" claim. Since diplomacy "cannot function in such an environment," nations must then resort to force.[48]

For these reasons, Kissinger views peace as a byproduct of order, rather than as an end in itself. Peace is not merely the absence of war; it has a positive content, viz., the conditions of order. If nations desire peace, they cannot seek it directly. Instead, they must focus their efforts on creating a stable structure of relations among nations. Kissinger regards it as ironic, but nevertheless instructive, that history was least peaceful during periods when leaders made peace their principal goal.

> Those ages which in retrospect seem most peaceful were least in search of peace. Those whose quest for it seems unending appear least able to achieve tranquility. Whenever peace—conceived as the avoidance of war—has been the primary objective of a power or group of powers, the international system has been at the mercy of the most ruthless member of the international community. Whenever the international order has acknowledged that certain principles could not be compromised even for the sake of peace, stability based on an equilibrium of forces was at least conceivable.[49]

Kissinger's concept of world order centers on two major conditions: the existence of a balance of power or (using the phrase he seems to prefer) an equilibrium of forces; and the acceptance of the international system by the major powers—an acceptance he terms "legitimacy." For the state system to be truly stable, both conditions must be present.

THE BALANCE OF POWER

Kissinger regards an equilibrium of forces as the minimal condition of international order. It provides order in international society in the same way that the centralization of power in the state gives order to domestic society. "The balance of power," Kissinger writes, "is the classic expression of the lesson of history that no order is safe without physical safeguards against aggression."[50]

The need for a balance of power arises from the nature of the international system. As discussed previously, the international realm is not an integrated society but a collection of very different states. Since the international system does not possess "the sanctions that prevail in domestic arrangements—courts and enforcement machinery,"[51] each nation must rely on its own power to safeguard its values and territorial sovereignty. "But," Kissinger cautions, "neither [is] power considered self-limiting; the experience of the conqueror had proved the opposite."[52] Drawing on the example of the Napoleonic wars, Kissinger stresses that because the international system requires each nation to rely on its own power, it is imperative that there be a balance of power among nations. This balance prevents the hegemony of one nation or group of nations in the state system.

Kissinger gives particular attention to the composition of the balance. He regards it as essential that a general equilibrium exists among the great states. Like many of the classical theorists, he views a balance among five states as the most stable.[53] Such a pentagonal balance produces the maximum amount of diplomatic flexibility, because every issue does not involve the survival of the other powers. Changes in the military balance can be offset by political realignments. "The guardians of the equilibrium of the nineteenth century," Kissinger observes, "were prepared to respond to change with counter adjustment."[54]

In addition to the general balance, Kissinger emphasizes what he calls the "particular" or "special" equilibrium. On this point, his views contrast with those of the classical theorists of the balance of power. The classical theorists, such as Comte d'Hauterive and Siour Favier, equate the *equilibres partiels* with the regional or local balances that existed in Europe and complemented the general European balance. The local balances in Italy, Germany, and the Baltic states are examples of these *equilibres partiels*.[55] For Kissinger, the particular equilibrium represents what today would be regarded as the "spheres of influence" of the great states. Within these spheres, each of the great states exercises a right to intervene in the affairs of lesser states.[56]

The significance of the particular equilibrium in Kissinger's work is twofold. First, it reveals his hierarchical conception of the state system; all power relations ultimately center on the great states.[57] The local balances among the weaker states are important in themselves, but, ultimately, their stability rests on the actions of the great states. Second, it indicates that he does not regard the balance of power as a mathematical equation. In contrast to those theorists of the balance who claim that it provides a precise distribution of power, Kissinger believes that the might of nations can never be calculated so exactly. Because nations are historical expressions rather than mere units in an equation, no balance—however perfectly established—will be stable if it is in conflict with the historical identities of the nations that comprise it. Kissinger's reflections on the balance of power reveal his historicist philosophy.

If the international order could be constructed with the clarity of a mathematical axiom, powers would consider themselves as factors in a balance and arrange their adjustments to achieve a perfect equilibrium between the forces of aggression and the forces of resistance. But an exact balance is impossible, and not only because of the difficulty of predicting the aggressor. It is chimerical, above all, because while powers may appear to outsiders as factors in a security arrangement, they appear domestically as expressions of a historical existence. No power will submit to a settlement, however well-balanced and however "secure," which seems totally to deny its vision of itself. No consideration of balance could induce Britain to surrender the maritime rights or Austria its German position, because their notion of "justice" was inseparable from those claims. There exist two kinds of equilibrium then: a general equilibrium which makes it risky for one power or group of powers to attempt to impose their will on the remainder; and a particular equilibrium which defines the historical relations of certain powers among each other.[58]

Kissinger shares this belief in the balance as more than a physical equation of power with Ranke. The latter expresses a highly "spiritualized" version of the European balance in his famous essay "The Great Powers," which emphasizes the élan of the major powers. Kissinger and Ranke both conceive of power primarily in terms other than its physical manifestation, including the rational form (doctrine) that shapes the manner in which power is employed and the national determination or will to employ power at all. Influenced by Spengler, Toynbee, and the historicist authors, Kissinger associates a nation's power with its morale or spiritual vitality—what Spengler refers to as a nation's "being in form."[59] In contrast, the realists approach power more empirically. For the most part, they equate a nation's power with the size of its armies and the number and destructive capacity of its weapons. Kissinger uses such historical events as Hannibal's victory over the Romans and the Napoleonic wars to refute this view. Physical power is never any greater than the strategic conception that informs it. Assessing power is not a mathematical exercise. The perception of a nation's leaders, the quality of its strategic doctrine, its psychological disposition to use power effectively—all these factors must be taken into account. Hence Kissinger's views on power lead him to refer to the balance of power as a psychological balance as much as a physical equilibrium.[60]

Kissinger's particular conception of power is linked to a positive view of the purpose of the balance of power. Other political theorists interpret the balance in negative terms; its major purpose is defined by what it prevents. Because a balance of power exists, no single nation can dominate the rest. In contrast, Kissinger sees the balance in more positive terms; it not only restrains would-be aggressor nations, but offers support for states that follow equilibrist policies. It is an often-overlooked corollary of the balance that a state that seeks to limit the power of other nations vis-à-vis itself likewise accepts its own power as limited with respect to other nations.

Several authors have called attention to the importance of "limits"—defined as the sense or realization by nations of their finiteness—in Kissinger's political thought.[61] This concern for limits arises from his historical studies, principally of Toynbee. Toynbee observes that the historical decline of nations can often be attributed to their loss of an inner sense of balance—to a sense of limits. This loss manifests itself in such forms as "suicidal militarism" or "the intoxication of victory," which cause a nation to overreach itself.[62] When Kissinger calls Castlereagh and Metternich "statesmen of the equilibrium,"[63] he offers a judgment not only about their political sagacity, but also about the historical soundness of their views.

In considering the effects of the balance of power, Kissinger stresses that it offers no absolute solution to the insecurity of the state system. Only partial and imperfect solutions are obtainable in the life of nations. No nation can transcend its condition of being one among many and therefore its security always depends in part on other nations. Nations can only achieve relative security through the balance of power. Most importantly, they must learn to accept this condition. "Absolute security for one power means absolute insecurity for all others,"[64] and it will thus never be sanctioned by other nations. Kissinger describes the fundamental condition of the state system as a paradox—the state system is most stable during periods when discontent with the conditions of stability is widely shared, although never to the point that any state renounces these conditions.

> Paradoxically, the generality of . . . dissatisfaction is a condition of stability, because were any one power "totally" satisfied, all others would have to be "totally" dissatisfied and a revolutionary situation would ensue. The foundation of a stable order is the "relative" security—and therefore the "relative" insecurity—of its members.[65]

Despite the importance he attaches to the balance of power, Kissinger regards it as a minimal condition of order. It is not in itself an adequate basis for order. To achieve such a basis, the balance must be transcended by political purpose. Kissinger regards the balance of power as inherently unstable and he supports his view with historical examples. Although he admires the statecraft of Bismarck, he faults the German leader for basing foreign policy solely on the balance of power. He labels Bismarck's statecraft as revolutionary, for the latter acted without any concern for ensuring that the international system was politically acceptable to the other major powers. Instead, the sole basis of order became the military equilibrium that Bismarck defined "not as harmony and mechanical balance but as a statistical balance of forces in flux."[66] Kissinger notes that "because of his magnificent grasp of nuances of power relationships, Bismarck saw in his philosophy a doctrine of self-limitation. . . . In the hands of others lacking his subtle touch, his methods led to the collapse of the nineteenth-century state system."[67]

Kissinger draws on his knowledge of the statecraft that preceded both world wars to offer his most conclusive statement regarding the balance of power and its relationship to international order:

> if a balance of power becomes an end in itself it becomes self-destructive. A country without strength will become the plaything of forces out of its control, but a country that makes its decisions only on military grounds will be dragged into adventures with consequences it cannot foresee. We have to learn from World War II, when a preponderance of strength in one country tempted it to attack, but we also have to learn from World War I, when a balance of strength produced a war because nobody got it under political control and put it in the service of foreign policy.[68]

What does Kissinger mean by subordinating the balance of power to political control? I believe the answer lies in what he refers to as the second condition of world order: international legitimacy.

INTERNATIONAL LEGITIMACY

In defining international legitimacy, Kissinger distinguishes it from legitimacy in a domestic society. Domestic authority derives its legitimacy from the fact that it both embodies and safeguards the traditions of the larger society. For example, in a democratic society, government institutions remain legitimate even though the public officials who run them change periodically. The institutions themselves reflect the society's view of a just order. But in international society, states have their own individual values that preclude a universal standard of justice. For this reason, Kissinger emphasizes that by legitimacy he means that the international order is accepted by the great states, not that it embodies shared values and traditions.

> "Legitimacy" . . . should not be confused with justice. It means no more than an international agreement about the nature of workable arrangements and about the permissible aims and methods of foreign policy. It implies the acceptance of the framework of the international order by all major powers, at least to the extent that no state is so dissatisfied that . . . it expresses its dissatisfaction in a revolutionary foreign policy.[69]

What causes a nation to accept the international order? Kissinger outlines three conditions for legitimacy. I have treated two of these in the previous section of this chapter. For a nation to regard the international order as legitimate, there must first be an equilibrium of power that guarantees its security. Second, the international order must not deny any major nation's vision of itself; no matter how exacting the general balance, it will prove inadequate if it is at odds with the historical aspirations of any one of the great states. Finally, the international order must be joined to what Kissinger calls a "legitimizing principle."

The legitimizing principle represents the prevailing values of the historical epoch—particularly its conception of how states should be organized. Kissinger, for example, describes the legitimizing principle of the nineteenth century as having changed from the dynastic conception of earlier periods to the modern emphasis on the nation. By the time of Versailles, no international order that did not recognize the racial and cultural unity of individual nation-states could be legitimate. It is in the name of the legitimizing principle that nations accept the arrangements of the international order. Hence, even though the international order does not manifest transcendent values such as justice, the values of the historical epoch do provide nations with a basis for a moral consensus. Kissinger writes that "it is the legitimizing principle which establishes the relative 'justice' of competing claims and the mode of their adjustment."[70]

Several features characterize a legitimate order. Foremost among these is the absence of fundamental schisms among the major powers. This is not to say that antagonisms do not exist, but they never call into question the basic order itself. "Wars may occur," Kissinger observes, "but they will be fought 'in the name of' the existing structure and the peace which follows will be justified as a better expression of the 'legitimate,' general consensus."[71] Furthermore, he states that it is only in a legitimate order that diplomacy can occur, for then a general framework exists that permits negotiators to decide among the relative interests of the different states.

Because this framework is taken for granted, relations among the great powers appear increasingly spontaneous. Issues do not involve self-conscious reflection about the general relations among states or the principles on which those relations are based. Rather, they concern only the specific matters being contested, and these are considered against the background of the principles of the legitimate order.

Kissinger suggests that "a legitimate order does not make conflicts impossible, but it limits their scope."[72] Because fundamental schisms do not exist, conflicts do not involve total war. When nations undertake total war, they seek to destroy the existing international structure and to render their enemies completely defenseless. In contrast, a limited war has specific political objectives, and these objectives can be reached—in fact, must be reached—within the existing structure. A nation waging limited war seeks to influence the enemy's will rather than to destroy his society. Limited wars are not small total wars, but political and psychological engagements. If total war eliminates the political element from conflict, limited war signifies its reintroduction.[73]

Similarly, the peace that follows a limited war is not punitive, but instead seeks to reestablish the equilibrium on which the legitimate order is based. Kissinger observes that it is the mark of a legitimate order that war is concluded by integrating the enemy into the established system. In the absence of a well-defined legitimacy, the totality of war generally leads to a retrospective peace that seeks to punish the defeated nation. Such a peace makes "a 'legitimate' settlement impossible, because the defeated nation, unless completely dismembered, will not accept its humiliation."[74]

A legitimate order also presents clear signs of political cooperation. I believe that this is what Kissinger means when he refers to transcending the physical balance in such a way that it is put in the service of political goals. Most theorists overlook this aspect of Kissinger's thought. In dealing with his conception of a legitimate order, they emphasize its minimalist political content. Legitimacy means no more than acceptance by the major powers. Kissinger associates this acceptance with a tangible agreement or mechanism that symbolizes the political collaboration of the major powers. The European concert system provided such a mechanism following the Napoleonic wars. This system involved the joint efforts of England, Austria, Prussia, Russia, and France to preserve the European social order and to forestall revolutionary challenges to the general equilibrium.[75]

THE REVOLUTIONARY CHALLENGE

It is part of the tragedy of human history that the conditions of stability are never permanent, and that the legitimate order must periodically face revolutionary challenges. In the most fundamental sense, the revolutionary challenge is a denial of limits. The revolutionary state universalizes its goals; it seeks to project its power and values without reference to other states. In contrast to the legitimate state, which accepts limits on its power and the particular application of its social values, the revolutionary state sees limits as a challenge to its existence. Kissinger points to the total nature of the revolutionary challenge when he quotes Metternich's personal assessment of the Napoleonic wars: "Napoleon and I spent years together as if at a game of chess; I to checkmate him, he to crush me together with the chess figures."[76]

A revolutionary challenge arises when one or more of the major powers rejects the existing international order and seeks to destroy it. Such was the challenge presented by Napoleon. The very fact of a revolutionary challenge calls into question the legitimacy of the international order. The relations among the major powers lose their spontaneity. "The essence of a revolutionary situation," Kissinger observes, "is its self-consciousness. . . . Principles in a revolutionary situation are so central that they are constantly talked about."[77] A sustained revolutionary challenge erodes the limits that characterize the legitimate order. Ultimately, legitimacy itself is destroyed, because the revolutionary power, when it is successful, overturns the physical safeguards and legitimizing principles of the previous system. Then diplomacy ends, for the central issue of a revolutionary period "is not adjustment of differences within a given system . . . but the system itself."[78] The revolutionary challenge replaces diplomacy with an arms race or total war.

Kissinger is mindful that social and economic changes give certain historical periods a revolutionary cast. But it is significant that he associates revolutionary challenges exclusively with the actions of one of the major powers. Once one power takes a position outside the accepted order, it transforms a legitimate system into a revolutionary one.

What factors cause nations to challenge the existing international order? Kissinger focuses on the revolutionary challenges posed by two states—Napoleonic France in the nineteenth century and the Soviet Union in the contemporary era. In both cases, ideology transformed the state domestically, making its existence incompatible with the other states in the international system. Both states sought to change the international order into one that was compatible with their own values— to make their domestic values into the basis for the legitimacy of a new order.[79] Kissinger is less clear regarding the origins of the transforming ideology. However, from his treatment it seems that he links these ideological changes as much to events in the international system as to the domestic circumstances of France and Russia.[80] He clearly takes this view regarding the revolutionary challenge posed by Hitler, associating it with the "retrospective" or punitive nature of the Treaty of Versailles.

For Kissinger, the revolutionary assumes the garb of two historical characters: the Conqueror (Napoleon) and the Prophet (Alexander).[81] Napoleon sought to overthrow the existing order by force, Alexander by a messianic religious appeal. Both claimed that they would replace it with a more perfect international society. Kissinger observes somewhat cynically:

Utopias are not achieved except by a process of levelling and dislocation which must erode all patterns of obligations. These are the two great symbols of the attacks on the legitimate order: the Conqueror and the Prophet, the quest for universality and for eternity, for the peace of impotence and the peace of bliss.[82]

The revolutionary state seeks to transform the existing order. Kissinger emphasizes the manner in which it accomplishes this transformation. The revolutionary state usually starts from a position of extreme weakness relative to the combined power of the other nations, yet it emerges as powerful enough to change existing patterns of military and political relationships. Kissinger stresses that the success of a revolutionary challenge results from two factors. First, the status quo mentality of the other powers keeps them from envisioning any unlimited challenge to the existing structure. In fact, they often mistakenly explain the revolutionary state's conduct as the sign of a specific grievance that can be resolved within the existing system. Second, the revolutionary state adopts a strategy of deliberate ambiguity; it presents each of its challenges as having only limited aims. In reality, of course, it seeks to smash the underlying structure of the international order.

An essential problem of statecraft is thus not only to defeat revolutionary challenges once they become explicit, but to forestall them. Kissinger notes, however, that the great powers have historically failed to meet either of these goals:

> history reveals a strange phenomenon. Time and again states appear which boldly proclaim that their purpose is to destroy the existing structure and to recast it completely. And time and again, the powers that are the declared victims stand by indifferent or inactive while the balance of power is overturned. . . . So it was when the French Revolution burst on an unbelieving Europe and when Hitler challenged the system of Versailles. So it has been with relations of the rest of the world toward the Soviet bloc.[83]

The final element of Kissinger's outlook on international politics concerns the role of statecraft. The leadership provided by great statesmen plays a prominent part in Kissinger's scheme because international order does not simply evolve by reason of an inner mechanism in the state system. Instead, order is established and maintained by the policies adopted by the leaders of the great states. These leaders must create order; they must also thwart revolutionary challenges to it.

The Role of Statecraft

The figure of the great leader dominates the historical landscape pictured in Kissinger's writings. The statesman is for Kissinger, as for

Spengler, "the center of action . . . history's commanding officer."[84] Part
of Kissinger's attraction to the Napoleonic era lies in its "dramatic contrast of personalities"[85] and the contrasting visions of order personified
by Napoleon (the revolutionary conqueror) and Metternich (the statesman). While American theorists emphasize "sociological" models of
shared decision making and policy formulation, Kissinger equates leadership with men of "marked individuality."[86]

Kissinger derives his views of the statesman and statecraft from his
study of such leaders as Metternich, Bismarck, and de Gaulle. In accordance with his historicist philosophy, he considers it essential to understand the statesman and his policies within the specific historical context
in which they are formed. Above all else, the statesman is a historical
character—a figure who lives in time, and whose understanding both
reflects and is limited by the era in which he exists. The statesman is also
part of a specific national culture that further defines the possibilities of
his leadership, including his understanding of the requirements of world
order. Kissinger observes that "not only geography and the availability of
resources trace the limits of statesmanship, but also the character of the
people and the nature of its historical experience."[87]

Kissinger's portrayal of the statesman embodies the historical and
philosophical themes that he explored in "The Meaning of History." His
views on leadership draw heavily on his idealist philosophy. The statesman's task is not merely to accept political reality but to shape and
transform it. Kissinger, for example, regards Bismarck's "insistence on
identifying his will with the meaning of events"[88] as a major factor in his
creative statecraft.

The statesman must also come to terms with the paradox of freedom
and necessity—a theme that dominates Kissinger's early work. In the
face of the limits imposed by his society and the inexorable development
of events, the statesman is compelled to act, to lead, to impart his vision
to his people. Even when he realizes that his efforts may end tragically,
the statesman must strive to shape events. Such was Metternich's fate
that he came to leadership at a time when the Austrian Empire had
become the lone remnant "of the great feudal structures of the medieval
period."[89] Metternich characterized his task as one of "shoring up decay-
ing buildings."[90] Kissinger, however, sees it as Metternich's failure that
he did not attempt to change the rigid social order of Austria. Instead,
Metternich settled for a manipulative diplomacy that enabled him to
master other leaders but not the fate of Austria. Because Metternich
settled for such a goal, he never achieved "the tragic stature he might
have, given the process in which he was involved."[91] Kissinger observes:

> Lacking in Metternich is the attribute which has enabled the spirit to
> transcend an impasse at so many crises of history: the ability to

contemplate an abyss, not with the detachment of a scientist, but as a challenge to overcome—or to perish in the process. . . . For men become myths, not by what they know, nor even by what they achieve, but by the tasks they set for themselves.[92]

The heroic picture of the statesman that emerges from Kissinger's works is mirrored in his description of the nature of statecraft. Choice is central to this description; in fact, Kissinger essentially equates statecraft with choice. He emphatically rejects the deterministic view that the statesman and his policies are products of vast impersonal forces. "A scholarship of social determinism," Kissinger observes, "has reduced the statesman to a lever on a machine called 'history,' to the agent of a fate he may dimly discern but which he accomplishes regardless of his will."[93] In contrast, Kissinger argues that the element of choice is inescapable in history. Great leaders usually confront great choices—choices that involve the survival of their nations. To some extent, their very greatness depends on these choices. In describing the statecraft of Castlereagh and Metternich, Kissinger emphasizes the central role of choice: "However self-evident the national interest may appear in retrospect, contemporaries were oppressed by the multiplicity of available policies, counselling contradictory courses of action."[94]

Choice, however, is not a "mathematical" exercise that considers every possible alternative. Kissinger regards the view that all alternatives have equal relevance as an illusion.[95] A nation's circumstances and historical experience mean that only some of these alternatives are politically acceptable. It is the statesman's task to recognize these, and, at times, to enlarge the nation's idea of what is politically acceptable.

Kissinger suggests that the statesman must often choose a course of action at the moment when he knows least about the immediate problem. The statesmen at Vienna, for example, did not fully understand the requirements of political and military stability in post-Napoleonic Europe nor its means of attainment at the time they decided Europe's fate. For these reasons, Kissinger defines the choice of the statesman as a "moral act," i.e., a choice derived not from objective facts about the available alternatives, but from the statesman's interpretation of events and his conception of the goals of his society.[96]

The elements of this "moral act" deserve closer study. The fact that the statesman must decide on policy in the absence of detailed knowledge is a central theme of Kissinger's writings. Paradoxically, he sees this situation not as an obstacle but as an ideal opportunity for creative statecraft. "When the scope for action is greatest, knowledge on which to base such action is small or ambiguous. When knowledge becomes available, the ability to affect events is usually at a minimum."[97]

Kissinger links the choice of the statesman to the act of "conjecture."

He defines conjecture as "the need to gear actions to an assessment that cannot be proved true when it is made,"[98] and he terms it a difficult and even tragic aspect of statecraft. I will discuss why he views it as tragic shortly. First, however, it is important to understand what conjecture entails. When Kissinger describes the statesman's decision-making role, he speaks at times of conjecture; on other occasions, he refers to the statesman's "intuition" or "vision of the future."[99] I believe that these concepts are synonymous in his thought. The statesman acts on the basis of his historical intuition or feel for the flow of history. It is because the statesman's "assessment" is intuitional and is not based on a calculus of facts that it cannot be proved true when made. Many of the German historicists also viewed intuition as an essential attribute of the great leader. Spengler characterizes it as the ability "to do the correct thing without 'knowing' it."[100] He writes:

> The born statesman is above all a valuer—a valuer of men, situations and things. He has the "eye" which unhesitatingly and inflexibly embraces the round of possibilities. . . . his talent is the very opposite of the man of theory. The secret pulse of all being is one and the same in him and in the things of history.[101]

The leader's conception of goals provides a second key element in Kissinger's description of the nature of statecraft. The statesman must articulate his nation's interests if he is to evoke the energies of his people. Just as importantly, he must remember that national goals that are badly conceived can lead to the destruction of his society. Graubard observes that beyond such elements as military and economic power, Kissinger links a nation's fate to one crucial factor—the quality of its political leadership. Although the state does not have a natural lifespan, its existence or decline depends on its leaders' conception of its national purpose.[102]

It is significant that Kissinger links the conception of national interest with the requirements of world order. For the major powers, the two are inseparable. Hence, the statesman's conception of national goals is rooted in a larger conception of world order—a conception concerning the international balance of power and the nature of the legitimacy that will enhance all the nations' interests.

Kissinger associates the conceptual element of statecraft with the statesman's creativity. National policy is primarily creative rather than consensual. Kissinger underscores this point by writing that truly "profound policy thrives on perpetual creation, on a constant redefinition of goals."[103] For him, the great statesman is a figure such as Bismarck—a man who breaks a mold or transcends the existing framework and creates a new pattern. The statesman does not so much solicit a consensus as provide the conceptual and moral basis on which a consensus can be built. The mark of his creativity is that he establishes the political framework within which the relations among states occur, rather than simply working within the existing framework. It is on this point that Kissinger faults Metternich. His leadership had a kind of sterility, because it consisted merely in the technical mastery of diplomatic practices. It was not creative or visionary. Evaluating Metternich's accomplishments, Kissinger writes: "Whenever Metternich operated within a fixed framework, when an alliance had to be constructed or a settlement negotiated, his conduct was masterly. Whenever he was forced to create his own objectives, there was about him an aura of futility."[104]

Because of the importance of creativity, Kissinger describes statecraft as a form of art. He refers to such statesmen as Bismarck and de Gaulle as having artistic sensibilities. Mastery depends on proportion and form, nuance and subtlety.

The artistry of statecraft finds expression in the practice of diplomacy. Beyond conceptualizing national policies, the statesman must see that they are embodied in practical measures. This involves political struggle, for it is not a given that other nations, or even his own, will accept his definition of the future. For this reason, the statesman must rely on his own political acumen and dialectical skills. Kissinger notes that "it is not sufficient to judge the statesman by his conceptions alone, for unlike the philosopher he must implement his vision."[105]

The problem of implementation confronts the statesman in both the international and domestic arenas. Internationally, the statesman must reconcile his vision of world order with the perceptions of the leaders of other nations. This is not a mechanical task, because nations disagree on the requirements of order and even on its very definition. A state's perception of its national security and the international order will depend on its relative power and geographical position, the quality of its leadership groups and government structure, and, most importantly, its historical beliefs and experience. Because nations are different, the perceptions of their leaders vary considerably. Even in a relatively homogeneous state system, the statesman faces obstacles in implementing his vision of world order. When the domestic social structures and ideologies of nations differ markedly, the task of implementation becomes almost impossible.

The acid test of policy, as Kissinger defines it, is obtaining domestic support. Here the statesman encounters the most obdurate resistance. Kissinger does not find it surprising that statesmen are most often opposed by their own people: "It was no accident, even if it was paradoxical, that in 1821 Metternich had greater difficulty with the Austrian than with the Russian ministers, and that in every negotiation Castlereagh had to fight a more desperate battle with his cabinet than with his foreign colleagues."[106]

Kissinger identifies two sources for this kind of domestic resistance: the governmental apparatus or bureaucracy and the national experience. The domestic bureaucracy is geared to executing existing policies. Its function is administration—the technical application of policy to concrete circumstances. Bureaucracy thrives on the routine performance of clearly defined tasks. It will therefore resist the changes introduced by creative statecraft. Because the statesman acts to transcend existing policy, he will encounter opposition from governmental administrators whose functions are linked to this policy.

The experience of the nation may also be at odds with the statesman's policies. It is difficult for a nation to accept the legitimacy of an international order that appears to supersede its own domestic values. The vision of the statesman must nevertheless be harmonized with the national experience. Kissinger regards this as part of the historical development of the nation. Until the statesman's vision becomes part of the national experience, he is regarded as an alarmist and is often excluded from leadership. Churchill and de Gaulle provide examples of the fate of leaders who go beyond the experience of their people.

> The statesman is therefore like one of the heroes in classical drama who has a vision of the future but who cannot transmit it directly to his fellow-men and who cannot validate its "truth." Nations learn only by experience; they "know" only when it is too late to act. But statesmen must act as if their intuition were already experience, as if their aspiration were truth. It is for this reason that statesmen often share the fate of prophets, that they are without honor in their own country, that they always have a difficult task in legitimizing their programs domestically, and that their greatness is usually apparent only in retrospect when their intuition has become experience.[107]

The fact that statesmen are rarely understood by their contemporaries provides what Kissinger describes as the tragic aspect of conjecture. The great leader can never prove his vision. Even if his words are heeded and his policies followed, he cannot prove that they prevented disaster.

In the face of domestic opposition, the statesman must educate his people to a broader conception of world order. Kissinger shares this perception with Spengler who also views the statesman as an educator.[108] Kissinger's studies of such leaders as de Gaulle and Adenauer emphasize that one of their principal roles involved teaching their people. "The statesman must . . . be an educator; he must bridge the gap between a people's experience and his vision, between a nation's tradi-tion and its future."[109] Leaders who fail in this role, e.g., Castlereagh and Wilson, fail to secure domestic approval of their policies because the people cannot comprehend them. Conversely, leaders who do not tran-scend the national experience, e.g., Metternich and most of America's leaders in the postwar era, also fail, because they condemn their nations to sterility in the face of historical change.

There are other aspects of statecraft that Kissinger regards as signifi-cant. The statesman must understand the "real relationship of forces and . . . make this knowledge serve his ends."[110] He must appreciate the nature of the environment (i.e., the real relationship of historical forces) and the historical epoch in which he finds himself. Is it a legitimate or revolutionary order? Are nations relatively satisfied with existing ar-rangements or is there a power that views the structure as a prison that it seeks to destroy? Unless the statesman answers these questions cor-rectly, his leadership will fail. Applying the diplomacy suited for a legitimate and stable period during an era of revolutionary change is a mistake filled with peril.

Finally, the great leader must institutionalize his vision. To ensure that his approach to international relations becomes the nation's approach, he must inspire a tradition. As Spengler observes, the act of statecraft involves creating a tradition "to bring on others so that one's work may be continued with one's pulse and spirit, to release a current of like activity that does not need the original leader to maintain it in form."[111] Kissinger associates a tradition with a group of followers who them-selves occupy or aspire to occupy influential foreign policy positions and who share certain elements of the statesman's doctrine. He writes that "one of the crucial challenges confronting a society is therefore the capacity to produce a leadership group capable of transcending the experience of that society."[112]

Kissinger indicates that the great leader is rare. Societies should con-sider themselves fortunate if such a figure appears once in several generations. Although Kissinger focuses on the great leader, he clearly recognizes that "mediocrity is the usual pattern of leadership."[113] Given the prevalence of mediocrity, it becomes essential that the great states-man instill his vision in those who succeed him. History will judge his success accordingly.

For Kissinger, the statesman is history's most prominent figure. His vision of order is crucial to international society; his leadership is equally crucial to his own society. He is immersed in an endless process that offers no respite. "The tides of history take no account of the fatigue of the helmsman. Posterity will reward not the difficulty of the challenge, only the adequacy of the response."[114] Only a dramatist could fully narrate the dimensions of the task that Kissinger sets for the great leader; only a poet could evoke the statesman's tragic stature.[115]

Henry Kissinger completed his doctoral program in 1954. He had spent the previous seven years in an intense, almost reclusive, study of history and philosophy. His education gave him the degrees needed to pursue an academic career. More significantly, the studies that culminated in "The Meaning of History" and A World Restored provided him with an intellectual orientation that distinguishes his thought and an idiom in which he continues to express himself today. It is important to recognize the impact of these two works, for they shaped his outlook toward the contemporary world and America's role in it.

Kissinger remained at Harvard for almost fifteen years, leaving it to enter the Nixon administration in 1969 as national security adviser. During this period, (with the exception of two years, from 1955 to 1957, which he spent working for the Council on Foreign Relations), he devoted himself to teaching and writing. He wrote and edited approximately forty articles and five books during this time. In sum, they contain a pervasive criticism of American foreign policy. At the center of this criticism is the theme of insularity that he used in A World Restored to characterize England's outlook on international relations. America, Kissinger believed, was as much an insular power in the contemporary period as England had been in the nineteenth century.

Then, as now, the leadership of each nation faced crucial decisions. Following the Napoleonic wars, it was Castlereagh's challenge to transcend the historical experience of his island nation. England had traditionally remained aloof from continental affairs—limiting its involvement to those occasions when the military balance was threatened. Kissinger regards it as Castlereagh's greatest accomplishment that he grew beyond the strictly English mentality. In deciding the fate of Europe at the Congress of Vienna, he "made his decision from the European, not from the insular, point of view."[116] That the English people never fully understood Castlereagh's vision only increased his heroic stature in Kissinger's eyes.

America faced the need for a similar act of transcendence in the modern period. Kissinger came of age intellectually at the same time that America was thrust into the role of world leadership. The decade following World War II was a period of transition. Kissinger believed that America's leadership was at a crossroads in the nation's historical experience—a crossroads no less momentous than that which Castlereagh faced. His writings aim at nothing less than exhorting the nation to transcend its historical experience—to break with the insular patterns that characterize American foreign policy.

In the pages that follow, I shall examine Kissinger's critique of the

American approach. I shall take the fact that he equates insularity with a national mentality as my starting point. Beyond the failures of specific policies or presidential administrations, Kissinger is concerned with a basic attitude that shapes the nation's thinking.[117] He sees the nation's insular mentality as the source of specific failures of leadership as well as failures of its political and military doctrine. I will address these failures in subsequent chapters.

PART 2
The American Approach to Foreign Policy

The Insular Approach of American Foreign Policy

The Haunted Decade

WE Americans recall the 1950s with ambivalence. The period evokes nostalgia for a time when life seemed simpler. Most Americans then were preoccupied with personal concerns. Values were widely shared, and social life provided a sense of permanence. Communities were relatively stable; it was not uncommon for several generations of a family to come from the same town or city. America had yet to be engulfed by the explosion of technology and the changes in communication and transportation that since then have so altered our lives.

A broad consensus supporting the nation's foreign policy accompanied these domestic conditions. It was a mark of the era that American leaders asked for and received bipartisan support for their foreign policy initiatives. Critics of the nation's diplomatic and military responses to the cold war focused on questions of method and style. The basic goal of American policy—the containment of Communism—remained unchallenged throughout the period.

In the truest sense, the 1950s was the decade before the deluge. The sixties and seventies fundamentally changed the nation's social existence. The civil rights movement and the protests of students and counterculture groups questioned many of the basic premises of our domestic society. The war in Vietnam compounded the turmoil of these years. Because we saw our involvement in Southeast Asia as an outgrowth of the nation's post–World War II policy of containment, this period marked the end of the general consensus concerning America's role in international politics. Beyond these political challenges, the sixties and seventies also witnessed profound demographic and technological changes.

Yet if Americans look back to the fifties with a sense of nostalgia, we also remember the decade as an era of complacency. Not all Americans were comfortable with the surface normalcy of the period. John Ken-

nedy's success in the pivotal election of 1960 lay in capturing this underlying mood of dissatisfaction with what was viewed as the economic and
military stagnation of the Eisenhower era. The nation, Kennedy argued,
was not only falling behind the Soviet Union in its global rivalry, it was
also failing to meet its own economic and social goals.

The ambivalence we now feel toward the 1950s mirrors an attitude that
was widely shared even then. The political commentator I. F. Stone
characterized the decade as the "haunted fifties."[1] Americans in this
period, however, were haunted by their future rather than the past. We
feared the changes that were occurring in the country—indeed, that had
to occur if we were to surmount the challenges presented by our global
responsibilities.

Thus, underlying the normalcy of what Eric Goldman termed the
"Eisenhower equilibrium"[2] was a general intuition that the nation was
embarking on a new era. Cracks began to appear in the surface of
American society—cracks that became the major fault lines of the next
decade. Issues involving racial equality and integration, the dissent of
American youth, and the role of government—particularly in the nation's economy—moved to the forefront. In the international realm,
America debated its support for the policies of the Truman era, especially its centerpiece of containment. Support for these policies would
symbolize the nation's commitment to playing a major role in international politics, and these policies involved a sharp break with the past.
The nation's responses to these issues continue to shape our domestic
and international policies today.

The Kissinger Critique

The fifties were also a crucial period for Henry Kissinger. Although his
earliest works concerned nineteenth-century cabinet diplomacy, he
wrote them with an eye for the issues that America was facing in the
contemporary age. The way in which the nation's leaders addressed
these issues provided the focus for Kissinger's criticism of American
foreign policy.

Kissinger believed that America's approach to foreign policy was seriously flawed.[3] This became especially significant in the post–World
War II era. Until that time, Europe had been the focal point of international politics. America's influence had been primarily economic. The
war, however, devastated European society and thrust America into a
position of world leadership. In Kissinger's view, the nation's approach
to foreign policy impaired its ability to provide this leadership. Emphasizing this idea, Kissinger wrote, "America has reached a turning point

in its relations with the rest of the world. The patterns of action of a secure past no longer work. . . . Whatever aspect of American foreign policy we consider, the need for new departures is apparent."[4]

Kissinger's criticism is fundamental. Although he advances his argument by referring to specific policies, such as the doctrine of massive retaliation, his purpose goes much further. He seeks to demonstrate that an underlying mentality accounts for the individual failures of American foreign policy. This mentality is actually a group of attitudes that shape the way the nation's leaders view international politics and the way they define national security. It is derived principally from the nation's historical experience, although it is also influenced by geography and culture. Because America is an island nation with respect to Eurasia, much like England is in relation to the European continent and Carthage was to Rome, Kissinger characterizes the American approach to foreign policy as insular.

Three initial points stand out about this characterization. First, Kissinger's emphasis on a national mentality to explain the patterns of American foreign policy illustrates his training as a historian. The scholars who most influenced him—Spengler, Toynbee, and the German historicists—all emphasized the concept of a unique national or civilizational character. In contrast to contemporary social scientists who regard the idea of national character as an unverifiable generalization,[5] historians tend to rely on this concept to differentiate nations. Moreover, some historians (and this is true of Kissinger) tend to regard national character as relatively immutable. They portray it as a distinct identity that remains fixed rather than as a set of national traits that change with shifts in the composition of the nation's society. Kissinger, however, is only interested in the American character insofar as it affects the practice of foreign policy.

Second, Kissinger writes about America's mentality and its insular foreign policy with the same detachment that marks the observations of such European students of America as de Tocqueville, Lord Bryce, and D. W. Brogan.[6] In this sense, he writes as an outsider. Although he often uses the term "we" when discussing the American approach to foreign policy, those familiar with his works and the nature of his critique might find this choice of pronoun incongruous, if not forced.

Third, Kissinger's characterization of America as insular is as much a disparagement of its views as it is a description of its geography. He portrays the nation's outlook on history and international politics as parochial and inward-looking. When he compares American statesmen to their European counterparts, he finds the former narrow in outlook and ill-prepared to exercise diplomatic leadership.

What does Kissinger mean by American insularity? It is important to realize that Kissinger is not repeating the customary criticism of America's "isolationist impulse."[7] His articles and texts were written a decade after the Truman Doctrine and the Marshall Plan were propagated, and several years after the Korean War and the formulation of NSC–68, which extended the perimeters of America's containment strategy. Because of these changes, Kissinger believed that America could never again isolate itself from the rest of the world—even though this desire remained strong and expressed itself in the 1950s in the Taft wing of the Republican party.

Instead, Kissinger emphasizes the manner in which America views both itself and the nature of international politics. He links insularity with a group of attitudes that give America a sense of "apartness" and historical "aloofness."[8] Changes in political alignment and weapons technology in the postwar era had forced the nation into the international community. According to Kissinger, America held onto a perception of separateness long after the geographic conditions of its apartness had passed. Similarly, it preserved a sense that it could transcend history—that it was different from other nations and was therefore not subject to the same historical processes that affected those states.

Kissinger attributes the failures of America's foreign and military policies to its insularity. These failures involve a reactive and "defensive conception of foreign policy."[9] Instead of formulating positive objectives, the nation defines its goals in negative terms. During the period in which Kissinger developed his criticism, America focused on limiting Soviet advances and preventing upheavals in Third World countries, rather than elaborating its own vision of world order. Because the nation possesses neither a defined policy nor a clear view of what it seeks to accomplish, its leaders normally wait for events to unfold so they can be sure they possess all the facts before they act. But, Kissinger argues, "by the time the facts are in, a crisis has usually developed or an opportunity has passed."[10] He identifies the major weakness of the nation's defensive and reactive approach: "Our policy . . . is geared to dealing with emergencies; it finds difficulty in developing the long-range program that might forestall them."[11]

Looking at the years immediately following World War II, Kissinger identifies an initial period of diplomatic creativity. American foreign policy during this era combined aspects of both its idealistic and pragmatic traditions, but it was at this time, according to Kissinger, that the nation had been most effective internationally.[12] He observes:

> When Dean Acheson said he was "present at the creation," he referred not only to the creation of our postwar foreign policy but to a new era in our own history. After two world wars in this century, the respon-

sibilities and burdens of world leadership proved inescapable. The United States had despite itself become the guardian of the new equilibrium. It is to the lasting credit of that generation of Americans that they assumed these responsibilities with energy, imagination, and skill. By helping Europe rebuild, encouraging European unity, shaping institutions of economic cooperation, and extending the protection of our alliances, they saved the possibilities of freedom. This burst of creativity is one of the glorious moments of American history.[13]

But Kissinger sees this creativity as having been short-lived. The challenges of this era were clear and of the kind that evoked the all-out response characteristic of Americans. Kissinger states that when the United States engaged in permanent peacetime diplomacy for the first time after 1945, "it did so under conditions that seemed to confirm [its] expectations."[14] The programs it fostered, such as the Marshall Plan and Point Four, "expressed our idealism, our technological know-how, and our ability to overwhelm problems with resources."[15] To some extent, America was projecting its own New Deal programs into the international arena, "expecting political conflict to dissolve in economic progress."[16] Moreover, America could still act unilaterally as it had in previous periods of isolation. The fact that it was the sole possessor of atomic weapons and that it produced nearly half of the world's gross national product meant that the United States was relatively free from the constraints that limited other nations.

Kissinger believed that this enthusiasm was bound to wane when problems became more complex and their solutions more ambiguous. Even during the creative stages of the postwar era, the country appeared to be psychologically unprepared to deal with protracted problems. As America's military and economic preponderance declined relative to other nations, it would no longer be able to indulge its penchant for total solutions. The nuclear age would also force the nation to give up the idea that its security could be absolute. These were the most profound implications of the period.

In offering these views, Kissinger returns to themes he developed in his historical studies. For the first time in its history, America confronted the necessity of limits. Its historical experience had not prepared it to live with this necessity. For most of its history, America had been free to develop its society and expand its territory without external challenges or restraints. In this setting, the nation developed a sense that its cultural values were superior to those of other countries and that its way of life had universal relevance. This notion is what is meant by the phrase "American Exceptionalism."[17]

Now, however, the nation would have to acknowledge that both its physical power and its social values were limited. For the first time, America would have to practice foreign policy like other nations—mindful of its own finiteness and of the fact that its choices of policies could have tragic consequences. Henceforth, it would also have to define its security in relative terms with respect to the Soviet Union, and to appreciate the significance of even marginal changes in the military balance.

America's conversion to a new foreign policy tradition would be a wrenching experience for the nation—one that contradicted its domestic experience. Part of the problem was that the need to transcend its insularity occurred at the very moment when it exercised unparalleled military and political influence in the world. Hence, its very achievements obscured its postwar challenges. Kissinger portrays this situation in Toynbeesque terms: the nation, having achieved great power, is content to "rest on its oars."[18]

The fact that America never adequately transcended its insular approach during this period represented a major failure of leadership. Kissinger believes that both the Truman and Eisenhower administrations formulated policies that perpetuated America's traditional outlook. Even the initially creative policies of the period had been justified on the grounds that they would eventually end the nation's involvement in foreign affairs. Similarly, the central doctrine of containment was offered to the American people as having a terminal point; political accommodation with the communist bloc would follow the military phase of containment. American foreign policy, observed some commentators during this period, amounted to "an attempt to make the world safe for American retreat from it."[19] In this vein, Kissinger writes that:

> our initiatives were explicitly justified as temporary measures to restore an underlying equilibrium. The Marshall Plan, our alliance commitments overseas, our international economic programs, were all conceived as dealing with temporary emergencies which once overcome would excuse us from permanent direct involvement abroad.[20]

To understand the nature of Kissinger's criticism, we must appreciate the factors that he believes led to America's outlook. The causes of American insularity and the specific attitudes they engendered are the subject of the next section.

The Sources of American Conduct

In his writings during the 1950s, Kissinger identified three major sources of America's insularity and the subsequent failure of its foreign policy. Characteristically, he singled out the nation's history—its autonomous development with little involvement in foreign affairs—as the primary source of its insular approach. The historical facts of the nation's development are not as important to Kissinger as the manner in which America interpreted its history. The philosophical basis of American society and culture provides a second factor responsible for its insular outlook. Kissinger emphasizes the relationship between the nation's views of reality (i.e., its dominant epistemological and metaphysical traditions) and the way these views shape societal institutions, including the practice of foreign policy. The third cause of American insularity is its geographic location. I will begin my analysis by taking up this element because it is the most tangible aspect of Kissinger's critique.

THE ISLAND POWER

In explaining the importance of geography in the nation's thinking—particularly with respect to the manner in which America defines its security—Kissinger draws heavily on the analogy to England that he develops in *A World Restored*. Most Englishmen have felt relatively immune historically from the military threats and the social and political upheavals that frequently embroiled other European states. While the English Channel gave the nation a sense of geographical remoteness, its navy fostered a sense of physical unassailability. This perception remained true until the early decades of this century, when the growth of German naval power challenged Britain's defense strategy.

Geography, Kissinger states, allowed England a condition of free security.[21] By this he means that it did not have to purchase its territorial security through constant vigilance and intervention in European affairs. Unlike the nations on the European continent, England's security only became endangered at the end of a long series of upheavals in which one nation began to dominate the continent. Such was the pattern with both Napoleon and Hitler. The Channel provided English leaders a natural barrier "behind which to assess developing events and across which to intervene at the moment of maximum advantage."[22]

England based its foreign policy on its conception of itself as an island power. It was a cardinal rule of English policy that it intervened in European affairs solely to defend against the "outward projection" or "forcible extension" of a hegemonic power across the Channel.[23] This policy explained England's classical role as the "balancer" in the European equation; it acted to prevent any country from achieving hegemony on the continent. Furthermore, England defined the European equilibrium as a mechanical equation of power, that is, a military balance among several nations. Kissinger considers this blindness to the link between the military equilibrium and its social and political legitimacy to be characteristic of an island power, an outsider.[24]

Kissinger sees America's outlook in the twentieth century as similar to that of England in previous eras. Historically, America's security had been linked to the safety afforded by two oceans. Like the English Channel, these oceans provided America with a sense of remoteness and distance that allowed it to assess developing events and gradually formulate a policy in response. This was especially true of the periods prior to America's entry into World Wars I and II; in both cases, the nation spent several years planning its participation. Like England, which acted only as a "balancer," America saw its purpose in both world wars as defeating the "outward projection" of European and Asian challenges. These attitudes meant that the nation only acted when a threat was a clear danger to the nation's security. As a result, the nation found itself ill-equipped to react to ambiguous challenges and unable to discern marginal transformations of the overall balance of power.

Kissinger believes that such attitudes are particularly unsuited to the contemporary era. Geography itself is no longer the significant factor it has been in the past. America became a world power during World War II—a conflict in which the importance of strategic air power was clearly demonstrated. The development of long-range missiles in the 1950s eliminated whatever was left of the safety net of geography. Now, America's security with respect to the Soviet Union would be involved at the very outset of any confrontation—not after a long series of upheavals. Moreover, the nature of nuclear weapons altered the relationship between territory and war. As John Herz points out, the destructiveness of atomic weapons and the speed of delivery systems eliminated the traditional meaning of territoriality, or what he terms the "hard shell" of nations.[25]

Kissinger argues that these strategic changes should have produced concomitant changes in our conception of national security. It could be expected that as the nature of war in the nuclear era became clearer and as our own safety became more imperiled, inhibitions about using strategic weapons would increase. It was also likely that nuclear stalemate would lead to diffuse forms of conventional military challenges. Kissinger observes that "the age of the hydrogen bomb is also the age of internal subversion, of intervention by 'volunteers,' of domination through political and psychological warfare."[26] America, however, did not respond to these new conditions.

Instead of developing the doctrines that would allow it to use power subtly and with discrimination, America clung to an insular conception of national security. Kissinger stresses that America has failed to devise an effective strategy for dealing with the "ambiguous" challenges of the modern era:

In determining what transformations to resist, our strategic doctrine has been inhibited, however, by the seeming lessons of our history. We have confused the security conferred by two great oceans with the normal pattern of international relations; we have overlooked that concepts of aggression developed in a period of relative safety may become dangerously inadequate in the face of a new type of challenge. A power favored by geography or by a great material superiority, as we have been through most of our history, can afford to let a threat take unambiguous shape before it engages in war. . . . And because many other states had to be attacked long before the threat to our security became apparent, we could always be certain that some powers would bear the brunt of the first battles and hold a line while we mobilized our resources. Thus we came to develop a doctrine of aggression so purist and abstract that it absolved our statesmen from the necessity of making decisions in ambiguous situations and of concerning themselves with the minutiae of day-to-day diplomacy.[27]

Kissinger labels American military thought in the 1950s as the "Esoteric Strategy,"[28] underscoring its lack of clarity. His criticism of America's military doctrine and the patterns of thought underlying it will be the subject of a later chapter.

AMERICA'S HISTORICAL ALOOFNESS

More than any other factor, a nation's historical tradition provides the formative influence on its leadership groups. Kissinger characterizes America as a "historically aloof" country—a phrase striking for both its directness and its ambiguity. How is it possible for a nation to be truly aloof from history? In actuality, it cannot; this circumstance, Kissinger believes, accounts for America's disillusionment in the modern period. The nation's historical experience, however, continues to encourage the belief that it can either dominate or escape history.

Kissinger describes two facets of America's aloofness. First, he equates it with the belief that the patterns of America's domestic historical experiences can be applied to international life. This assumption affects the nation's understanding of international politics, the role of power and conflict among nations, and the purposes of diplomacy. I will address each of these elements shortly.

A second facet of America's aloofness involves its belief in its superiority, especially in contrast to European nations. This "exceptionalism" has many components. Kissinger emphasizes that it has left the nation with a sense of omnipotence, i.e., with a belief that it is not constrained by the limits that apply to other countries. He underscores this point by calling attention to the nation's indifference to the role of tragedy in history. From his historical studies of Spengler and Toynbee—particularly their writings on civilizational breakdown—Kissinger concludes that national power is finite. He observes that every civilization that has existed ultimately declined. Often, this decline is precipitated by a great national tragedy. The realization of its own mortality, however, is not part of America's outlook:

> Another factor shaping our attitude toward foreign affairs is our lack of tragic experience. Though we have known severe hardships, our history has been notably free of disaster. Indeed, the American domestic experience exhibits an unparalleled success, of great daring rewarded and of great obstacles overcome. [American leaders] simply cannot believe that in the nuclear age the penalty for miscalculation may be national catastrophe. They may know in their heads, but they cannot accept in their hearts, that the society they helped to build could disappear as did Rome or Carthage or Byzantium, which probably seemed as eternal to their citizens. These characteristics make for an absence of a sense of urgency, a tendency to believe that everything can be tried once and that the worst consequence mistakes can have is that we may be forced to redouble our efforts later on. The irrevocable error is not yet part of the American experience.[29]

America's historical aloofness is rooted in its actual historical experiences. Kissinger acknowledges that America's origin is fundamentally different from that of other nations. At a specific moment in time, the nation "was created as a conscious act of men dedicated to a set of political and ethical principles they believed to be of universal applicability."[30] Further, Kissinger observes, the American federal union was constructed from states similar in size, cultural background, and language; these entities shared a common historical experience and "had no tradition of sovereignty in the conduct of foreign relations."[31] America's roots thus differ markedly from other nations'—particularly those of Europe. There, distinct nations were formed as a result of centuries of historical evolution. Cultural and linguistic differences were pronounced. More significantly, each nation regarded its own history as the major source of its national identity.[32]

America's development also contributed to its historical aloofness. Kissinger observes that from Waterloo to 1914, two oceans and the English navy shielded the United States from involvement in international affairs.[33] For most of the nineteenth century, the nation was preoccupied with its domestic growth. America's continental expansion increased its autonomy from the state system; its domestic experiences not only absorbed its energies, they also provided a model of what could be accomplished by unfettered national effort.

Kissinger stresses that the manner in which the nation's historical experiences became part of its consciousness accounts for its insular foreign policy. America's own development from a harmonious union of states, as well as its political and ethical principles, foster the belief that a natural amity among nations characterizes international life. In the American tradition, "peace is the 'normal' pattern of relations among states," and peace "is equivalent to consciousness of harmony."[34] Because of this dominant outlook, Americans came to believe that conflict among nations must result from factors extrinsic to the state system. "Crises," to quote Kissinger, "must therefore be caused by personal ill-will rather than by objective conditions."[35]

America's belief in the universal relevance of its own democratic values caused it to repudiate the dynastic rivalries of Europe. Americans profess a Wilsonian faith that as states become more democratic, the natural amity of the international system will be enhanced. Citizens will curb the impulsiveness of their leaders. A moral perspective thus supplants historical understanding. Americans tend to judge other nations in normative terms rather than in relation to the national interests of the states involved. Similarly, they justify their own international conduct on the basis of moral and legal imperatives. Kissinger observes that although our entry into World War I was necessitated by our own geopolitical interests, we interpreted our involvement as supporting democratic principles.[36] "It is part of American folklore that, while other nations have interests, we have responsibilities; while other nations are concerned with equilibrium, we are concerned with the legal requirements of peace."[37]

Related to America's belief in the harmony of international relations and its moralistic bent is its deprecation of power. Because states have no fundamentally antagonistic interests, a nation's use of power to advance its own interests is seen as an aberration. As a result, American leaders find it difficult to think in terms of power or to use the nation's power creatively. Kissinger observes:

> To be sure, American expansion, both economic and geographical, was not accomplished without a judicious application of power. But our Calvinist heritage has required success to display the attribute of justice. . . . As a nation, we have used power shamefacedly as if it were inherently wicked. . . . Our feeling of guilt with respect to power has caused us to transform all wars into crusades, and then to apply our power in the most absolute terms. We have rarely found intermediary ways to apply our power and in those cases we have done so reluctantly.[38]

According to Kissinger, America's attitudes toward power lead to two serious shortcomings in its statecraft. First, Americans have little understanding of the structural relationships of international politics—particularly the requirement to maintain an equilibrium of power. Kissinger points out that "in American discussions of foreign policy, even through much of the twentieth century, the phrase 'balance of power' was hardly ever written or spoken without a pejorative adjective in front of it—the 'outmoded' balance of power, the 'discredited' balance of power."[39] American leaders tend to define peace as a negative condition, i.e., the absence of war. A more historical perspective would allow them to understand peace as a derivative of structural arrangements of power in the state system. Kissinger observes that peace results not from a final settlement or a static condition, but from a relatively stable balance of power.

Second, the reluctance to think in terms of power and structure causes American leaders to divorce diplomacy from power. Traditionally, the nation regards negotiations and the use of force as two discrete elements—force begins when nations stop talking. Americans demonstrate little ability for using force to advance specific political objectives. "Any attempt to treat foreign and military policy as separate problems," Kissinger warns, "usually leads to the atrophy of both."[40]

America's separation from international politics fosters a characteristic suspiciousness toward the very practice of diplomacy.

> Negotiations were treated less as a means of reconciling our ideals with our interests than as a trap to entangle us in the endless quarrels of a morally questionable world. Our native inclination for straightforwardness, our instinct for open, noisy politics, our distrust of European matters and continental elites all brought about an increasing impatience with the stylized methods of European diplomacy and with its tendency toward ambiguous compromise.[41]

American leaders couple their suspicions with an overly pragmatic approach to diplomacy. They regard statecraft as an intermittent undertaking rather than as a historical process. Diplomacy, Kissinger observes, is "treated as episodic—a series of isolated problems to be solved on their own merits."[42]

America's physical autonomy from the state system for much of the nineteenth century contributed to its preoccupation with domestic matters and to the primacy it gives domestic politics. Americans tend to liken complex international issues to domestic problems and try to treat them with the same manageability. Because international issues rarely have the manageability of domestic issues, Kissinger sees this attitude as the source of the impatience that Americans have demonstrated in response to protracted problems.[43]

AMERICA'S PHILOSOPHICAL TRADITION

The final element that contributes to the nation's insular character is its dominant philosophical outlook. Kissinger believes that this outlook markedly influences American culture and society. Throughout his writings, he calls attention to a "deep-seated philosophical attitude which was all the more pervasive for rarely being made explicit."[44] This attitude shapes the way Americans perceive reality and determines how they study both the physical and social sciences—including politics. Kissinger's particular concern is the manner in which this philosophical attitude affects the nation's conduct of foreign policy.

According to Kissinger, the American outlook reflects "the impact of Newtonian thinking."[45] He equates the Newtonian perspective with two primary beliefs: first, that reality is external to the observer; and second, that knowledge about reality is obtained through recording and classifying data.[46] The Newtonian universe is orderly and intelligible; it can be compared to a giant machine composed of interacting parts. Mechanical laws that are scientifically discoverable explain the relationship of these parts. This epistemological outlook generates a perception of reality as given and unchangeable—as something external to which the observer must adapt. It also leads to an emphasis on methodological certainty to ensure that reality is correctly perceived.

The Newtonian perspective has been particularly dominant in Anglo-American societies. Why different cultures adopt certain philosophical perspectives is a matter beyond the scope of this study. Kissinger, however, clearly relates the insular mentality to Newtonian thought. In particular, he condemns the extension of the scientific outlook into the social realm. Although the emphasis on causation, laws, and methodological certainty has helped men understand nature, Kissinger believes that man himself must be dealt with in terms of his inner subjectivity and uniqueness. He frequently praises the political dynamism of less technical societies, which he terms pre- or non-Newtonian cultures.[47] Here the "realities" of political and social life are viewed as more malleable. In these societies, changing political conditions is often synonymous with changing the people's perceptions of these conditions.[48]

Kissinger connects the Newtonian perspective with both empiricism (which he views as dominant in English and American societies) and pragmatism (which he regards as particularly American). Empiricism relies on scientific principles and the objective verification of truth. Kissinger defines empiricism as a philosophical perspective that demonstrates "a greater concern with the collection of facts than with an interpretation of their significance."[49] He links pragmatism to this empirical perspective. The test of knowledge in pragmatic philosophy is its "instrumental quality," i.e., its ability to solve some problem. It is through "experience" that its use is demonstrated. Kissinger notes that "pragmatism is based on the conviction that the context of events produces a solution."[50]

Kissinger rejects the philosophical outlook represented by empiricism and pragmatism. He considers both approaches devoid of metaphysical content; both are concerned mainly with "juxtapos[ing] surface data."[51]

Two generations of Americans have been shaped by the pragmatic conviction that inadequate performance is somehow the result of a failure to understand an "objective" environment properly. . . . The interaction of several minds is supposed to broaden the range of "experience," and "experience" is believed to be the ultimate source of knowledge. Pragmatism, at least in its generally accepted forms, produces a tendency to identify a policy issue with a search for empirical data. It sees in consensus a test of validity. Pragmatism is more concerned with method than judgment. Or, rather, it seeks to reduce judgment to methodology and value to knowledge.[52]

Kissinger sees danger in this perspective, because it makes man a passive observer who merely reacts to external events. The quest for empirical data and methodological certainty lies at the core of this passivity. Kissinger's preference for Kantian idealism led him to regard reality as fundamentally "idea-ist" and therefore in a sense internal to the observer. Reality consists primarily of acts of will and ideas. Man does not merely adapt to events, he actually shapes their occurrence and his underlying perception of reality. "Certainty . . . is conferred at least as much by philosophy as by fact; it derives from the imposition of purpose on events."[53] Summarizing the essence of his own philosophy, Kissinger writes that "matter can defeat only men who have no spirituality to impart to it."[54]

Empiricism and pragmatism reinforce the lessons America drew from its history and geography. For example, the nation's empirical bias supports its tendency to take threats seriously only if they present explicit danger. The aggressive conduct of a would-be enemy must be demonstrated or "verified," usually through a process in which other nations are defeated in such a way as to lead to an erosion of the international balance of power. Pragmatism also contributes to this reactive and defensive approach to foreign policy. Kissinger observes that "problems are dealt with as they arise. Agreement on what constitutes a problem generally depends on an emerging crisis, which settles the previously inconclusive disputes about priorities."[55]

America's empirical bias also influences the way it interprets history. This bias produces an overly positivistic view of history as a succession of discrete events, rather than as a fluid process. It supports the view of states as "similar phenomena," i.e., primarily as constituted by legal and economic institutions. American leaders demonstrate little understanding of what Kissinger terms the "ethical basis"[56] of states, which arises from their unique cultures and historical development.

More importantly, Kissinger indicates that America's Newtonian mentality fosters a leadership style and an administrative structure that are particularly ill-suited to the practice of foreign policy. He disparages this "bureaucratic-pragmatic"[57] approach throughout his career. The relationship between America's bureaucratic-pragmatic style of leadership and the failures that it has produced will be discussed in more detail in the next chapter. For the present, I will limit my remarks to a few observations that convey the essence of Kissinger's criticism.

Kissinger regards the bureaucratic organization of the nation's foreign policy as directly related to its empirical-pragmatic bent. Issues, which for Kissinger are historical and political in nature, are treated technically. The tendency is to divide problems into separate parts that are treated discretely by "experts" in highly specialized fields. This approach supposedly ensures that all the information known about an issue will be collected and that problems are dealt with objectively. The solutions to these problems are derived from a consensus created among semi-autonomous departments. Such an approach is designed to guarantee the validity of the policy proposed.

Kissinger attributes the bureaucratic-pragmatic style to psychological bias as much as philosophical conviction. In America, "the committee approach to decision-making is often less an organizational device than a spiritual necessity."[58] Kissinger finds much that is wrong with such a mechanistic treatment of foreign policy. The bureaucratic style distorts the essence of policymaking. It diminishes innovation. Bureaucratic conservatism leads to "the avoidance of risks rather than the boldness of conception."[59] Planning consists of projecting the present into the future. The bureaucratic style fragments policy into separate elements—such as arms control, international trade, and so forth—without establishing interrelationships among them. Kissinger indicates that this kind of fragmentation leads to "a hiatus between grand strategy and particular tactics."[60]

Kissinger emphasizes the fact that bureaucratic organization detracts from foreign policy leadership. If bureaucracies can be counted on to execute routine functions, they perform a valuable role, for they free leaders to deal creatively with substantive problems. Yet the dilemma of policymaking in America is that it depends on bureaucracy to such an extent that administration replaces leadership. Because policymaking is associated with organizational consensus, more time is spent ensuring the smooth operation of the bureaucracy than deciding on the substance of policy. For this reason, Kissinger writes that in America the "spirit of administration" supplants leadership or what he alternately describes as the "spirit of policy."[61] Coordination of specialized functions takes precedence over the main task of the leader, which is to "infuse and occasionally to transcend routine with purpose. Administration is concerned with execution. Policy-making must address itself to developing a sense of direction."[62]

The American Century

America emerged from World War II as the most powerful nation in the international state system. Because it was the sole possessor of atomic weapons and because other nations had been devastated by the war, it found itself in a position of military supremacy that had few historical parallels. The world economic system designed at Bretton Woods—a system that had as its centerpiece free trade and the U.S. dollar—confirmed America's economic dominance. Added to this physical primacy was America's significance as a society to imitate—especially to the countries that were beginning to emerge from colonial status. The United States, particularly in contrast to the Soviet Union, provided a model that new societies could profitably emulate. Zbigniew Brzezinski describes America's unique postwar appeal:

> Americans have seen their society as the wave of the future, and as an embodiment of libertarian values of universal pertinence; much of the world—be it poor immigrants or activist nationalist leaders—saw America much the same way. . . . World War II and its immediate aftermath were thus high watermarks of the American appeal. As a consequence, American foreign policy operated from a philosophical base and with a mass appeal that provided unique assets and were probably as important to the post–World War II American paramountcy as were its military might and its relative gross national product to the rest of the world.[63]

Given this dominance and appeal, it is little wonder that distinguished commentators in the 1950s referred to the contemporary period as the American century. It was against this background that Kissinger evaluated America's insular approach. He thought it ironic that the same values that fostered the nation's success now imperiled its future. He observed that "rarely before—and never in our history—has every accomplishment so much contained the seeds of its own failure or every advance so much threatened to turn into a roadblock."[64] The nation's relative achievements obscured the full importance of the challenges it faced. Kissinger noted that one looks in vain throughout the fifties for any fundamental criticism of the main trends of American foreign policy.[65]

Kissinger regards the 1950s as a turning point in the nation's history. In many ways, it was as much a crucial decade as the 1850s. Then, the issues at stake involved the future course of the nation's domestic life; now the issues focused on its role as a world power. Yet, unlike the 1850s, the nation could not afford a disaster like the Civil War before it would depart from its traditional outlook. In the nuclear era, America could no longer remain an insular power.

Drawing on his historical studies, Kissinger described the challenges faced by America in the 1950s in an idiom reminiscent of Spengler and Toynbee:

> . . . the tragic aspect of history is that creativity is constantly in danger of being destroyed by success. . . . The United States is at a point in its historical development where it has mastered much of its physical environment. We can, therefore, easily lose our adaptability in our satiety. The price we pay for this will be all the higher for not having to be paid for a while. Earlier in our history, circumstances imposed the need for innovation. We must now work on treasuring our creativity. Any society faces a point in its development where it must ask itself if it has exhausted all the possibilities of innovation inherent in its structure. When this point is reached, it has passed its zenith. From then on, it must decline, rapidly or slowly, but nonetheless inevitably. Only a heroic and deliberate effort can arrest narcissism and the collapse which starts at the moment of seemingly greatest achievement. America is now at such a critical juncture.[66]

Kissinger described the challenges of the period in such dire terms because he regarded the failures of American policy as massive. He asked Americans to "grasp the measure of . . . [this] decline"[67] by comparing the world in the middle to late fifties to the one that existed a decade before. In 1945, the United States held an atomic monopoly. Its conventional military strength was still formidable. Communism held sway in only one country, which had been desolated by the war. The Eastern European nations were not yet politically in the Soviet orbit, and the outcome of the Chinese civil war was still to be decided. The new nations beginning to emerge in Africa and Asia sought both inspiration and assistance in the West. Kissinger emphasized that every one of these conditions had been overturned, and each had been decided in a way favorable to the Soviet Union.[68]

The very nature of the issues that occupied America's attention defined the range of its failures: "Is there or is there not a missile gap? Is Communism gaining ground in the underdeveloped nations? Is there any hope for democracy in the new nations? Is NATO still meaningful a decade after its inception? Can the arms race be ended before it consumes humanity?"[69] Kissinger summarized America's condition:

> Our margin of survival has narrowed dangerously. . . . Whatever the answers, the [above] questions are a testimony to the deterioration of

our position. When our ability to survive is being doubted, when Communist penetration has become a major concern even in the Western Hemisphere, when we enter negotiations with an agenda almost every item of which was placed there by Communist pressure or initiative, only self-delusion can keep us from admitting our decline to ourselves.[70]

In addressing this deterioration of America's world position, Kissinger focuses his own criticism on three areas in which he believes the nation's approach has produced its most serious failures. The first is American leadership itself. He regards American leadership as passive and stagnant—particularly under the Eisenhower administration. Such attitudes, he warns, would "doom us to sterility"[71] in an era marked by revolutionary change. A second area of concern is the nation's military strategy—or more precisely, its lack of coherent strategy. In *Nuclear Weapons and Foreign Policy*, Kissinger underscores the fact that we had not yet decided the relationship between nuclear and conventional weapons, and all-out and limited war. As a consequence, American military doctrine amounted to improvisation in response to crises. America's political failures, especially with respect to its European allies and the developing nations, provide the third focus for Kissinger's criticism. He believes that each of these factors contributed to strategic reversals vis-à-vis the Soviet Union.

These elements will be discussed in the following pages. The failures of American leadership provide the subject of the next chapter.

4
Reflections on American Leadership

Leaders

OF the four books that Richard Nixon has written since leaving the presidency, his work *Leaders* is by far the most animated. Nixon provides profiles and reminiscences of such statesmen as Churchill, de Gaulle, and Adenauer—leaders whom he claims have shaped the modern world. "In the footsteps of great leaders," Nixon writes, "we hear the rolling thunder of history."[1]

Nixon's romanticized views of leadership are strikingly similar to Kissinger's ideas. This similarity, in fact, extends to their choices of the same men—particularly de Gaulle—as the leaders who have dominated the contemporary era. As with other aspects of their political outlooks and foreign policy, Nixon draws his ideas on leadership from personal observations, while Kissinger bases his ideas on historical and philosophical scholarship. As Roger Morris suggests, these ideas—"contempt for the establishment and for the bureaucracy, and an insistence on a single iron leadership in foreign policy"—better explain Nixon's and Kissinger's centralization of policymaking in the White House than does both of their psychological inclinations toward secrecy and evasiveness.[2]

The study of leadership was an abiding—at times, all-consuming—interest of both Nixon and Kissinger. Stephen Graubard suggests that *A World Restored* is in effect an extended essay on the nature of leadership. Graubard observes that "Kissinger's preoccupation with the theme [of leadership] was long-standing; those who encountered him early in the 1950s were quickly made aware of the consuming nature of his interest in political leadership. Whether speaking of Truman, Churchill, or Adenauer, or listening to someone else interpret the strengths and weaknesses of these or any other of a dozen world leaders, he showed a keen appreciation for political talent."[3]

From my earlier treatment of Kissinger's writings, it is possible to distinguish three strands of thought that shape his views on leadership. It is important to consider these, at least briefly, for they provide the basis for his criticism of American leaders in the fifties and sixties.

The first of these elements is Kissinger's philosophical commitment to activism. In "The Meaning of History," Kissinger concludes that despite the limits of objective necessity, man can shape events through acts of will. As Graubard observes, Kissinger's undergraduate thesis "showed his intense commitment to a philosophy that made the individual the responsible agent. . . . Kissinger's concern was with action; ultimately, with the individual."[4] Because of the impact that the leader can have on events, Kissinger sees him as personifying this kind of activism. The great leader is, as Sidney Hook suggests, the event-making man: "The hero in history is the individual to whom we can justifiably attribute preponderant influence in determining an issue or event whose consequences would have been profoundly different if he had not acted as he did."[5] Kissinger's activist bias is so strong that he suggests that great leaders are not necessarily those who succeed in their designs, but rather those who attempt great things. Even in their failures, the latter derive a stature that is all the more formidable for being tragic.[6]

An emphasis on character provides the second element in Kissinger's outlook on great leaders. By character, I mean primarily strength of will and force of personality. "Nothing great is done without great men," de Gaulle writes, "and these are great because they willed it."[7] For Kissinger, the great leader is distinguished not primarily by intelligence or oratory, but by his character. Strength of will, not conceptual clarity, is the sign of the leader's desire to leave his mark on events—to bracket the age. All of those who Kissinger regards as history's great leaders were men of "marked individuality" and almost demonic strength of will.

Finally, Kissinger's idea of the great leader is elitist. Only a handful of men have possessed the creativity and vision needed to shape history. Leadership can never be exercised by the mass, but only by the rare individual "musically attuned to history."[8] It is not accidental that Kissinger's writings about leadership bear a distinctly antipopulist strain, similar to that found in the works of other European intellectuals such as Spengler and Ortega y Gasset.[9] Nor is it by chance that he deprecates the public diplomacy practiced by Congress and the press as a barrier to great leadership. With few exceptions, Kissinger derives his ideas on great leaders from the aristocratic tradition of cabinet diplomacy—a tradition in which a few men determine the fate of nations.

In addition to his emphasis on leadership, Kissinger's writings are marked by a profound antipathy toward governmental bureaucracies. Kissinger stresses that great leaders and bureaucracies stand in diametrical opposition. This opposition provides another theme underlying his criticism of the American leadership style. Kissinger regards it as a normal condition that the statesman will be opposed by the "experts" in his government. This conflict results from the leader's efforts to change an existing policy in which the bureaucracy has vested interests. Kissinger characterizes this struggle as one between the "spirit of policy" (which is synonymous with the creativity of great leadership) and the "spirit of bureaucracy" (which is synonymous with the routine administrative functions of government). He describes the differences between the two:

> The essence of policy is its contingency; its success depends on the correctness of an estimate which is in part conjectural. The essence of bureaucracy is its quest for safety; its success is calculability. Profound policy thrives on perpetual creation, on a constant redefinition of goals. Good administration on routine, the definition of relationships which can survive mediocrity. Policy involves an adjustment of risks; administration an avoidance of deviation. Policy justifies itself by its relationship of its measures and its sense of proportion; administration by the rationality of each action in terms of a given goal.[10]

For Kissinger, the opposition between great leadership and bureaucracy is part of a more fundamental conflict—one that he first dealt with in his studies of Toynbee and Spengler. In chapter 1, I discussed what Kissinger terms the inextricable element of history—the conflict between "inspiration and organization." Inspiration is linked to the vital and creative aspects of a society's development; organization with an erosion of this vitality. Societies decline when their organizational structure becomes so complex and rigid that they lose their capacity for innovation. Hence, in contrasting great leaders with governmental bureaucracy, Kissinger is in effect contrasting the deeper spirit that allows for creative development with the forces that weaken this capacity.

It was against this background that Kissinger formed his opinion of American leaders. The criticism that he voiced of American leaders in the Eisenhower years was substantially the same as that which he offered of the Kennedy and Johnson administrations.[11] Deep-seated patterns rather than individual political figures attracted his interest.

American Leadership in the Contemporary Era

Kissinger believes that America lacks a leadership elite that can effectively assume the highest government positions concerned with foreign policy. In an early article entitled "The Policymaker and the Intellectual," he observes that "the stagnation of our policy is often ascribed to the fact that our best people are not in government service. But the more serious and pertinent question is how qualified our eminent men are for the task of policymaking in a revolutionary period."[12]

Kissinger's criticism focuses on two areas. First, he regards senior American officials as lacking the knowledge and political sensitivity needed for foreign policy leadership. He voices this criticism in the 1950s in writings about Secretary of State John Foster Dulles and Secretary of Defense Charles Wilson. A decade later, he makes essentially the same points about Dean Rusk and Robert McNamara.[13] "Our leadership groups," Kissinger writes, "are . . . better prepared to deal with technical than with conceptual issues. Projected on the Washington scene, they often lack the background to cope with a developing political and strategic situation. . . . The absence of a conceptual framework makes it difficult for them even to identify our problems or to choose effectively among the proposals and interpretations with which our government is overloaded."[14]

Kissinger identifies this lack of substantive knowledge with a neglect of history. For the most part, America's eminent men tend to regard the study of historical and political issues "as an extracurricular activity that does not touch the core of their concerns."[15] American leaders, Kissinger suggests, demonstrate "a relatively low valuation of historical factors."[16] In addition to their unfamiliarity with contemporary issues, most senior officials lack a framework for thinking about these issues historically, i.e., by analogy to past eras. Kissinger contrasts their mastery of technical problems with their failure to understand historical processes and to appreciate the interrelationship of seemingly discrete events. He calls attention to this absence of political and historical sensitivity in terms of how Americans interpret, or fail to interpret, specific events. He notes, for example, that "even with the perspective of a decade there is little consensus about the relationship between the actions culminating in the Suez fiasco and the French decision to enter the nuclear field."[17]

The second aspect of Kissinger's criticism involves the character of American officials. When he contrasts American leaders to the statesmen (such as Bismarck and de Gaulle) whose forceful personalities he admires, he judges the former as lacking conviction and assertiveness. Their "insecurity" reflects a societal belief that truth grows out of a consensus of several minds rather than the historical intuition of a single leader. American leaders, Kissinger observes, operate with the illusion that they can avoid personal judgment and responsibility. Similarly, American leaders downplay the importance of conjecture in leadership—i.e., the ability to base decisions on an intuition of the outcome of events, rather than on a factual assessment of those events. In fact, Americans usually associate the conjectural element of policymaking (which Kissinger regards as an essential aspect of true leadership) with dogmatism.[18]

The problem [of American leadership] is magnified by the personal humility which is one of the most attractive American traits. Most Americans are convinced that no one is ever entirely "right," or, as the saying goes, that if there is disagreement each party is probably a little in error. The fear of dogmatism pervades the American scene. But the corollary of the tentativeness of most views is an incurable inner insecurity. Even very eminent people are reluctant to stand alone.[19]

Given these views, it is understandable that no American statesman figures in Kissinger's writings as an example of a genuine leader. The most serious implications of his criticism, however, become clear in the comparisons he makes between American and Soviet leaders. Kissinger sees even such a figure as Khrushchev (whom the Soviets came to regard as an adventurer) as more politically astute than American officials were during the Eisenhower years. He attributes many postwar Soviet successes to their leadership. He gives particular credit to the formative influences that Soviet leaders encounter on their rise to power.

Whatever the qualities of Soviet leadership, its training is eminently political and conceptual. Reading Lenin or Mao or Stalin, one is struck by the emphasis on the relationship between political, military, psychological, and economic factors, the insistence on finding a conceptual basis for political action and on the need for dominating a situation by flexible tactics and inflexible purpose. And the internal struggles in the Kremlin ensure that only the most iron-nerved reach the top.[20]

One cannot read Kissinger's *Nuclear Weapons and Foreign Policy* without recognizing that he regards Soviet leaders as modern day Clausewitzian thinkers whose formidable skills are responsible for a military and political strategy superior to that of the West. Paradoxically, the society of the commissar produces leaders of marked individuality and strength of character—leaders animated by a philosophy whose activism is affirmed by the Marxist credo that history should not merely be understood, but changed. In contrast, American society, which emphasizes individualism, fosters the "organization man"[21] as its most eminent political leader. "Against the Politbureau, trained to think in general terms and freed of problems of day-to-day administration, we have pitted leaders overwhelmed with departmental duties and trained to think it was a cardinal sin to transgress on another's field of specialization. To our leaders, policy is a series of discrete problems; to the Soviet leaders it is an aspect of a continuing political process."[22] In the most telling of all comparisons, Kissinger characterizes the contest beween American and Soviet leaders as one between amateurs and professionals. He emphasizes that even a mediocre professional will usually defeat an excellent amateur because the latter cannot react quickly or consistently enough to the gambits of the professional.[23]

Kissinger holds American leaders responsible for the failures of the nation's foreign and defense policies. Yet he also emphasizes that American officials are ill-prepared to perform many of the roles essential to genuine leadership. For example, both Presidents Truman and Eisenhower failed in the role of educator. As I noted earlier, Kissinger stresses this aspect of statesmanship in A World Restored. The leader must educate his nation so that his people can bridge the differences between their traditional outlook and the demands of the future. Both Truman and Eisenhower, however, justified the policies of the cold war as temporary measures.[24] They created the impression that active and sustained involvement in world affairs would not be necessary in the future. In particular, Eisenhower's emphasis on budgetary restraints, his exclusive reliance on strategic nuclear weapons for defense, and his efforts to foster a "spirit of normalcy" served, in Kissinger's view, to obscure the fundamentally different nature of the postwar period.[25]

An even more serious fault is what Kissinger describes as a reliance on personalities as a basis for negotiations. To illustrate this point, he quotes Eisenhower who, prior to the 1955 Geneva summit conference, commented that "our many postwar conferences have been characterized too much by attention to detail, by an effort apparently to work on specific problems rather than to establish the spirit and attitude in which we shall approach them."[26] Kissinger characterizes this "evasion of concreteness, the reliance on personalities; [and] the implication that all problems can be settled with one grand gesture"[27] as fatuous. He looks on this approach not as an expression of policy but as a tacit acknowledgment of its absence.

The effects of this approach were even more pernicious. For one thing, it misconceived the nature of the cold war, portraying it as merely the product of personal distrust rather than as a conflict resulting from fundamentally dissimilar national and ideological interests. Kissinger emphasizes that such an outlook would ultimately demoralize the West; how could nations justify to their citizens the sacrifices that the cold war demanded if differences with the Soviet Union were merely a matter of distrust. This personalistic approach also led Americans to make concessions to the Soviets; the reliance on personal summitry made agreements ends in themselves.

Most importantly, Kissinger believes that the American approach to negotiations failed to come to grips with the revolutionary nature of the Soviet Union—a point he first develops in A World Restored.[28] As a result, the Soviet Union used the summits at Geneva in 1955, Camp David in 1959, and Paris in 1960 to appeal symbolically to the uncommitted nations of the Third World. By cleverly manipulating the agenda of those summits, the Soviets appeared in the guise of international peace-makers, while the United States was viewed as intransigent. Writing during the second Eisenhower administration—a period during which American diplomacy emphasized personal summitry—Kissinger points out that while Americans sought to address the Soviet leaders, the Soviets addressed the people of the world.[29] As a consequence, Kissinger believes it a *tour de force* that:

> The power which has added 120 million people to its orbit by force has become the champion of anticolonialism. The state which has utilized tens of millions of slave laborers as an integral part of its economic system appears as the champion of human dignity in many parts of the world. Neither regarding German unity, nor Korea, nor the satellite orbit have we succeeded in mobilizing world opinion. But Formosa has become a symbol of American intransigence, and our overseas air bases a token of American aggressiveness. . . . As a result the international debate is carried on almost entirely in the categories and at the pace established by the Soviets.[30]

Why does America lack leaders who can think conceptually about international issues? Kissinger finds the answer to this question in the nature of American society itself. He attributes the failure of America's leadership to the core values of its "business" culture.[31]

THE BUSINESS EXECUTIVE AS LEADER

Kissinger emphasizes that American society customarily draws its senior public officials from those who achieve prominence in the private sector. In an obvious reference to its pragmatic nature, he observes that America is a society that prides itself on its business character. "As a result, the typical Cabinet or sub-Cabinet officer in America comes either from business or from the legal profession."[32]

Even allowing for the action-intellectuals in the Roosevelt "brain trust" in the 1930s, Kennedy's "new frontiersmen" in the 1960s, and such national security advisers as Zbigniew Brzezinski and Kissinger himself, the business and legal communities have dominated senior governmental positions in America. At no time was this truer than in the Eisenhower years—the years during which Kissinger first voiced his criticism of American leadership. Charles Wilson, Eisenhower's first secretary of defense, had been the president of General Motors. His successor in 1952, Neil McElroy, was the president of Procter and Gamble. Similarly, George Humphrey, the influential secretary of the treasury, had been chairman of the board of M. A. Hanna Corporation, a large industrial holding company. (Because Eisenhower relied on budgetary restraints in determining defense procurements and strategy, his secretary of the treasury helped to shape national security policy.)[33] Although Secretary of State John Foster Dulles had been Thomas Dewey's chief foreign policy adviser, he was an attorney by education and had spent most of his career as a lawyer specializing in international cases at the premier Wall Street firm of Sullivan and Cromwell.

Although the Eisenhower administration exhibited the business-legal pattern in the extreme, representatives from these groups have controlled the inner councils of American foreign policymaking for most of the post–World War II era. In his book *The Cold Warriors: A Policy-Making Elite*, John Donovan emphasizes the presence in successive administrations of figures like Paul Nitze, John McCloy, Robert Lovett, and Clark Clifford.[34] All played prominent roles in formulating postwar American foreign policy, and all had similar backgrounds in large law firms or financial and banking institutions.[35] This same phenomenon continues to operate today in the presence in government of such men as former Secretary of Defense Casper Weinberger and Secretary of State George Shultz.

Kissinger worked with many of America's most eminent business executives and attorneys during his association with the Council on Foreign Relations from 1956 to 1957 (an association that resulted in *Nuclear Weapons and Foreign Policy*) and later with the Rockefeller Brothers Fund. Why does he attach such importance to the dominance of business executives and lawyers among American leaders? Kissinger emphasizes that these very groups are the most ill-prepared to exercise foreign policy leadership. Ironically, he regards their qualifications as competent managers as irrelevant to the tasks involved in directing America's foreign policy. "Very little in the experience that forms these men produces the combination of political acumen, conceptual skill, persuasive power, and substantive knowledge required for the highest positions of government."[36]

The business executive is principally a manager. Because American corporations are highly diverse entities, their smooth operation depends on the administration of specialized functions. As a consequence, business leadership involves the job of coordinating routine functions that are largely technical in nature. This way of life emphasizes a pragmatic approach to problem-solving. The businessman deals with problems as they arise and considers them largely in terms of existing conditions. Kissinger believes that the legal profession shares this approach. Most business executives face enormous workloads. Kissinger links this phenomenon to the high degree of specialization in business and the requirement that executives be familiar with all aspects of their organization.

Kissinger compares, or more aptly, contrasts, the requirements of political leadership and the skills of the American business executive. He associates political leadership with establishing an overall direction for society and inspiring others with a vision. He sees the business executive, however, as an administrator who coordinates the work of the individuals and divisions of his corporation. The leader often transcends the existing organization; the business executive takes the smooth operation of the existing organization as a sign of his success. The leader shapes the future; the businessman solves problems on their own merits and waits to see how events develop. Kissinger contrasts the leader's decisive handling of political issues with the executive's tentativeness—a tentativeness based on a career of dealing with technical problems requiring specialized skills. Kissinger sees the leader as a man of substantive knowledge—particularly historical and philosophical understanding. "The American business executive (or the lawyer coming from a business background) is," according to Kissinger, "rarely familiar with the substance of the problems into which he finds himself projected largely because, in the rise through the administrative hierarchy, the executive is shaped by a style of life that inhibits reflectiveness."[37]

When the business executive enters government, he typically becomes dependent on the bureaucracy that he has been appointed to lead. Because he lacks almost all of the skills for a senior government position as well as knowledge regarding foreign policy, the executive relies "to an increasing extent on his subordinates' conception of the essential elements of a problem."[38] This dependency leads him to see leadership as administration and coordination—the same functions he performed in private life. Decision making turns into a group effort.

Kissinger attacks this conception of leadership. Given the high degree of specialization in contemporary society and the great transformation that occurred in American foreign policy after World War II,[39] bureaucracy was inevitable. Kissinger suggests, however, that it was not inevitable that senior officials would depend on the bureaucracy for their conceptions of policy or that decision making would become synonymous with consensus. The result of this dependency is what Kissinger calls the bureaucratic-pragmatic style—a style he associates with an abnegation of true foreign policy leadership.

Before discussing the bureaucratic-pragmatic style and its shortcomings, I wish to consider Kissinger's views on the role of American intellectuals in foreign policy. Having judged American business executives as lacking the knowledge needed to formulate policy, he turns his attention to that group that claims historical and political reflection as its domain.

THE ROLE OF AMERICAN INTELLECTUALS

As an associate professor of government at Harvard, Kissinger was familiar with scholars who served as advisers to senior government officials. Even in the days before the Kennedy administration called on such resident intellectuals as McGeorge Bundy and Arthur Schlesinger, Jr., Harvard had made its presence felt in Washington. Kissinger's graduate adviser, William Yandall Elliott, for example, was generally absent from campus a few days each week, traveling between Cambridge and Washington, D.C. Kissinger observed other scholars in advisory roles through his work with the Special Studies Project of the Rockefeller Brothers Fund.

As much from these observations as from his own reflection on the role of the intellectual in society, Kissinger judges American intellectuals to be failures. He faults them for accepting the role of technical problem-solver for issues identified by the policymaker instead of defining which issues are significant. In short, "the contribution of the intellectual to policy is . . . in terms of criteria that he has played only a minor role in establishing. . . . He is asked to solve problems, not to contribute to the definition of goals."[40]

More importantly, Kissinger suggests that American intellectuals lose creativity when they move into government. In their attempt to offer expert advice, they become proponents of the existing policy (for therein resides their expertise), rather than charting new courses.[41] Why does this occur?

As in his critique of the business executive, Kissinger links the short-comings of American intellectuals to the nature of American society. The empirical bent of American culture creates enormous demands for expert advice. "Every problem which our society becomes concerned about . . . calls into being panels, committees, or study groups supported by either private or governmental funds."[42] Permanent research organizations, think tanks, and planning staffs abound. Given such organizational pressures, many notable scholars are drawn into an existence incompatible with the contemplative life that is the source of true scholarship.

As a result, intellectuals with a reputation soon find themselves so burdened that their pace of life hardly differs from that of the executives whom they counsel. They cannot supply perspective because they are as harassed as the policymakers. All pressures on them tend to keep them at the level of the performance which gained them their reputation. In his desire to be helpful, the intellectual is too frequently compelled to sacrifice what should be his greatest contribution to society—his creativity.[43]

Kissinger links the roles that American intellectuals assume to their own self-image. In a "pragmatic" culture such as America's, the pursuit of knowledge for its own sake—speculative wisdom—is not highly regarded. The sciences and "practical" endeavors take precedence over such disciplines as history and philosophy. American intellectuals, Kissinger believes, often suffer "feelings of insecurity or even guilt" because of their choices to pursue the scholarly life. To assuage these feelings, they frequently attempt to apply their knowledge in advisory roles.

There are many who believe that their ultimate contribution as intellectuals depends on the degree of their participation in what is considered the "active" life. It is not a long step from the willingness to give advice to having one's self-esteem gratified by a consulting relationship with a large organization. And since individuals who challenge the presuppositions of the bureaucracy, governmental or private, rarely can keep their positions as advisers, great pressures are created to elaborate on familiar themes rather than risk new departures.[44]

In Kissinger's view, American intellectuals become extensions of the bureaucratic organizations that they seek to advise, thus increasing the dependency of senior officials on that bureaucracy. Rarely are they included in policymaking at the level at which decisions are made. Instead, they serve as technical specialists, offering solutions to specific problems. Their status as experts proves inimical to innovation. Too often, Kissinger believes, intellectuals in government turn into administrators, distinguished from their bureaucratic colleagues only by having come from the academic community.[45]

The Bureaucratic-Pragmatic Style

In a 1966 article entitled "Domestic Structure and Foreign Policy," Kissinger elaborates on leadership themes that he first explored as an undergraduate.[46] His central point is that the leaders of any society epitomize its values. In their rise to senior positions, leaders are influenced by their society's beliefs. Hence, Kissinger observes, "the mediating, conciliatory style of British policy in the nineteenth century reflected, in part, the qualities encouraged during careers in Parliament and the values of a cohesive leadership group connected by ties of family and common education."[47]

In the contemporary period, Kissinger identifies three types of leaders: the ideological, the revolutionary-charismatic, and the bureaucratic-pragmatic type. He associates the first group primarily with the Soviet leadership, because of the continued influence of Marxist-Leninist thought in that society.[48] He includes in the second category such Third World figures as Castro of Cuba, Nyerere of Tanzania, and Sukarno of Indonesia—men who became symbols of national independence. Kissinger finds examples of the third group—the bureaucratic-pragmatic type—in all modern, industrialized nations, but he suggests that American leaders exhibit this style more than any other national group. Contrasts abound between these types, but none is more significant to Kissinger than the lack of dynamism and conceptual ability that sets American leaders apart from their ideological and revolutionary counterparts. Even the Third World revolutionary figure, because of his activism, philosophical orientation, and political sensitivity, provides a more powerful model of leadership than the American pragmatist.

Kissinger ascribes the failures of American leaders to their dependency on the bureaucracy. I have already examined many of the shortcomings of the bureaucratic-pragmatic style, that is, the loss of creativity, the emphasis on the technical nature of problems and problem-solving, and the reactive nature of policy. The specific manner in which American foreign policy exhibited this style in the postwar period will be discussed shortly. Before proceeding, however, I think it important to consider Kissinger's criticism within the context of American political scholarship.

The phenomenon of bureaucratic politics as a basis for American foreign policy is a subject that has occupied many prominent theorists. Graham Allison, I. M. Destler, Morton Halperin, and Roger Hilsman, among others, come readily to mind.[49] Kissinger's views are distinguished by the fact that they are highly critical of bureaucratic decision making. In contrast, most other theorists present the bureaucratic model in a purely descriptive way. This model regards the formulation of foreign policy as a series of political bargains and trade-offs; the policy that emerges usually represents a compromise among the different interests of the policymakers.[50] It would not be untrue to say that most American political scientists view the bureaucratic model as a more sophisticated way of understanding political decision making than the approach that sees the nation as a unitary actor.

It is also important to recognize that the bureaucratic model contains an implicit outlook in relation to leadership. Leadership is viewed "legislatively," as the act of building coalitions and consensus among relatively equal groups, rather than "hierarchically," a mode in which direction flows unambiguously from the top down.[51] Almost all of the theorists of bureaucratic politics owe an intellectual debt to Richard Neustadt, whose work *Presidential Politics* describes the model of bureaucratic leadership. Here, leadership is associated with the political maneuvering of a Gulliver-like figure hemmed in by the restraints of the system. "Presidential power," according to Neustadt, "is the power to persuade. . . . Underneath our images of President-in-boots, astride decisions, are the half-observed realities of President-in-sneakers, stirrups in hand, trying to induce particular department heads or Congressmen or Senators, to climb aboard."[52]

Such a view of leadership is, of course, diametrically opposed to Kissinger's. American leaders during the fifties and sixties provide clear examples of the bureaucratic model.

THE EISENHOWER YEARS

The Eisenhower administration—particularly with respect to the operations of the National Security Council (NSC)—exhibited the bureaucratic-pragmatic style of leadership in its clearest form. The NSC had been established in 1947 as part of the legislation that organized the Department of Defense and the Central Intelligence Agency. Its main purpose was to advise the president on foreign affairs and national security by integrating domestic, foreign, and military considerations into one perspective. In 1968, both President-elect Nixon and Kissinger agreed that the NSC machinery had functioned poorly during the Eisenhower years—obscuring options and providing little substantive advice. Roger Morris recalls the early conversations between Nixon and Kissinger regarding the NSC: "He [Nixon] had watched Ike . . . being manipulated and subverted by the bureaucracy with their special interests. He had seen the homogenized 'position' papers slowly wind their way to the top, giving the Chief Executive no choices other than what 'they' wanted."[53]

The Eisenhower presidency prided itself on its administrative style and spirit of teamwork. In what amounts to almost a parody, Marion Irish characterizes the essence of Eisenhower's leadership as "The Organization Man in the Presidency."[54] Applying the concepts of William Whyte's pioneering sociological work, she observes that the Eisenhower administration displayed a passion for anonymity and a dilution of individual responsibility and leadership that reflected the patterns typical of modern organizational life.[55] Irish's point is that the machinery of decision making replaced personal conception and choice during the Eisenhower administration: "Editorializing on 'the changing of the guard' in January 1953, *The New York Times* observed . . . that President Eisenhower was 'looking for men who could administer, not for a brain trust, not for philosophers.' "[56]

Kissinger notes that Eisenhower relied almost exclusively on the NSC for formulating foreign policy. As we have seen, senior leaders during this period were drawn largely from the business community. With the exception of Dulles, almost none of the cabinet officers who made up the NSC had knowledge of the foreign policy issues that they were asked to resolve. Partly in response to this lack of experience, but largely as a result of Eisenhower's administrative background in the military, the NSC became a highly structured and formal institution that relied on committee and subcommittee work. In addition to the periodic NSC meetings, policy proposals were considered by an NSC Planning Board. The NSC Planning Board consisted of representatives at the assistant secretary level from the Departments of State, Defense, Treasury, the Bureau of the Budget, and the Office of Defense Mobilization, as well as advisers and observers from the Joint Chiefs of Staff, the Central Intelligence Agency, the Atomic Energy Agency, and the Department of Justice. It was the function of the NSC Planning Board to distill departmental policy papers and eliminate disagreements prior to their submission to the NSC itself. After the NSC ratified a policy, it depended on an operations coordinating board to implement its decision.

Kissinger believes that this reliance on the NSC machinery for foreign policy formulation contributed to the passivity and stagnation of the Eisenhower years. More than any single factor, the practice of using bureaucracy to create policy accounted for Eisenhower's failure. Kissinger elaborated on several of these failures in his writings, including the lack of an effective military doctrine to deter Soviet advances in the Third World, and the inability of the Eisenhower administration to derive diplomatic benefits from turmoil in the Soviet Union, such as at the time of Stalin's death. I address several of these shortcomings in subsequent chapters. Kissinger maintains that although the NSC machinery can be used for fact-finding and the bureaucracy for implementation, neither should be used for policy conception. Only the leader with substantive mastery of the immediate political issues and the deeper historical processes can make policy.

In practice, the elaborate formalism and attention to procedure of Eisenhower's NSC contributed very little of value to the formation of policy. Kissinger observes that the NSC substituted the consensus of semiautonomous departments for creative policy. "In effect, it was somewhat ridiculous—there were many documents which were really diplomatic treaties between the various departments, and which enabled each department to do what it had wanted to do in the first place."[57] The bureaucratic approach did, however, contribute to the rigidity of American foreign policy. Once the system disgorged a policy, senior officials were reluctant to begin the decision making process all over again, even if the policy had become outdated and needed to be changed.

Emphasizing the vacuousness of the Eisenhower NSC process, Kissinger states that he knew of no negotiating position for the U.S.-Soviet summits of 1955, 1959, or 1960 "existing before a date for the conference was set."[58] He observes further: "In my experience I do not recall a single instance in which, when a decision had to be made at a high level, a policy planning paper was discussed."[59] Hence, crisis situations such as Suez in 1956, in which the United States intervened to prevent the combined forces of France, England, and Israel from overturning Nasser's control of the Suez Canal and ousting the Egyptian president, and the U.S. incursion in Lebanon in 1958 in order to stabilize its pro-Western government, were dealt with outside the formal NSC process.

> The drawback of the NSC as it was run under President Eisenhower was that it was terribly formalistic. One way to tell they really weren't doing anything was to take their papers, write down the opposite of what they had said, and see that this involved no policy choice. One is not saying anything by advocating that it is in the American interest to have a pro-American government in country X. No one would argue that it is in our interest to have an anti-American government there. It turned into a series of abstract platitudes which were not very effective.[60]

The sterility of the NSC process as it functioned under Eisenhower created a need for "outside" advice. Kissinger's own book, *Nuclear Weapons and Foreign Policy*, was widely read and highly regarded by such senior officials as Vice-President Nixon—even though it was extremely critical of Eisenhower's defense policies. Similarly, the papers of the Rockefeller Brothers Fund, collected under the title *Prospect for America*,[61] were conspicuous for the advice that Republicans outside of government were offering to the senior hierarchy of a Republican administration. "Crucial policy advice," Kissinger noted at the time, "is increasingly requested from ad hoc committees of outside experts, as, for example, the Gaither Committee on national defense, the Draper Committee on economic assistance, or the Coolidge Committee on arms control."[62]

Although American theorists have largely accepted the bureaucratic-pragmatic model, the process of foreign policy decision making became so stultified during the Eisenhower years that others offered criticisms similar to Kissinger's. George Kennan, in an article entitled "America's Administrative Response to Its World Problems," criticized the excessive growth of government machinery during this period.[63] The result of this growth was a hodgepodge of recommendations that make policy the lowest common denominator on which officials can agree. Kennan condemned the flight from individual judgment that gave "the governmental apparatus an inflexibility, an inertia, a sluggishness, and an incoherence in communication that renders it an inferior instrument in the hands of the senior officials of government."[64] Similarly, Hans Morgenthau, in an article called "Can We Entrust Defense to a Committee?" urged the creation of an office called the first secretary of the government in order to avoid the shortcomings of the committee approach to decision making.[65] Because the NSC was not an independent entity with an independent outlook, but only a composite body representing the views and interests of the agencies that comprised it, Morgenthau believed that it institutionalized parochialism and ensured a lack of innovation. Dean Acheson, W. W. Rostow, and Paul Nitze put forth similar views.[66] The Jackson Subcommittee on National Policy Making echoed these criticisms when it reviewed the nation's policy formulation process. As Roger Hilsman explains, "the subcommittee harshly criticized the heavy undergrowth of interdepartmental committees clustered around the NSC and particularly the cumbersome Operations Coordinating Board."[67] Senator Henry Jackson referred to the Eisenhower NSC approach to policymaking as a facade.

What distinguishes Kissinger's criticism from that of the others is his insistence on viewing the bureaucratic approach in the context of American culture. The empirical and pragmatic bias of American society and the primacy of businessmen in its leadership elite ensure that political processes will be treated administratively. Even Morgenthau, with whom Kissinger agrees on many issues, envisioned that the failures of the NSC could be corrected by organizational changes as opposed to fundamental changes in national attitudes.[68]

THE KENNEDY-JOHNSON YEARS

Both Kennedy and Johnson worked outside the formal NSC structure. Kissinger observes that Kennedy dismantled the Eisenhower machinery and "substituted for it a sort of nervous energy and great intellectual activity."[69] Under Johnson, however, neither structure nor intellectual excitement was present. Increasingly, American foreign policy became Vietnam policy. In 1968, both Nixon and Kissinger denounced Johnson's "Tuesday lunches" (which became the administration's primary foreign policy body) as "talkfests" with little substantive content. Kissinger, however, wrote very little else about the leadership style of the Johnson administration. Because of this and because Johnson's foreign policy in other areas was largely a continuation of Kennedy initiatives, I will emphasize Kissinger's criticism of the Kennedy approach.[70]

According to Roger Hilsman, a close Kennedy adviser and the assistant secretary of state for Pacific affairs, Kennedy intended to make the State Department the "key element in the national security policy-making machinery."[71] The State Department, however, never fulfilled the president's expectations. Early in the administration, the most important foreign policy issues were assigned to interdepartmental task forces. The Berlin task force was headed by Paul Nitze, then assistant secretary of defense for international security affairs; the Vietnam task force was chaired by Deputy Secretary of Defense Roswell Gilpatric. Hilsman relates that following the Bay of Pigs fiasco, the Department of State never again exercised foreign policy leadership in the Kennedy administration.

The failure of the State Department lay in part with its Secretary, Dean Rusk. Generally unassertive, Rusk typically deferred to the institutional positions of his own department. This lack of activism and the slow pace of the State Department's machinery displeased the Kennedy hierarchy. The Department's deeper failure, however, lay in its excessively bureaucratic approach—an approach that John Franklin Campbell describes in his book *The Foreign Affairs Fudge Factory.*[72] Hilsman relates that Kennedy's criticism of the State Department was that it "is slow in acting, requiring endless 'clearances' from the different bureaus and offices before taking action; that it is frequently indecisive in the actions it does take; and that it often fails to provide the strong overall leadership to the other departments and agencies that is needed if the United States foreign policy is to be effective and consistent."[73]

As a consequence, Kennedy relied heavily on Secretary of Defense Robert McNamara for foreign policy advice. Regional secretaries such as Hilsman, Averell Harriman, and G. Mennen Williams cultivated direct ties to the president. According to I. M. Destler, McGeorge Bundy, Kennedy's NSC adviser, served mainly to ensure a flow of information to the president and to communicate Kennedy's wishes to the bureaucracy.[74]

The end result was that, although Kennedy's style was less formal than Eisenhower's, it was scarcely more effective. Its major failure, according to Kissinger, was its excessive pragmatism. The "ad hoc" bent of Kennedy and his advisers—even intellectuals such as Bundy and Theodore Sorensen—meant that policy was never fully conceptualized, except in response to emergencies. The journalist Joseph Kraft underscored this point, noting that the Kennedy style treated everything on a case-by-case basis. Such an approach, Kraft wrote, "does not contribute to the systematic elaboration of coherent programs expressing broad . . . public policies."[75] Kissinger observes that:

The drawback under the Kennedy administration was that there really was no regular process of getting things done, except on crisis issues. . . . It was a somewhat amorphous process. . . . Kennedy used the NSC primarily as a sounding board; it rarely made important decisions. He had something called the Committee of Principles which met when concrete decisions had to be made—such as the Berlin crisis. There was no regular staff work for these meetings, it was all done on an ad hoc basis.[76]

Kissinger disparages the pragmatic "crisis management" approach of the Kennedy administration. He questions why emphasis was placed on managing crises, rather than on forestalling them. Although Kissinger acknowledges that Kennedy acted decisively in the Cuban Missile Crisis in October 1962, he believes that it was America's own tentative reactions in other areas, such as Berlin, and its initial hesitation in responding to the Soviet arms build-up in Cuba that "tempted the Soviets into so rash, so foolhardy an adventure as establishing missile bases on an island only ninety miles from our shores."[77]

Although the Kennedy administration was less formal than its predecessor, it could at times be equally bureaucratic. Despite the adaptation of systems-management approaches and quantitative techniques, Kissinger believes that McNamara never really gained control over the Defense Department. In fact, he suggests that it was the reliance on these techniques, with their corresponding denigration of political insight, that became McNamara's principal shortcoming. Kissinger indicates that McNamara gained control over the procurement process in the Pentagon at the cost of losing control over major defense policy decisions.[78] McNamara's systems-management approach produced the Skybolt Affair in 1962. The Defense Department cancelled the Skybolt missile program because of budget constraints. Eisenhower, however, had promised to share the missile with Britain; the latter counted on Skybolt for its future nuclear deterrent force. Kissinger regards this episode as the most salient example of the failures of the bureaucratic approach to foreign policy.[79]

Leadership and Insularity: A Summary

Kissinger associates the failures of America's leadership with the deeper patterns of insularity. Because American leaders lack substantive knowledge about foreign policy and a conceptual basis for action, they adopt a reactive approach to policy formulation. Events must usually unfold to a point where a crisis is clear before decisive action is possible. Even then, the policy that results from the bureaucratic process typically represents a compromise on which several governmental departments agree rather than a coherent plan for action.

Kissinger relates the origin of America's leadership failures to American culture itself. The pragmatic bent of American society gives rise to a leadership class whose skills are narrowly manipulative rather than conceptual. The procedures of bureaucratic organizations are an outgrowth of the nation's empirical approach, that is, its specialization and search for methodological certainty.

In Kissinger's criticism of American leaders, one detects an underlying element of satire. The social dominance of the businessman and the prevalence of commercial values in America have long been disparaged by some American and European writers. The figure of George Babbitt in Sinclair Lewis' *Main Street*, characterized by his uncritical acceptance of the philosophy of business and his Midwest provincialism, exemplifies this view. Similarly, Kissinger disparages the intellectual shallowness of American leaders. Either they appear to lack even the rudiments of political and historical understanding, or they seem to possess an intelligence that is only quantitative and analytical. Kissinger portrays Eisenhower, for example, as a likable but ineffectual military hero whose attempts at diplomacy were both fatuous and naive.

It would, of course, be a mistake to regard Kissinger primarily as a social critic. He sees in the failures of American leadership the reasons for the erosion of America's power and world position. He holds America's leaders and their insular conception of defense responsible for the mistaken military policies that are the subject of the next chapter.

The Need for Doctrine in the Nuclear Age

The Historian as Strategist

THE MATURING SCHOLAR

HENRY Kissinger established his scholarly reputation as a strategist of limited nuclear war and as a critic of American military doctrine in the post–World War II era. His first book, *Nuclear Weapons and Foreign Policy*, was widely read by the general public and earned him the prestigious Woodrow Wilson Award in 1958. Most of the articles that he wrote in the 1950s deal with military issues, ranging from preventive nuclear war to defense of the so-called "grey areas" in Africa and Asia. His much-acclaimed work, *The Necessity for Choice*, which was published at the beginning of the Kennedy administration, contained several sections on military strategy. It is understandable that this area of Kissinger's scholarship frequently overshadows his earlier writings on the philosophy of history and nineteenth-century European diplomacy, and his later publications on the Atlantic alliance.[1] Many still regard him primarily as a defense analyst—one of the original theorists whose writings introduced Americans to the significance of nuclear weapons and their effect on foreign policy.

Kissinger's work on defense issues and national strategy also introduced him to a world vastly different from that of the academy—the world of America's business, government, and military elites. He had written his honors thesis and doctoral dissertation at Harvard as solitary tasks, roaming in silence among the shelves at Widener Library. In contrast, *Nuclear Weapons and Foreign Policy* resulted from his association with the Council on Foreign Relations in New York from 1955 to 1957. Kissinger acted as a study director for a discussion group that met under the council's sponsorship to consider the implications of nuclear power and the new weapon systems then being developed. This group included some of America's most distinguished leaders—individuals with extensive government service, military experience, and scientific and technological acumen.[2]

During this same period, Kissinger was also associated with the Special Studies Project of the Rockefeller Brothers Fund. Chaired by Nelson Rockefeller, this group examined the prospects for American foreign and domestic policy over the next decade. Like the Council on Foreign Relations, the Special Studies Project included on its several panels some of the nation's most prominent men and women. Stephen Graubard observes that from 1956 until 1958 "Kissinger played a major role in the study, in his capacity as Director of Special Studies, but also as principal author of the paper published by Panel II on 'International Security: The Military Aspect,' which appeared in January 1958; it was, in effect, an abbreviated version of *Nuclear Weapons and Foreign Policy*."[3]

Kissinger gained immensely from his exposure to the American Establishment. He came away from these years with literary success, status as an accomplished scholar, and a connection to the Rockefeller family that facilitated his own rise to power. Beyond these tangible benefits, Kissinger derived an understanding of the way in which American leaders perceived issues of national security. As Graubard states, "what interested him was not isolated facts, which he might have learned from reading or private conversations, but the words and arguments that were used. What kind of evidence did such men introduce to support their conclusions?"[4] Although many of these conclusions provided the basis of the defense policies that the nation followed in the cold war, Kissinger regarded them critically. He recognized, however, that they were characteristically American in both their successes and shortcomings.

As Stephen Graubard observes, Kissinger's interest in national security issues continued after his return to Harvard as a lecturer in government in 1957. In addition to teaching, he helped establish and became head of the Defense Studies Program.[5] The program was centered around Government Seminar 259, "Defense Policy and Administration," which Kissinger taught. Under its auspices, he brought to Harvard senior military and governmental leaders for weekly discussions. Because of the way Kissinger organized the seminar, these discussions covered more than the scientific and technical aspects of defense studies. Kissinger approached military issues—even those involving nuclear weapons—in terms of their relationship to the purposes of foreign policy and to the practice of diplomacy.

During this period, Kissinger also served as the associate director of Harvard's Center for International Affairs. The center had been created in 1958 under the directorship of Robert Bowie, who also had a keen interest in defense issues and whose name was later associated with Kennedy's ill-fated proposal for a multilateral nuclear force for NATO.

Kissinger conducted a number of courses and study groups under the center's direction. Here, too, the focus was on national security and military policy. Through the center, Kissinger met public officials and military figures, both American and foreign, who studied at Harvard as fellows for a year. The center also exposed Kissinger to other members of Harvard's social science faculty—men whose ideas he used to buttress his own thinking on defense policies. Graubard notes, for example, that Kissinger "came to have great respect for Thomas Schelling, whose elegant theories had large implications for strategic thinking."[6] Edward Mason, an economist like Schelling, influenced Kissinger's ideas regarding the developing nations. The center's arms control and defense studies group included such prominent thinkers as Saville Davis, Arthur Schlesinger, Jr., Max Milliken, Jerome Wiesner, Jerrold Zacharias, and Morton Halperin. Such seminal works on defense policy as Robert Levine's *The Arms Debate*[7] and Schelling and Halperin's *Strategy and Arms Control*[8] were written under the center's auspices. Years later, Kissinger reflected that even as secretary of state, in the area of national security he relied heavily on the concepts and theories to which he had been exposed at Harvard in the 1950s.[9]

Kissinger's name was often linked with other defense theorists of the period such as Herman Kahn, Albert Wohlstetter, and Donald Brennan.[10] All these men added to the intellectual ferment of the fifties with pioneering works on the nature of thermonuclear war and the meaning of deterrence. More specifically, Kissinger was identified not only as an analyst of the overall nuclear balance, but as an advocate of a particular kind of defense—a capacity for limited war, both nuclear and conventional. Kissinger believed that limited nuclear and conventional defense should be as central to American military policy as strategic nuclear weapons. This was the principal message of *Nuclear Weapons and Foreign Policy* and of the articles that he wrote during this period. It was the basis of his critique of American military doctrine.

In advocating a strategy of limited war, Kissinger was part of a wider circle of thinkers both in and out of government who were criticizing American military policies. The Eisenhower administration's defense strategy, the "New Look," relied primarily on nuclear retaliation. These policies were intensely debated. Opponents called attention to both the increasing political restraints on using nuclear weapons, and to the multidimensional nature of the threat posed by the Sino-Soviet bloc. Books such as Bernard Brodie's *Strategy in the Missile Age*[11] and Robert Osgood's *Limited War*[12] articulated the need for a limited war fighting capability. In 1962, Morton Halperin compiled an annotated bibliography citing some 328 works on the subject of limited war, most of which had been written during the Eisenhower years.[13] Indeed, this arms debate figured prominently in the work of the Gaither Committee in 1957 which assessed the overall U.S. military posture,[14] and, within government, in the budgetary and strategy conflicts among the individual U.S. military services described by General Maxwell Taylor in his book *The Uncertain Trumpet*.[15]

It should be noted that, in his writings throughout the 1950s, Kissinger like other defense strategists of the time referred to the Sino-Soviet bloc as constituting a unified threat. Although he was sensitive to their separate national interests and historical antagonisms, he was less attentive to the growing rift between the two Communist powers. The irony in this should not go unnoticed since much of Kissinger's acclaim as a statesman is associated with his use of the Sino-Soviet rift to obtain leverage vis-à-vis both China and the Soviet Union. I have chosen not to discuss the implications this outlook had for the advocacy of limited war because this subject is widely discussed in much of the literature on the Vietnam war. However, the pitfalls of Kissinger's doctrine of limited war in the context of a perceived global (Sino-Soviet) threat should be mentioned. For Kissinger, limited war signified a highly controlled effort with specific political goals. In less skillful hands, the doctrine had the potential for leading to the kind of "indiscriminate globalism" that Kissinger rejected.

THE CONTINUITY OF HISTORICAL THEMES

Although Kissinger's thought on defense strategy paralleled that of others of the period, there are important distinctions that need to be made. These should not go unnoticed, because they are part of the underlying unity that connects his thought on national security issues to his historical and philosophical writings. These distinctions fall into three areas: first, his treatment of nuclear weapons; second, his particular emphasis on limited war; and third, the relationship of his writings to the theory of containment.

Nuclear Weapons and Foreign Policy is primarily a work of history—albeit a history of the contemporary period—written by a historian-strategist. Kissinger's purpose in the book is to explain the challenge of the nuclear age—specifically, the revolutionary impact of modern weapons on both military strategy and diplomacy. He contrasts the present age with the past when traditional modes of warfare were commensurate with the political purposes served by war. Now man would have to provide this commensurability by learning to use power "subtly and with discrimination."[16] Kissinger uses analogies to advance his argument. For example, he sees parallels between the present and previous periods in which new weapons initially outpaced doctrines necessary to control their use.

The need for doctrine to translate power into policy is a major theme of his work. When he describes the strategy of the Sino-Soviet bloc in the 1950s, he labels it revolutionary, for its goals were unlimited and could only be accomplished by overturning the existing international order. He finds historical parallels to the Sino-Soviet strategy in the challenges posed by Napoleon and Hitler.

In contrast to many works that appeared during the period, Kissinger's book cannot be regarded as a technical treatise on nuclear weapons. He offers few descriptions of these weapons, and he rarely uses the scientific terms associated with nuclear power. He deals with deterrence with little reference to the mathematical and probability analyses used by many theorists at the time. Although Kissinger was familiar with these approaches, he emphasizes the psychological factors that might influence an opponent's thinking and ultimately deter him from using nuclear force.

For these reasons, Kissinger was disparaged by others working in the field of nuclear weapons as a "popularizer."[17] As Graubard observes, Kissinger chose a relatively unconventional theme in *Nuclear Weapons and Foreign Policy* and discussed it in a highly idiosyncratic manner.[18] In part, Kissinger attempts to bridge the worlds of science and politics.[19] His thesis is that technology—however advanced or qualitatively different from that of the past—should never be considered apart from its political significance. Hence the need for doctrine to translate the power of nuclear weapons into political goals. While many theorists treated subjects such as deterrence and arms control in a highly technical way, Kissinger emphasizes the interrelationship among such areas as nuclear weapons, limited war, and diplomacy. Graubard writes that "Kissinger expected that the field would probably soon become highly specialized, and that this would exclude the kind of thinking that he deemed most important. Without disparaging technical research, Kissinger wanted to assert the importance of another kind—of the kind he was doing."[20] The historical and philosophical emphasis of *Nuclear Weapons and Foreign Policy* makes it accessible to the nontechnical student. Graubard observes:

> Though the book might be thought difficult—it was so described by a number of commentators—it was not technical. Any layman who wished to could read and understand it. This was what Kissinger intended. He had written it not for himself or for a small coterie of friends and experts who would have a special reason for being interested in the subject. Kissinger had taken a theme that was only beginning to be defined—the political, diplomatic, and military implications of thermonuclear weapons—and had written a book that

any conscientious lay reader could master if he made the effort to do so.[21]

Kissinger's historical and philosophical themes are drawn largely from his earlier writings. The Clausewitzian integration of force and diplomacy is, of course, a subject he first explored in *A World Restored*. Similarly, his analogy between England and the United States as "island powers" with similar perceptions of national security and reactive conceptions of defense is a theme that he carries over from his doctoral dissertation to his writings on nuclear weapons.

In *Nuclear Weapons and Foreign Policy*, Kissinger uses an idiom that echoes the philosophical speculation of his undergraduate thesis. He begins by referring to Nemesis, the goddess of retribution. Part of man's fate historically has been a paucity of physical power; now, in the nuclear age, his dilemma was that he had a superabundance of power that could result in his own destruction. Kissinger here draws on his study of Toynbee. In *A Study of History*, Toynbee showed how frequently Nemesis was involved in historical occurrence—particularly in the guise of the creative advances of one generation becoming the cause of decline in the next. Kissinger emphasizes the need for doctrine to transform physical power (even the power of nuclear weapons) into a political instrument. As I indicated in chapter 2, he shares this "spiritualized" conception of power with such historians as Spengler and Ranke. Finally, Kissinger stresses the need for choice in the nuclear age. He fears that the power of nuclear weapons would ultimately paralyze the will of our leaders, leaving them unable to provide a coherent defense. The belief in the necessity for action and the indispensability of choice that he developed in his studies of Kant animate his efforts to formulate a doctrine for using nuclear weapons.

The second difference between Kissinger and other theorists of nuclear weapons involves his writings on limited war. His advocacy of developing both nuclear and conventional capabilities for limited war arose from several factors. Kissinger believes that the most likely challenges in the contemporary period would be below the level of an all-out strategic conflict with the Soviet Union. Despite its bitter legacy, he suggests that Korea provided a better model for American military planning than World War II. He also maintains that as the Soviets gained strategic parity, our exclusive reliance on nuclear weapons to deter all forms of aggression would become implausible. Would a future American president risk the destruction of U.S. cities because of a limited Soviet military action in West Germany? The task of American military strategy, Kissinger stresses, was to devise intermediary steps that would avoid the dilemma of choosing between doing nothing in the face of communist aggression and risking all-out nuclear war.

Other authors also supported developing capabilities for limited war. Bernard Brodie discussed limited war in the context of our overall strategy in the nuclear age. Robert Osgood, whose book on limited war was published in the same year (1957) as *Nuclear Weapons and Foreign Policy*, expressed ideas very similar to Kissinger's. In fact, Osgood's work is superior in portraying limited war historically. He discussed it as a specific mode of warfare with a unique environment and tactics and a highly developed relationship between ends and means.

Kissinger's writings on limited war are distinguished, I believe, by his treatment of the American character and its insular perceptions of national security. Specifically, he views the nation's insularity as the principal obstacle to its formulation of a limited war doctrine. Other writers such as Osgood call attention to the American approach to warfare, highlighting its emphasis on technology, industrial production, and the principles of total war. Kissinger's treatment of this phenomenon is more fundamental. I will discuss the relationship that he establishes between America's insularity and its military shortcomings later in this chapter. Kissinger regards these shortcomings as a key to the erosion of our geopolitical position in the period after 1945.

> Many of our problems in the postwar period have been produced by our failure to accept the doctrinal challenge [of limited war]. . . . Above all, we have a penchant for considering our problems as primarily technical and to confuse strategy with the maximum development of power. One of the paradoxical lessons of the nuclear age is that at the moment when we are acquiring an unparalleled command over nature, we are forced to realize as never before that the problems of survival will have to be solved above all in the minds of men. In this task the fate of the mammoth and the dinosaur may serve as a warning that brute strength does not always supply the mechanism in the struggle for survival.[22]

Kissinger's works on limited war are also distinguished by his emphasis on the use of tactical nuclear weapons. For the most part, other authors discuss limited war with respect to conventional military strength. In this respect, Kissinger occupies a position somewhere between the "utopian" theorists who emphasize strategic air power and primary reliance on nuclear weapons and the "traditionalists" who stress conventional military forces for land and sea defense.[23] Kissinger later recanted his belief in limited nuclear war,[24] but part of the impact of *Nuclear Weapons and Foreign Policy* resulted from his discussion of this strategy. It should be mentioned that Kissinger's reappraisal of limited nuclear war arose from several factors, including the growth of the Soviet nuclear arsenal and the impact of arms control negotiations—both of which decreased the likely use of nuclear weapons even in a limited fashion. No factor, however, was more important in Kissinger's later reformulation than the fact that the U.S. military services had been unable to define the nature of a limited war or to agree on a common doctrine for its propagation.

CONTAINMENT AND AMERICAN FOREIGN POLICY

The third major difference between Kissinger and other strategists of the period involves the goal of American foreign and defense policy during the cold war, containment. As Louis J. Halle indicates, containment "was a word and a concept" whose efficacy lay in the fact that its doctrinal implications fitted the nation's capabilities and perceptions at the end of World War II.[25] It provided an intellectual mooring for American leaders who had been set adrift by the breakdown of our wartime alliance with the Soviet Union.[26] For the most part, other strategists writing at the same time as Kissinger accepted, either implicitly or explicitly, the doctrine of containment as the basis of American policy. To the extent that these theorists differed with official American policy, they disputed the various forms that containment assumed, such as the New Look of the Eisenhower administration which emphasized the use of strategic air power to contain Soviet advances, rather than the substance of the policy itself.[27]

In contrast, Kissinger argues against containment as the cornerstone of postwar American policy. He regards it as the clearest manifestation of America's insularity. Although Kissinger never made the comparison explicit, there is a striking similarity between the policy of containment and English policy during the Napoleonic era—a policy known as the Pitt Plan. Kissinger discusses the Pitt Plan in *A World Restored*. Castlereagh's transition from an "English" to a "European" outlook involved his disavowal of this policy. The Pitt Plan called for ringing France with "secondary powers, each with a barrier of fortresses to absorb the first French onslaught."[28] Contained behind these defensive barriers, France could be expected to moderate its expansionist policies until, over time, it accepted the European order. Kissinger sees in the Pitt Plan the "mechanical conception of international relations"[29] characteristic of an insular power which made no allowances for changing relations among the other European powers, or for the various forms that expansion could take other than "pure" aggression. Kissinger also observes that the Pitt Plan conceived threats to the European equilibrium solely in military terms, whereas the continental powers viewed France's major challenge as political and ideological, i.e., the attempt to transform Europe through the revolutionary ideas of the French Republic.

Containment, Kissinger believes, grew out of this same kind of mechanical conception of policy. Its reliance on defensive barriers and evolutionary changes in the Soviet Union amounted to what Walter Lippmann characterized as "holding the line and hoping for the best."[30] Kissinger advances three major arguments against containment. The first argument criticizes its separation of the political and military dimensions of foreign policy. Kissinger describes this separation in the following way:

> The notion that war and peace were separate and successive phases of policy has been at the root of our post-war policy. It came to expression in the dominant Western policy of the post-war period: the policy of Containment. This was based on the assumption that a substantial effort to rebuild Western strength had to *precede* any serious negotiations with the Soviet Union. Conferences would be futile until the Communist countries found themselves confronted by preponderant strength all around their periphery. "What we must do," said Secretary Acheson, "is to create situations of strength; we must build strength; and if we create that strength then I think the whole situation in the world begins to change. . . . With that change there comes a difference in the negotiating position of the various parties and out of that I should hope that there would be a willingness on the part of the Kremlin to recognize facts . . . and to begin to solve at least some of the difficulties between East and West."[31]

Kissinger traces this separation of power and diplomacy to George Kennan's famous "X" article in *Foreign Affairs* in 1947, and to the diplomacy of Dean Acheson and John Foster Dulles. He believes that this separation of foreign policy and military power led to "the atrophy of both."[32] Kissinger stresses that this division caused us to lose critical opportunities for meaningful negotiations with the Soviets. One such opportunity was at the very beginning of the cold war. It was then that our atomic weapons offered the most relative strength we would ever enjoy vis-à-vis the Soviets. Kissinger repeatedly quotes from what he terms "a major much-neglected speech"[33] that Churchill delivered in Llandudno, Wales, in October 1948. On this and other occasions in the late forties, Churchill called for diplomatic confrontation with the Soviets, lest their growing military strength erode any basis for negotiations.[34] Kissinger sees another missed opportunity in the period after Stalin's death in 1953—a period that he describes as one of maximum confusion and fluidity in Soviet leadership groups.[35] He thinks it paradoxical that the United States had been on the diplomatic and military defensive during years in which the Soviets were beleaguered by leadership changes, economic difficulties, and unrest in their East European satellites.[36] Kissinger also believes that our failure to correlate military and political objectives led to much of the frustration the nation experienced in Korea.

The second failure of containment involves its military form. Kissinger equates the military aspects of containment with a defensive and reactive conception of security—with "holding the line." This defensive conception expressed itself in our reliance on nuclear weapons and on efforts to construct a global network of pacts and alliances. Massive retaliation and "pactomania" were opposite sides of the same coin. Both, Kissinger argues, were vulnerable to Soviet efforts to alter the global balance of power through a strategy of ambiguity. In the face of challenges, no single one of which would involve our vital security, our reliance on nuclear weapons and collective security would ultimately paralyze our will. Furthermore, he argues that deterrence and containment were essentially incompatible. While deterrence could establish a strategic stalemate, it was relatively ineffectual in containing advances below the strategic level. While containment required the demonstration of strength, deterrence rested on the premise that strength need not be demonstrated.

> During this period, it became increasingly apparent that the guiding notion of our strategic planning—the concept of deterrence—could not support the key assumption of the containment theory that strength would more or less automatically lead to negotiation. Deterrence is tested negatively by actions which do not happen. But, unless there is aggression, our strength is not demonstrated and can supply no incentive to negotiate.[37]

The third failure of containment was political. The belief that "time was on our side" fostered a diplomatic passivity that relied, as Lippmann noted, on "hoping for the best." Kissinger observes that containment was based on the premise that the Soviet Union, once hemmed in by defensive barriers, would "mellow," largely through an evolutionary process that was economic in nature. This same belief in economic evolution shaped our political relations with Western Europe and with the new nations of the Third World. Such a doctrine was a sterile response to the revolutionary nature of the times. History, Kissinger points out, contains no guarantee of eventual success, but must be shaped by active diplomacy and leadership.[38]

I will discuss Kissinger's criticism of the political failures of containment in chapter 6. In the following pages, I will deal with its military side and what Kissinger refers to as America's "esoteric strategy."

The Challenges of the Postwar Era

THE REVOLUTIONARY AGE

Kissinger sees the period after 1945 as a revolutionary age. His analysis of the military challenges facing the United States must be understood in this context. As I demonstrated in chapter 2, the distinction between a revolutionary and a legitimate period is fundamental to Kissinger's conception of international politics. The nature of the age determines the structure of the international system, defining the reasons why nations compete, the role of diplomacy, and the scope of conflict.

Drawing on his description of a revolutionary age in *A World Restored*, Kissinger interprets the competition between the United States and the Soviet Union in the cold war period as one that involved ultimate goals—the nature of international society itself—rather than adjustments within the system. Because the values of each society were fundamentally incompatible, their dispute ultimately involved the existence of their domestic social systems in their present forms.

The nature of this dispute also meant that the international system lacked a framework for reconciling competing demands. This made diplomacy especially problematical. Diplomatic practices in a revolutionary period are vulnerable to attempts by revolutionary powers to isolate the status quo nations morally. Kissinger regards such an attempt as the basis of Soviet diplomacy. Its major purpose—even in periods of détente—was to demonstrate that the values of American society were antagonistic to those of the world community, especially those of the emerging nations of Africa and Asia.

Conflict in a revolutionary period is unlimited in scope. It is the mark of a revolutionary power that it rejects the conditions of relative security inherent in the international system. Kissinger was familiar with the political and historical arguments that allegedly explained Soviet conduct after 1945. These arguments depicted Eastern Europe as a "cordon sanitaire," which the Soviets constructed to block the historical routes of invasion that Hitler's Germany had most recently used. Kissinger rejects these arguments, which implied that Soviet goals were limited in nature. He believes that Soviet insecurity could only be assuaged by a world order in which all other powers, including the United States, were largely defenseless. The distinguishing feature of a revolutionary power such as the Soviet Union "is not that it feels threatened—such feeling is inherent in the nature of international relations based on sovereign states—but that nothing can reassure it. Only absolute security—the neutralization of the opponent—is considered a sufficient guarantee, and thus the desire for one power for absolute security means absolute insecurity for all the others."[39]

The Soviet challenge, therefore, existed on two planes—the ideological and the military. Before turning to a discussion of the latter, it is important that we consider two other factors that, for Kissinger, contributed to the revolutionary temper of the age. The nature of military power in the nuclear era and the emergence of the Third World nations both played an important role in defining the character of the postwar period.

Kissinger believes that nuclear weapons require man to adjust his definition of power. Security, for example, can no longer be equated with the impermeability of a nation's territory. No matter how much power a nation possesses, it cannot prevent cataclysmic damage to its society. In the past, the military equilibrium depended on the preservation of territorial limits and the prevention of territorial expansion by one power at the expense of others. In the contemporary period, territory no longer serves as a measure of power. Nations such as the Soviet Union and China gained more from their acquisition of nuclear weapons than from any conceivable territorial addition. "In other words," Kissinger writes, "the really fundamental changes in the balance of power have all occurred within the territorial limits of sovereign states. Clearly, there is an urgent need to analyze just what is understood by power—as well as by balance of power—in the nuclear age."[40]

Yet Kissinger regards the most significant impact of nuclear weapons to be that they eroded the traditional relationship between military power and foreign policy. Because power was no longer commensurate with many of the goals that nations sought, leaders found it difficult to translate power into policy. Kissinger points out that this situation makes diplomacy in the modern period uniquely intractable, because traditional pressures can no longer be used to break diplomatic stalemates. The most important consequence, however, is that this inability to balance power and policy might ultimately demoralize a nation. Kissinger feared that America faced just this possibility in the cold war.

The dilemma of the nuclear period can, therefore, be defined as follows: the enormity of modern weapons makes the thought of war repugnant, but the refusal to run any risks would amount to giving the Soviet rulers a blank check. At a time when we have never been stronger, we have had to learn that power which is not clearly related to the objectives for which it is to be employed may merely paralyze the will. No more urgent task confronts American policy than to bring our power into balance with the issues for which we are most likely to contend.[41]

The emergence of new nations from areas previously under European rule also fueled the revolutionary temper of the postwar period. Kissinger asserts that historically the integration of even a single state into the international system, such as Prussia in eighteenth-century Europe, necessitated fundamental changes. Power relationships had to be adjusted. Economic patterns were altered. Basic shifts occurred in traditional alliances. In the contemporary period, these problems were compounded by the number of states to be assimilated and by their radically different societies and cultures. Furthermore, Kissinger indicates, the emerging nations of Africa and Asia continued "to inject into their policies the revolutionary fervor that gained them independence."[42]

For Kissinger, calling the postwar period revolutionary was tantamount to saying that the conditions of world order were missing from international life. The schisms caused by the ideological struggle with the Soviet Union and by the egalitarian demands of the new nations meant that the international system lacked a basis for legitimacy. A significant number of Third World nations did not accept the postwar structure of political and economic relations. Writing in the 1950s, Kissinger indicated that the Sino-Soviet bloc exploited this turmoil as a basic instrument of its strategy. He also believed that the communist bloc would strive to overturn the other basic condition of world order—the military equilibrium. The most formidable challenge to American defense, Kissinger wrote, arose from a "Soviet strategy of ambiguity which seeks to upset the strategic balance by small degrees and which combines political, psychological, and ideological pressures to induce the greatest degree of uncertainty and hesitation in the minds of the opponent."[43] It is to this challenge we now turn.

THE NATURE OF THE MILITARY CHALLENGE

Kissinger's assessment of the threats posed by the Sino-Soviet bloc and the implications for American military strategy accounted for much of the success that *Nuclear Weapons and Foreign Policy* enjoyed. In this and other works of the period, Kissinger provides a lucid analysis of the multidimensional challenges posed by Soviet strategy.

The strategic problem of the United States had two aspects: the central relationship between the United States and the Soviet Union, and the defense of the Eurasian continent. The first, Kissinger writes, involved deterrence—"to create a level of thermo-nuclear strength to deter the Soviet bloc from a major war, or from aggression in areas which cannot be defended by an indigenous effort."[44] It is significant that Kissinger pays less attention to strategic deterrence in *Nuclear Weapons and Foreign*

Policy than to America's military policy in the Third World countries of the Eurasian land mass. It is with the publication of *The Necessity for Choice* in 1961 that Kissinger fully elaborates his views on deterrence.

The reason for this omission is that until the Soviet Sputnik was orbited in 1957 and the alleged "missile gap" emerged in 1958, Kissinger regarded the strategic balance as relatively stable. Although the United States had strategic superiority in the initial period of the cold war, Kissinger believed that nothing could prevent the Soviet Union from increasing its supply of nuclear weapons. To this extent, he decried calls for "preventive" or "pre-emptive" war against the Soviet Union as a bankrupt policy and a "fit of frustration."[45] He considered such calls characteristic of an insular nation that seeks to cut the "Gordian knot" of complexity involved in international relations.[46] Kissinger believed that the likely outcome of growing Soviet power would be the creation of a nuclear "stalemate."

> Thus for the first time in military history there is the possibility of a stalemate despite an absolute superiority in number of weapons and in technology; and when this point has been reached the American strategic problem is transformed. The Red Army may have been immobilized by the American atomic monopoly, but it may be liberated by the Soviet capacity to retaliate on Washington. It is argued by some that the atomic stalemate is nothing new, that it has in fact existed on the Eurasian continent since 1949. But this is surely not the same as saying that it has been part of the American consciousness since then, and this is the crucial factor in determining willingness to engage in a general war. The stalemate on the Eurasian continent has been maintained solely by the relative freedom of action of the United States. That is precisely why our nuclear arsenal is no better than our willingness to use it, and this is in danger of being reduced as the Soviet nuclear capacity grows.[47]

It was only in the wake of the growing Soviet missile capacity that Kissinger turns to the problems of deterrence. Like Albert Wohlstetter,[48] he came to regard the U.S.–USSR balance as more precarious than the condition implied by the word "stalemate." Given both the capabilities and volatility of new weapons technology, there was no longer an "automaticity" about the strategic equilibrium. Depending on the nature of a nation's retaliatory forces, an opponent might be tempted to a "first strike."

Even during this period, Kissinger's writings on deterrence are relatively meager. He still believed that the overall balance, however delicate, could be stabilized by ensuring that the retaliatory forces of both sides were mutually invulnerable. Kissinger acknowledges that, even with invulnerable second-strike capabilities, a balance made up of two powers would never possess the flexibility of the classical European system. Although he enters into the theological debates involving "finite" deterrence and "counterforce" strategy,[49] he emphasizes the psychological dimensions of deterrence. He focuses on the political implications of mutual invulnerability and the relationship between deterrence and arms control.[50]

Kissinger has always emphasized the second aspect of America's strategic problem, i.e., America's military policy in Eurasia, particularly in the peripheral countries. His writings on defense issues in the fifties and early sixties focus on the Sino-Soviet challenge in these areas.

Kissinger's analysis originates in what he regards as an unalterable geopolitical reality. America is an island power—endangered by the possible hegemony of one power over the opposite land mass. Kissinger first makes this observation with respect to England in *A World Restored*.[51] Not even the nuclear age could alter its significance. Kissinger offers the following analysis in an early article:

> We have a strategic interest in Eurasia . . . namely, the geopolitical fact that in relation to Eurasia the United States is an island Power with inferior resources at present only in manpower but later on even in industrial capacity. Thus we are confronted by the traditional problem of an "island" power—of Carthage with respect to Italy, of Britain with respect to the Continent—that its survival depends on preventing the opposite land-mass from falling under the control of a single Power, above all one avowedly hostile. If Eurasia were to fall under the control of a single Power or group of Powers, and if this hostile Power were given sufficient time to exploit its resources, we should confront an overpowering threat. At best we would be forced into a military effort not consistent with what is now considered the "American way of life." At worst we would be neutralized and would no longer be masters of our policy.[52]

The Soviet Union, unmistakably, was the "avowedly hostile" power striving to control Eurasia. Kissinger treats the reader of *Nuclear Weapons and Foreign Policy* to a description of the Soviet Union as a revolutionary power that is largely paraphrased from his doctoral dissertation. His intent is to show that the danger presented by the Soviet Union is, like that of Napoleon and Hitler, a total danger. He emphasizes that America, as both an insular and a status quo power, is particularly ill-suited to grasp the magnitude of the Soviet challenge. Historically, Kissinger observes, status quo powers have been at a profound psychological disadvantage. They tend to believe that the goals of the revolutionary state are limited (for therein lies their own notion of peace), and that the revolutionary power can be integrated into the international system that it seeks to destroy. Kissinger stresses that this belief explains the American approach to the Soviets and the historical success of revolutionary powers in altering the balance of power.

> The revolutionary power [the Soviet Union], therefore, gains a subtle advantage. If it displays any degree of psychological skill, it can present every move as the expression of limited aims or as caused by a legitimate grievance. The status quo powers [America and Europe], on the other hand, cannot be sure that the balance of power is in fact threatened or that their opponent is not sincere until he has demonstrated it, and by the time he has done so it is usually too late. However the physical balance may be weighted at first against the revolutionary power, this handicap is more than made up by the psychological advantage conferred by the absence of self-restraint.[53]

Kissinger believed that the Sino-Soviet bloc aimed at isolating the United States—both physically and morally—from the European land mass. The central area of contention was, of course, Europe. Kissinger felt reasonably assured that the NATO region could be defended, although even here, as I will discuss shortly, he believed that American strategy adversely affected NATO defenses. The key thrust of Sino-Soviet action, Kissinger maintains, would be in the peripheral areas of the Eurasian continent. These countries, grouped around the periphery of China and the Soviet Union, were characterized by former Secretary of the Air Force Thomas Finletter as the "grey areas"—a phrase that Kissinger adopts for both its psychological and geostrategic connotations. The countries in this group were outside the sphere of influence of the major powers, but their alignment with the Soviet Union would dramatically alter the global equilibrium. "The particular danger zone," Kissinger states, "is the arc which stretches from the eastern border of Turkey around the periphery of Eurasia."[54] In this region, he notes that Iran, Afghanistan, Burma, Thailand, and Indochina (Vietnam, Laos, Cambodia) lacked sufficient forces to put up an initial defense.[55] Sino-Soviet penetration of this area would have a major geopolitical effect in the Middle East, the Indian subcontinent, and northeast Asia.

But how could the Soviets accomplish such a geopolitical transformation without triggering a western response—including a nuclear attack by the United States? Kissinger believes that such a transformation was highly possible, given American attitudes and its military doctrine, and what he refers to as the Sino-Soviet "strategy of ambiguity."[56]

THE STRATEGY OF AMBIGUITY

The Sino-Soviet bloc presented challenges in such a manner—particularly in the "grey areas"—that no single challenge appeared conclusively to warrant an American response. In fact, Soviet strategic thought envisions that if challenges were presented in such an ambiguous fashion, pressures would mount in democratic societies for solutions short of war or for the end of wars that might have already started.[57] Soviet strategy steadfastly avoids an all-out showdown. "Rather," Kissinger writes, "the Soviet concept is one of seeking to manage the inevitable flow of history, to bring about the attrition of the enemy by gradual increments, and not to stake everything on a single throw of the dice."[58] Kissinger addresses this aspect of Soviet conduct and the difficulties it presents for American policy in an article in *Foreign Affairs* in 1956.

> unless we maintain at least an equilibrium of power between us and the Soviet bloc we will have no chance to undertake any positive measures. And maintaining this equilibrium may confront us with some very difficult choices. We are certain to be confronted with situations of extraordinary ambiguity such as civil wars or domestic coups. Every successful Soviet move makes our moral position that much more difficult: Indochina was more ambiguous than Korea; the Soviet arms deal with Egypt more ambiguous than Indochina; the Suez crisis more ambiguous than the arms deal. There can be no doubt that we should seek to prevent such occurrences.[59]

In the modern age, however, America would find the forms of aggression chosen by the Soviets difficult to counter, even with conventional forces. The contemporary period would see the growth of guerrilla warfare, insurgencies, and domestic coups. Kissinger believes that this situation places decision-makers under great stress, for the impetus to use their most potent weapons is countered by the realization that these weapons are not suited to the form of aggression they face. How can nuclear weapons prevent political changes in societies deemed vital to American security?

Kissinger writes at length about Sino-Soviet strategy. It is evident that he finds communist strategic thought politically and psychologically astute. He traces its strength to three interrelated factors. The first is the Soviet assessment of the physical balance of power vis-à-vis the United States. Kissinger believes that the Soviets understood the implications of the growing stalemate in nuclear weapons. They believed that this stalemate would inhibit America from using nuclear weapons in peripheral areas. Further, Kissinger points out, Soviet diplomatic strategy in the early years of the cold war had largely offset our overwhelming strategic power. Thus, even during a period in which no physical stalemate existed with respect to our use of nuclear weapons, there existed a psychological stalemate every bit as potent.

The second element that contributes to the strength of Sino-Soviet strategic thought involves its emphasis on psychological insight. Soviet strategic thought aims at exploiting the psychological weaknesses of democratic societies. Kissinger notes that Soviet leaders are not only versed in the elements of their own doctrine, "but have consciously sought to press the psychological vulnerabilities of their opponents into their service."[60] Hence, the Soviets alternate acts of belligerency with peace offensives—appealing to the American belief that peace is the normal condition of international politics. Similarly, wars of national liberation in the "grey areas" are justified in terms designed to appeal to the West's sense of democratic legitimacy. Kissinger offers particular praise for Mao's psychological subtlety and mastery of the psychological aspects of war.

The political-ideological component of Sino-Soviet strategy also contributes to its strength. Kissinger views Leninist thought as responsible for the Soviets' ability to use flexible tactics while maintaining a doctrine that was largely unchanging. This doctrine postulates a ceaseless conflict with the noncommunist world, although the form of this conflict would vary. Kissinger sees the influence of Clausewitz in Leninist thought. The political and military realms are inextricably linked in Sino-Soviet strategy. Kissinger cites Lenin's insight that "war is part of the whole. The whole is politics. . . . Appearances are not reality. Wars are most political when they seem most military."[61]

Together, these three aspects of Sino-Soviet thought produced a strategy of extreme ambiguity. Its purposes were to disguise the full nature of the challenges that were being posed and to paralyze America's will to resist. What response did the nation make to these challenges? Kissinger finds the answer in what he calls America's "Esoteric Strategy."

The Esoteric Strategy

THE NEW LOOK

America faced several choices regarding its defense strategy as the Soviet challenge developed in the period after 1945. Advocates at one end of the spectrum favored a return to something like America's prewar isolationism. They wanted the nation to restrict its concerns to the Western Hemisphere and to depend largely on its air and sea power. Changes in the balance of power in other areas of the globe did not endanger American security. Support of this neoisolationism was offered as late as 1950 in former President Herbert Hoover's "Gibralter" speech, and in the "Great Debate" of 1951 regarding stationing additional troops in Europe. At the opposite end of the military spectrum were proponents of preventive war. The United States should force a military showdown with the Soviets while we still possessed strategic superiority. Preventive war theories, however, received little support within government, a fact demonstrated by Secretary of Defense Louis Johnson's resignation in the fall of 1950. Johnson was one of the few officials who supported this position.[62]

Containment became America's official postwar strategy. Containment rejected both isolationism and preventive war in favor of a policy of long-term counterforce designed to block further Soviet expansion. The military forms of containment were elaborated in NSC–68 and NSC–162. The latter became the basis for what was known as the New Look of the Eisenhower administration. The New Look operated under most of the same premises as NSC–68, with the exception that it placed greater reliance on nuclear air power. Thus, American military strategy possessed a basic continuity throughout the Truman and Eisenhower years. Because Kissinger's criticism of American military policy focuses on the New Look, I will highlight this doctrine in the following discussion.

In assessing American military doctrine, Kissinger observes that its basic premises have remained unchanged, despite the nation's changing strategic position vis-à-vis the Soviets. Writing about the New Look in 1955, he notes that "it is surprising how little affected American strategic thinking has been by the fact that within just a few years the U.S.S.R. will have the capacity to deliver a powerful attack with nuclear weapons on the United States."[63] Kissinger believes our policies were not reassessed because of "the general agreement about the main lines of American strategy" represented by the public statements of Secretary of State Dulles and Vice President Nixon.[64]

What was the New Look? Primarily, it involved the belief that America's nuclear retaliatory capacity would deter both general and limited war with the Sino-Soviet bloc. The threat of "massive retaliation" would inhibit Soviet aggression more effectively than any other military posture. The corollary of this position was that conventional forces above a certain level do not add appreciably to the nation's strength. Consequently, strategic air power and nuclear arsenals should be emphasized over ground forces.

Alliances were used to buttress the New Look. Between 1945 and 1957, the United States created a system of alliances involving forty-four sovereign states. With these alliances, the United States sought to surround the Soviet Union with nations that it would shrink from attacking for fear of American nuclear retaliation.

American officials such as Secretary of State John Foster Dulles and Secretary of the Air Force Thomas K. Finletter recognized that the Sino-

Soviet bloc had both more manpower and the advantage of internal lines of communication and supply to support limited wars in the "grey areas." As a result, they believed that America "must not exhaust itself in a 'war of attrition' in peripheral areas" where it was at a strategic disadvantage.[65] Samuel Huntington provides the following analysis of the military basis of the New Look. Huntington's reference to American leaders in the quotation is to Admiral Arthur Radford, the chief of naval operations, who testified before the Senate on the Department of Defense requested appropriations for 1955.

> The Korean War was over. American leaders publicly rejected the idea that the United States would become tied down in a similar conflict in the future. The overwhelming superiority of the Soviets in manpower meant that "there is no local defense which alone will contain" the Communists, and hence the free world "should not attempt to match the Soviet bloc man for man and gun for gun."[66]

The basis for the New Look resided only partly in military doctrine. The Eisenhower administration believed that the communist threat to American security was as much economic as military. Unless a proper balance existed between a strong economy and defense expenditures, the nation would spend itself into ruin. For this reason, Eisenhower imposed a budgetary ceiling for defense in each year of his presidency and used this figure to plan both the level of armed forces and their composition. Although NSC–68 (1950) had described the growth of the communist threat as leading to a year or several years of crisis in the near term, Eisenhower saw America's confrontation with the Soviets as a condition that would continue over the "long haul." This belief enhanced the need for a military-economic balance. Reliance on nuclear weapons was deemed the best way to create this balance.[67] Huntington describes the economic concepts behind the New Look:

> The economic collapse which the [Eisenhower] administration feared could take two forms. Sustained excessive military programs could cause a spiraling inflation which would eventually lead to disaster. Or, the setting of a specific target date for the peak of the defense effort could cause a subsequent slump which, in turn, might lead to a disastrous depression. The New Look program was designed to avert both possibilities: the military program was to be reduced to avoid the danger of inflation and collapse; stabilization for the "long haul" would avoid the danger of peaking and depression.[68]

These were the major elements of the Eisenhower defense strategy. Kissinger discusses each at length. Beyond the specifics of the New Look, however, he discerns a characteristically American outlook toward defense policy in general. He sees the principles of all-out war as basic to American military thinking. These principles led him to dub the Eisenhower strategy "esoteric."

THE PRINCIPLES OF ALL-OUT WAR

Kissinger traces the roots of American military thinking to "a theory of war based on the necessity of total victory."[69] Americans historically viewed war more in moral than strategic terms. For this reason, war was thought to involve an all-out effort aimed not only at crushing the opponent's will but destroying him physically.

This conception of war and victory is, to a certain extent, inherent in all democratic nations. Leaders in a democracy must arouse its citizens against an opponent before they can declare war. Because of the nature of the acts that occur in war, this kind of popular antagonism develops its own momentum, often eroding the government's control and eliminating its diplomatic options. Only total victory can assuage such pitches of feeling.

Kissinger recognizes these general tendencies in democratic societies. He gives greater emphasis, however, to America's particular historical experience in explaining its military outlook. America first took an active role in international politics in the twentieth century—the century, in Raymond Aron's apt description, of total war.[70] Kissinger describes the changes in military thought that occurred:

> with the outbreak of World War I, war suddenly seemed to become an end in itself. After the first few months of the war, none of the protagonists would have been able to name an objective other than the total defeat of the enemy. . . . During World War I a gap appeared between military and political planning which has not since been bridged. The military staffs had developed plans for total victory, because in such plans no political limitations interfere with the full development of power and all factors are under the control of the military. But the political leadership proved incapable of giving these military objectives a political expression in terms of peace aims.[71]

This gap between military power and political purpose, coupled with the nation's moralistic outlook, provide the two pillars of the theory of all-out war. In fact, they reinforce each other. It is precisely because war is approached in moral terms that it becomes unthinkable that political interests should fetter the military effort. Kissinger believes that this strain of thought is deeply rooted in the American conscience. He suggests that during the nineteenth century—a period of limited wars—America provided an exception to that rule, fighting its civil war as a total war in both scale and aims.[72]

Kissinger also associates the nation's commitment to all-out war with its search for final solutions in international politics. Having been isolated throughout much of its history from the limits imposed by the international state system, America rebels against the imperfect and partial adjustments that are the essence of international life. Its idea of war mirrors the same escape from complexity that marks its diplomacy.

Robert Osgood observes that "more than any other great nation, America's basic predisposition and her experience in world politics encourage the dissociation of power and policy."[73] Kissinger's use of the term "esoteric" to describe American military thought refers to this dissociation of power and policy. Kissinger draws on his historical studies—particularly those of European history—for the basis for his criticism of American doctrine. Only during brief periods in Europe, such as the religious wars in the sixteenth century and the French Revolution, were wars based on purely military considerations. Kissinger points out that "far from being the "normal" form of conflict, all-out war constitutes a special case. It comes about through the abdication of political leadership or when there exists so deep a schism between the contenders that the total destruction of the enemy appears the only goal worth contending for."[74]

Two other elements support the American doctrine of all-out war. The first involves the belief that once a war begins, victory resides in the full development of America's military and industrial potential. Strategy is equated with the ability to mobilize industry and to outproduce the opponent. A corollary of this belief is that until a war actually begins, our forces-in-being "need only be large enough to avoid disaster."[75]

The second of these elements concerns the nature of the threat. Kissinger believes that American military thought defines threats as acts of "pure aggression."[76] Danger to national security is usually seen to result from an unambiguous act of hostility, either taken directly against the United States or against its allies. Such acts of "pure aggression" warrant a total response. The attack on Pearl Harbor clearly reinforced this belief. Kissinger suggests that the nation carried its fear of a surprise attack as the most likely form of aggression into its postwar thinking.

Kissinger depicts American military doctrine as the legacy of both its insular character and its experiences in World Wars I and II. Thus America's military doctrine in the period after 1945 was a "new look" only in the sense that nuclear weapons were a new instrument of warfare. The doctrine governing their use, however, remained unchanged from previous periods.[77] Kissinger observes:

> If our military doctrine in the immediate postwar period had difficulty in coming to grips with our most likely dangers, it had few doubts about the strategy for conducting any war that might break out. A war

would be global and it would be won by our superior industrial potential. Since war would start with a surprise attack, our best defense lay in "our ability to strike back quickly with counteroffensive, to neutralize the hostile attack at its source . . . by striking at the vitals of the aggressor." The doctrine of massive retaliation was far from new at the time Secretary John Foster Dulles proclaimed it.[78]

The Need for Doctrine

THE MAGINOT LINE

How relevant was America's military thinking to the postwar Soviet challenge? In an analogy to which he repeatedly returns, Kissinger suggests that the doctrine of massive retaliation had become America's "Maginot line." "To seek safety in numerical superiority or even in superior destructiveness," he writes, "may come close to a Maginot-line mentality—to seek in numbers a substitute for conception."[79]

During the fifties, Kissinger came increasingly to believe that our strategic doctrine contributed to a paralysis of policy. He compares our situation to that created by French strategic thought in the 1930s.

> In 1936, the French General Staff possessed no doctrine for any conflict except all-out war and it believed in no strategy save the defensive. It failed to provide for any contingency except a direct attack on the Franco-German border. Nor did it anticipate that the strategic balance might be upset by small stages, each of which, in itself, did not seem "worth" all-out war. As a result, when Hitler remilitarized the Rhineland, French leadership was paralyzed. It recoiled before the consequences of full mobilization, but its strategic doctrine provided for no other military measures. . . . The penalty for doctrinal rigidity was military catastrophe.[80]

Kissinger maintains that American military strategy was leading—indeed, had led—to this same paralysis. Kissinger believed that America's reliance on nuclear weapons, particularly in the "grey areas," had become implausible. With the growth of the Soviet nuclear arsenal and its delivery capability, nuclear war had become a "double-edged sword."[81] America would be inhibited from using these weapons for the same reasons that they were supposed to deter Soviet aggression. Moreover, it was fundamental to the psychological aim of Sino-Soviet strategy to orchestrate challenges such that none seemed "worth" all-out war. American strategy, i.e., its "doctrinal rigidity," thus offered the Sino-Soviet bloc frequent opportunities for eroding the global balance.

Kissinger also believes that American military strategy was incompatible with its policy of alliances. Both with respect to NATO and the "grey areas," a fundamental inconsistency existed between "a reliance on nuclear war and political commitment to regional defense."[82] American strategy remained unclear as to whether an attack against Thailand, for example, would initiate an effort to defend Thailand locally or to wage an all-out war against the Sino-Soviet bloc. Moreover, Kissinger argues, the doctrine of massive retaliation sapped the strength of our alliances. Our allies would either feel that they had no military role to play in a nuclear war or would themselves recoil from such a war, preferring surrender.[83] In making these points, Kissinger again draws on the comparison to French strategic thought.

> Thus the French system of alliances in the interwar period broke down, when put to the test, because its political purpose and the military doctrine on which it was based were inconsistent with each other. The political purpose of the French system of alliances was to assure the integrity of the small states of Central and Eastern Europe. Militarily, this implied an offensive strategy on the part of France, because only by forcing Germany into a two-front war could the latter's pressure on the Central European powers be eased. But with the building of the Maginot line the condition of military co-operation between France and its allies disappeared. . . . In every crisis, France was torn between its political and military commitments, and its allies were forced to choose between suicidal resistance or surrender.[84]

Kissinger believes that America's position continually eroded throughout the cold war. The nation repeatedly recoiled before the consequences of using its nuclear weapons. American paralysis was evident, for example, in Indochina in 1954. Our reliance on massive retaliation did nothing to prevent the loss of North Vietnam following the fall of Dien Bien Phu. In fact, Kissinger regards it as a contributory factor, for we lacked both a doctrine and a capability to intervene. He also calls attention to the ineffectiveness of nuclear weapons in situations like the Suez crisis of 1956 and Soviet penetration of the Middle East by means of the sale of arms to Egypt in 1955. (In order to accomplish this penetration, the Soviets acted as an intermediary since the arms were actually provided on favorable terms by Czechoslovakia. This episode, likewise, allowed Nasser to demonstrate his capacity for independent action by rebuffing the West.) Other theorists pointed out that our strategy offered us no options for assisting the uprisings that occurred in Soviet satellites, such as Hungary.

Kissinger, however, reserves his greatest criticism of American strategy for the Korean War. Although he regards its lessons as plain, he frequently laments America's failure to absorb them. The war in Korea,

Kissinger observes, "caught us completely unprepared, not only militarily but above all in doctrine."[85] Korea was not outside the U.S. defense perimeter, but it fitted none of the concepts of our strategic thought. This war did not originate as a surprise attack against the United States. It did not involve Europe or an all-out conflict between the United States and the Soviet Union.[86] Almost in parody, Kissinger writes that "it has been remarked more than once that, had the Korean War not actually taken place, we would never have believed that it could."[87]

Kissinger believes that throughout the Korean War, American action was stymied by an incongruity between our vision of reality and what really transpired. Our actions were inhibited by "the consciousness that this was not the war for which we had prepared."[88] Rather than realigning our thought, we tried to interpret Korea as an all-out struggle. General MacArthur viewed it as a prelude to a showdown with China, while others in the Truman administration saw it as a feinting action prior to an all-out Soviet strike in Europe. The result, Kissinger believes, was frustration in the military execution of the war as well as a failure either to grasp or achieve the political goals for which the war was being fought.

Thus, American strategy led either to outright paralysis—as witnessed in Indochina in 1954—or to a situation in which doctrine had to be improvised in the face of a military crisis, as witnessed in Korea. The effect, according to Kissinger, was the gradual transformation of the global balance in favor of the Soviet bloc. At first, American strategy faltered in the "peripheral" or "grey areas." Yet the implications of its strategy were such that over time America would no longer be able to distinguish between "peripheral" and "vital" areas. At that point, it would be in danger of suffering the same fate as France, whose Maginot line has come to symbolize the fact that military failure is, first of all, a failure of doctrine.

THE PRIMACY OF DOCTRINE

Kissinger's views on America's "esoteric strategy" and the *cul-de-sac* to which it was leading were part of a more fundamental critique. Although he refers to American military strategy in his writings, his essential theme is that the New Look was a strategy in name only. More than anything else, America needed to develop a doctrine for using military power that was appropriate to the nuclear age.

Characteristically, Kissinger cites several historical examples to underscore the importance of a clear and coherent security doctrine. He compares the superior strategy of the Roman legions to that of the Macedonian forces, and describes Napoleon's genius in defeating the armies of Europe with a military doctrine based on mobility and the use of artillery. "All these," Kissinger writes, "were victories not of resources but of strategic doctrine: the ability to break the framework which had come to be taken for granted and to make the victory all the more complete by confronting the antagonist with contingencies which he had never even considered."[89] Kissinger often quotes from the writings of Lenin and Mao to illustrate the importance the communist bloc gives to doctrinal questions.

Kissinger's emphasis on strategic doctrine arises from his "spiritualized" conception of power. Drawing on the German historicists, he regards strategic conceptions as the primary element of power, rather than material resources. The maximum development of power is not enough. In the absence of a clear doctrine, our power alone could not prevent the Soviets from seizing the initiative. "It is the task of strategic doctrine," Kissinger explains, "to translate power into policy. Whether the goals of a state are offensive or defensive, whether it seeks to achieve or to prevent a transformation, its strategic doctrine must define what objectives are worth contending for and determine the degree of force appropriate for achieving them."[90]

Hence, strategic doctrine gives political form to raw power. Kissinger also sees it as performing other important roles. It identifies the most likely challenges a nation will face in advance of their occurrence. Strategy allows issues of national security to be handled without improvising in the midst of a crisis. Strategic doctrine provides a basis for using weapons and criteria for selecting particular weapons over others.

American doctrine was inadequate in all of these areas—particularly in correlating power and political purposes. Kissinger believes that this situation has resulted from the nation's reliance on all-out war. The principles of all-out war stress only military factors and advocate the maximum development of physical power.

This reliance on all-out war developed from certain characteristics in American society—characteristics Kissinger regards critically. One such tendency has been referred to as the "material bias"[91] of American thinking. As a result of this bias, Americans emphasize the development of the "tools" of war. They equate doctrine with the procurement of essential "hardware." The material bias of American military thought[92] actually inverts the relationship between weapons and strategy, substituting weapons for a conception regarding their use. As a nation, Kissinger points out, "we added the atomic bomb to our arsenal without integrating its implications into our thinking."[93]

A corollary of America's emphasis on physical power is its fascination with technology. Kissinger observes that the nation responded to the periodic crises of the cold war with a "flight into technology: by devising ever more fearful weapons."[94] Americans were more accustomed to technological innovation than to the development of strategic doctrine.[95] Both the nature of the arms race and America's historical experience contributed "to the notion that strategy is identical with technical analysis of weapon systems, obscuring the fact that both the development and the use of weapon systems are impossible without strategic doctrine."[96]

The reliance on all-out war also impeded effective collaboration among the military services. Because the nation lacked a clear doctrine, the services defined their own. This led to both overlapping missions as well as redundant weapon systems. Moreover, each service stressed its own form of all-out war strategy. The cumulative effect was to reduce the nation's capability for fighting conventional wars—the arena where the most likely challenges to American security lay.

LIMITED WAR

The doctrine that Kissinger advocates to meet the Sino-Soviet challenge combined elements of both deterrence and defense. He supports reliance on nuclear weapons to deter the Soviets from a strategic strike against the United States. He also advocates a capacity for local defense—as an insurance should deterrence fail, as well as from a belief that Soviet challenges will most likely occur on this level of engagement. Kissinger believes that the capacity to wage limited war offered us the best chance to bring about strategic changes favorable to our side.[97] The capacity for local defense is what is referred to as the doctrine of limited war.

Kissinger believes that the nature of the nuclear age made limited wars more likely. This belief seems contradictory in the context of his political thought. As I indicated in chapter 2, Kissinger associates limited war with a legitimate international system. How then could he advocate a doctrine of limited war in the modern revolutionary era? Were not Soviet goals unlimited?

Kissinger acknowledges that the present system lacks legitimacy. Yet he believes that both the United States and the Soviet Union have an overwhelming interest in keeping wars limited. The destruction involved in thermonuclear war offered an opportunity to establish limits in both the military and diplomatic realms.[98]

But if neither an agreed legitimacy nor a stable power relationship exists today, they may be outweighed by a third factor, the fear of thermonuclear war. Never have the consequences of all-out war been so unambiguous, never have the gains seemed so out of relation with the sacrifices.[99]

The doctrine of limited war maintains that the political and military elements of war are inseparable, and that the political element has primacy. All-out war seeks to destroy the enemy; decisions are based "purely" on military factors. In contrast, limited wars are fought for specific political objectives, which by their very existence "establish a certain commensurability between the force employed and the goal to be attained."[100] Limited wars are planned and occur according to clearly defined ground rules that express this commensurability. Finally, political leadership is never more essential than during a period of limited war. Leaders must define the goals that will shape military plans and capabilities. Diplomacy does not cease during a limited war, but instead it achieves an unparalleled intensity, because it must articulate the political reasons for using force.

Kissinger lists four types of limited war. His examples are designed to show that limited war is doctrinally superior to the strategy of massive nuclear retaliation. Limited war enables us to plan for contingencies other than direct U.S.–USSR confrontation, particularly in the "grey areas." It allows us to exercise our power and to avoid the "choice between all-out war and a gradual loss of position, between Armageddon and defeat without war."[101]

These four types of limited war can be reduced to two: those that explicitly involve both the United States and the Soviet Union from the outset, and those that begin without both major powers involved but which have the potential for involving them. Almost every confrontation in the postwar era fits this description—Korea; the Suez Crisis in 1956; wars involving secondary powers such as Israel and Egypt, and India and Pakistan; the Cuban crisis in 1962; Indochina in both 1945 and the war in Vietnam; and also military actions by the Soviets in Eastern Europe and by the United States in the Western Hemisphere.

Kissinger suggests that limited war takes a specific form in the nuclear age. War can, of course, be limited in the sense that it is confined to a specific geographical area. Kissinger, however, does not accept this definition, because even such a "local" war could threaten the very existence of one of the participants. Similarly, he suggests that neither limitations on total weapons nor limitations on their targets provide an adequate definition of limited war. Instead, Kissinger describes limited war as restricting all of these elements—the geographical area of the war, the weapon systems used, and the targets attacked. The limits imposed in each of these areas are determined by the specific political objectives that give the war its purpose. These limits represent the orchestration of force to "affect the opponent's will, not to crush it, to make the conditions to be imposed more attractive than continued resistance."[102]

In addition to examining the doctrinal aspects of limited war, Kissinger stresses developing the capabilities needed to fight such wars. Foremost among these capabilities is a leadership group able to relate together the political and military aims of war. Kissinger was not optimistic on this point, because American leaders have not previously demonstrated either a capacity for diplomatic subtlety or for employing force for purposes short of total victory.

Kissinger also believed that the reorganization of the American military could add to the clarity of our strategic doctrine. He regards it as an anomaly that, in the age of nuclear weapons and intercontinental missiles, our military services were still organized around forms of "locomotion." Because of the way they moved, the army was responsible for land defense, the navy for the seas, and the air force for the air. Such a division of roles and missions created overlapping and often contradictory strategies. Kissinger suggests that the traditional military services be retained for training purposes. "But for all other purposes two basic organizations would be created: the Strategic Force and the Tactical Force. The Strategic Force would be the units for all-out war. . . . The Tactical Force would be the Army, Air Force, and Navy units required for limited war."[103]

To this force structure for limited war, Kissinger proposed adding both nuclear and conventional weapons. His reasoning was straightforward. Using tactical nuclear weapons was a strategy most advantageous to our side. Such a strategy demanded an officer corps that could assume the initiative in fluid situations. Kissinger judges the American military to be superior to the Soviets in this area. Moreover, "the ability to wage limited nuclear war seems more suitable than conventional war because it poses the maximum *credible* threat. If we possess a wide spectrum of nuclear weapons then the aggressor's risks are increased, and because limited nuclear war greatly complicates the problem of controlling territory, aggression may seem less attractive."[104] This was the major argument for limited nuclear war. Kissinger, however, also maintained that we should not have to improvise a strategy in a crisis, if the Soviets were first to use limited nuclear weapons.

I want to emphasize that Kissinger's advocacy of limited nuclear war rested in part on his belief in the rationality of the United States and the Soviet Union and on the controllability of nuclear weapons. Although he later changed both views, he stressed that the so-called "firebreak," or resort to full-scale nuclear war, need not occur when tactical nuclear weapons were first used on the battlefield. A limited nuclear war would not automatically deteriorate into an all-out war because, presumably, both powers would retain a capacity for strategic retaliation. This threat of retaliation and possible nuclear destruction would deter either power from escalating the conflict even if one of them were faced with defeat.

What of the superior numbers of the Sino-Soviet bloc and the internal lines of communication in the "grey areas" provided by the geographic position of these nations? Kissinger believes that American strategists overstated this argument. They erroneously identified power and quantitative factors.

> Now to underestimate an adversary may be disastrous, but to overestimate his resources may lead to a needless paralysis of policy. Absolute numbers are important, but only the part which can be effectively utilized is strategically significant. In these terms Chinese manpower is limited by the Soviet-Chinese capacity to equip and train it, and Chinese effectiveness by the difficulty of communication and supply. The vision of hordes of Chinese streaming into the "grey areas" is unrealistic.[105]

Kissinger believed that our development of a capacity for limited war must be accompanied by a concomitant effort to train and equip indigenous armies in the "grey areas."[106] These indigenous forces, coupled with politically stable governments, would ensure that Sino-Soviet aggression was apparent to the world community. The existence of these armies and governments would provide America with sufficient prerequisites for taking local action. Because of its maritime strength, America could develop strategic reserves in peninsular and island nations "rimming" the "grey areas," such as Malaysia and the Philippines. These strategic reserves could buttress "nuclear defense forces in the three critical countries: Iran (to help Turkey and Pakistan cover the Mideast), Pakistan (to strengthen Afghanistan and to back up Iran and Burma), and the Indo-Chinese states (to protect Malaya and Thailand)."[107]

Kissinger believed that the doctrine of limited war, joined to a political and economic program, would give us the best chance to advance our strategic interests. He provides several examples. He argues that decisive American leadership and unilateral intervention in Indochina after the fall of Dien Bien Phu in 1954 would have offered significant political benefits. "And had this unilateral action been accompanied by a political proposal, such as a political trusteeship committee for Indo-China under Asian chairmanship and a guarantee of China's southern boundary, it would have done more to demonstrate our determination and moderation than any number of formalistic declarations."[108] Similarly, Kissinger believes that the correct application of force and diplomacy during the Korean War would have caused the Chinese to question the value of their Soviet alliance. In time, the doctrine of limited war might even offer opportunities to reduce the Soviet sphere—as in the case of Yugoslavia's disaffection over the Trieste issue.[109]

Finally, Kissinger believes that the capacity to deploy forces to the "grey areas" would make our power tangible to the uncommitted nations. Kissinger even suggests that in some instances the "majesty" of our military power would impress these nations at least as much as the moral appeal of our political doctrine. "The power chiefly visible to the newly independent states," he writes, "is that of Soviet or Chinese armies on their borders. The United States must counter with a twentieth-century equivalent of 'showing the flag,' with measures which will permit us to make our power felt quickly and decisively, not only to deter Soviet aggression but to impress the uncommitted with our capacity for action."[110]

Kissinger's writings on American military doctrine struck a responsive chord in the nation. His thoughts were widely quoted by senior public officials. Both Eisenhower and Nixon praised *Nuclear Weapons and Foreign Policy*. The major impact of Kissinger's thought, however, can be seen in the Kennedy administration's strategy of "flexible response" and in the development of forces for limited war and for counterinsurgency warfare. Kissinger's works, along with those of other strategists, had created a receptivity to this doctrinal change. In this sense, his writings fulfilled the responsibility that he had assigned to intellectuals in American society—that of challenging unquestioned assumptions and providing the philosophical basis for changes in public policy.

Yet even though American leaders were prepared to alter their views regarding limited war, this did not mean that traits deeply ingrained in the national character would also be altered. In his writings about America's involvement in Vietnam, Kissinger returns to themes that he had elaborated in the fifties. The form of war had changed—from all-out to limited war—but the American outlook regarding war remained the same.

Kissinger's interest in defense strategy seemed to decline in the early sixties. He did not stop writing in regard to this area, but his writings took on a different focus, becoming part of a critique that was more political than military in nature.

What accounted for this change? The Kennedy administration implemented a military doctrine that represented the type of defense efforts that Kissinger had advocated. There was no reason to continue his critique now that the substance of his criticism had become national policy. Furthermore, the Kennedy administration included in senior positions many of Kissinger's Harvard associates. In 1961, he himself became a part-time consultant on German policy to the National Security

Council. Undoubtedly, these associations as well as the administration's acceptance of a new military doctrine caused him to limit his criticism.

In the next chapter, I will examine Kissinger's criticism of American foreign policy. The relationship he draws between our policies and the ideas Americans have about political evolution is central to this criticism.

6

American Foreign Policy: Themes of Political Evolution

The Enduring Philosophical Challenge

THE SOVIET UNION AND COMMUNISM

AMERICA confronted several challenges after World War II for which its history had not prepared it. None, Kissinger believes, was more fundamental than the philosophical challenge presented by Soviet communism. "The most singular feature of Soviet foreign policy," he writes, "is . . . Communist ideology, which transforms relations among states into conflicts between philosophies."[1]

The danger in this conflict was that communist philosophy would prove more relevant to the contemporary age than Western values. The global balance and the consensus supporting international society would shift in favor of political systems antithetical to American principles. This danger was at issue particularly with respect to the new nations in Africa and Asia. America faced being spiritually isolated from the world community—a danger Kissinger regards as more serious than a military defeat. "Americans, for the first time in our history, would live in a world where we were foreign in the deepest sense, where people would share neither our values nor our aspirations, where we might meet hostility everywhere outside of North America."[2]

Kissinger does not minimize the role of Russian nationalism and its legacy of expansion in both Europe and Asia. "Over centuries the strange Russian empire has seeped outward from the Duchy of Moscow, spreading east and west across endless plains where no geographical obstacle except distance set a limit to human ambition, inundating what resisted, absorbing what yielded."[3] The vastness of Russia has also lured invaders from both east and west. Because of the nation's expansionist drive and insecure history, Russian leaders identified security not only with pushing back surrounding countries but with dominating them.[4]

Communism gives Russian expansionism an ideological cast. International conflict traditionally involved an attack against the territory of an enemy state. Nations sought to gain an advantage in physical power, not to alter the social structure of their opponents. In the contemporary era, Soviet leaders seek to gain an advantage in global power precisely through altering the social structure of other nations. Subversion and domestic revolutions have become common forms of aggression. Kissinger observes that the ideological challenge of communism extends "the arena of international struggle . . . to include the internal policies and social structures of countries, mocking the traditional standard of international law that condemns interference in a country's domestic affairs."[5]

Soviet leaders claim that communist philosophy can be applied to all nations despite cultural and historical differences. They believe that communism provides a society superior to that of other philosophical and economic systems. Communist philosophy states that a society's economic relations shape its legal and cultural institutions. In the predominantly capitalist societies of the West, the working class is said to be exploited by those who own the means of production. The values and institutions of these nations are regarded as inhumane, because they reinforce this exploitation. In communist societies, class distinctions are supposed to be overcome—the workers become the owners of the means of production. Thus, the economic basis for all forms of social injustice is ended. For these reasons, capitalism is characterized as a temporary stage of human society—a stage to be transformed by the progressive forces of communism.

Communism also entails a specific philosophy of history. It provides its adherents with an understanding of historical evolution. Marx defined historical epochs by the way economic production is accomplished. Changes in the mode of production create new economic classes and social and political relations. History evolves through a dialectical process that is economic or materialist in nature. World communism is the final stage of this process.

Communist philosophy and its promise of a utopian society are fundamentally at odds with western values. Kissinger stresses the importance of this philosophical challenge, but he also criticizes the Manichean outlook of many American leaders, who describe the conflict between the Soviets and the West solely as a struggle between the forces of darkness and light. Although he gives this conflict an ideological cast in his own writings, he never divorces the Soviet challenge from its geopolitical strategy.

To the extent Kissinger clarifies the specific points of opposition involved in this philosophical conflict, he emphasizes the different beliefs that the West and the communist world hold regarding the individual and the role of the state. Kissinger notes that in western societies, "individual freedom of conscience and expression is the proudest heritage of our civilization."[6] He attributes the West's emphasis on human dignity to features unique to its history. Foremost among these is its Greco-Roman heritage, the source of most western ideas of law and justice.[7] Kissinger also calls attention to the emphasis on the individual conscience that emerged from the Protestant Reformation, the notion of "spiritual inwardness" that attracted him to Kantian thought.[8]

In contrast, the individual in communist thought possesses neither spiritual significance nor transcendent importance. The materialist bias of Marxist philosophy denies the existence of a soul or mind.[9] The individual derives his identity and social conscience from his economic class.

The second distinction that Kissinger makes between western values and Soviet communism concerns the relationship between society and the state. Kissinger notes that western political development has been marked by social pluralism. The state and society are regarded as distinct entities. The political sphere is by no means all-encompassing. Western nations produce a variety of social institutions—the family, religious groups, educational establishments, businesses, and so forth. Kissinger writes that "a pluralistic society contains many structures, all subject to more or less continuous change. In such a society parts of the intellectual, cultural, and political framework are dying while others are being reborn."[10]

Unlike western political thought, communism proclaims the absolute unity of the political and social realms. The Communist party, representing the "dictatorship of the proletariat," has absolute authority over the political and economic life of the nation. Its control also extends to social and cultural activities. For this reason, political values in communist societies prevent the evolution of true social pluralism. All institutions must be subordinated to the Communist party, for the party defines the prevailing orthodoxy.

Kissinger stresses that the philosophical struggle between the West and Soviet communism has affected the international system. For Kissinger, world order has two foundations: first, a military balance among the great powers; and second, legitimacy—a general political acceptance of the international system by the major states. The Soviet Union challenges both. Its military strategy sought to overturn the global balance and achieve a "correlation of forces" favorable to the Sino-Soviet bloc.[11] Its communist philosophy sought to establish its values and social structure as the basis for international legitimacy.

THE STRUGGLE FOR LEGITIMACY

As discussed in chapter 2, the concept of legitimacy occupies a central role in Kissinger's political philosophy. Legitimacy, as Kissinger defines it, means that the major powers accept the international system. Although legitimacy appears to be based solely on a consensus of the major powers, Kissinger makes it concrete by linking it to what he calls the "legitimizing principle." The legitimizing principle represents the prevailing values of the historical epoch. It is in the name of the legitimizing principle that nations accept the international order.

Thus the philosophical struggle between communism and the West may be stated as follows: which side will define the legitimizing principle for the modern era? Defining the legitimizing principle entails, first of all, determining what type of international system is judged morally acceptable. I stress morally because the legitimizing principle is derived as much from a consensus among the majority of nations as from the realities of global power.[12]

The legitimizing principle also defines the range of acceptable conduct within the international system. In the past, declaratory policies of terrorism—particularly terrorism aimed at the major powers—would have been widely challenged. Groups espousing such policies and nations supporting such groups might expect to suffer retribution from one or more of the major powers. In the postwar period, however, some states justify such forms of hostility as a legitimate act of national liberation.

The legitimizing principle shapes the spirit that animates international organizations. The League of Nations and the United Nations have exhibited a changing consensus on issues reflecting changes in the legitimizing principle. The legitimizing principle also determines the acceptability of international agreements. The international community would condemn a treaty significantly at odds with the legitimizing principle of the era.

Against this background, the significance of defining the legitimizing principle is clear. A nation that failed to convince the international community of the relevance of its values would live in a world hostile to its very existence. Kissinger envisions the possibility of an America endangered by the direction of global change.

> If the West can be humiliated over a period of time, the new nations, whatever their moral preference, will consider Communism the wave of the future. The success of Moscow and Peiping will have the same kind of attraction as the accomplishments of Europe in the nineteenth century. No amount of economic assistance will avail against the conviction that the West is doomed.[13]

The tragic irony of America's spiritual isolation would be that the nation that throughout its history had thought of itself as different from other countries would now be different in reality. But its difference would be a mark of alienation, not of esteem. Its values and way of life would lack dynamism and would no longer serve as a model for other countries.

AMERICA IN THE WORLD ARENA

World War II and the destruction of Europe thrust America into world leadership. Whatever the inadequacies of its historical preparation, only the United States possessed the strength and resources required to play this role. America had to fill the military vacuum created by the British inability to support Greece and Turkey in 1947. Secretary of State Acheson characterized the task of American policy after 1945 as providing "strength at the center"[14]—a task to which there was no alternative. If the nations outside the communist orbit were "to be pulled together into a workable system, the leadership must come from the United States."[15]

Kissinger's writings on American foreign policy in the cold war stress this theme of leadership at the center. American stewardship was indispensable in three areas. First, America alone could defend the values of the West against the Soviet challenge, while engaging the Soviets in agreements conducive to world order. The United States would have to define the purposes of the West as well as the issues for which we were willing to contend. Policies that offered moral distinctions between the West and the communist bloc did not, in Kissinger's view, preclude negotiations.[16] Indeed to the extent to which both systems were fundamentally antagonistic, the need for diplomatic contacts, especially in areas such as arms control, was even greater. America's responsibility as the leader of the West thus included conducting effective negotiations with the Soviets.

The second area of concern to American foreign policy involved the nations in Africa and Asia that had recently emerged from colonialism. Kissinger regards upheaval in these areas as essentially political. Because most of the new nations lacked stable social and political institutions, "their forms of government all too frequently place a premium on demagoguery and encourage the emergence of some form of Caesarism."[17] Kissinger believed that American foreign policy had to demonstrate the relevance of western political values to the societies being formed within these nations.

The third area in which American leadership was essential concerned the Atlantic alliance. At issue was the future orientation of the continent, whether it would seek its political identity in a union of European states or in an Atlantic partnership with the United States. The form of Europe's future political unity was also at stake—would it be a confederation of sovereign nations that preserved the identity of each or a supranational entity advocated by many American leaders. NATO, which Kissinger regards as the cornerstone of American foreign policy, also needed to adjust to changes in strategic relationships. The role of American forces in Europe, the contribution of European allies, the degree of reliance on nuclear and conventional forces—all of these issues contributed to the disarray in NATO and demanded clarification.

How did America respond to these three challenges? This was the central question that concerned Kissinger in his study of postwar American foreign policy. The following section will deal with this subject.

American Foreign Policy and the Cold War

AMERICAN LEADERSHIP

In one of his early articles, published in 1956, Kissinger warns that American foreign policy is at an "impasse."[18] America had failed in each of the areas in which the Soviets contested with it for supremacy. These failures "led to a crisis in our system of alliances and to substantial Soviet gains among the uncommitted peoples of the world."[19] Kissinger identifies the cause of the impasse in American policy: "For several years, we have been groping for a concept to deal with the transformation of the Cold War from an effort to build defensive barriers into a contest for the allegiance of humanity."[20]

Kissinger's reference to defensive barriers was his way of describing America's containment policy. In chapter 5, I discussed the military features of containment. Its political component determined America's diplomatic relations with the Sino-Soviet bloc. Kissinger regards containment as a defensive barrier, because it amounted to "a frozen attitude seemingly fearful of diplomatic contact."[21] The proponents of containment maintained that Soviet society must undergo a basic transformation before negotiations would be possible with the communist world. To be sure, interludes of personal diplomacy during the Eisenhower administration such as the Geneva Summit in 1955 and the Camp David Summit in 1959 had occurred. But, according to Kissinger, these periods of "flexibility" were as sterile as our overall "rigidity." They were based on the delusion of American leaders that Soviet society had been transformed—hence, that defensive barriers could be lowered.

Kissinger links America's failure to confront the Soviet bloc diplomatically with its attempt to seal off the Soviets politically through a worldwide system of multilateral and bilateral alliances. These alliances provided the military and political barricades behind which America waited for the Soviet system to change. The United States, Kissinger notes, treated these alliances as proof that the world as a whole perceived the Soviet threat the way we did. "The pacts, the alliances, the aid programs have come to seem self-evident guideposts along an unalterable route, ends in themselves requiring no justification beyond their obvious utility for dealing with the Soviet threat."[22]

Kissinger equates containment with political passivity. America interpreted its purposes negatively. Instead of erecting defensive fortresses, the goal of our policy should have been "to demonstrate Soviet intransigence and thereby create a climate of opinion for common action. . . . [America] has conceived its tasks as primarily technical: to create an adequate defense force. But in fact the problem has proved to be principally psychological: to bring about a climate of opinion that would support such a force."[23]

Creating such a "climate of opinion" required an activist foreign policy. America, however, approached the cold war with the belief that history guaranteed the eventual success of its political and economic system.[24] Foreign policy, therefore, need only concentrate on "holding the line."[25] But as Kissinger pointedly asks, "What would have been Western history if the knights who defeated the Arabs at Tours had surrendered because they believed in the historical inevitability of the triumph of Christianity?"[26] He rejects America's false confidence:

> Equally worrisome is our interpretation of the process in which we find ourselves engaged. Throughout a decade of almost continuous decline the notion that time was on our side has been at the basis of much of our policy. Our attitudes have therefore tended to remain passive. When history contains a guarantee of eventual success, survival can easily become the primary goal. Creativity, innovation, sacrifice pale before tactical considerations of dealing with day-to-day concerns. A powerful incentive exists for deferring difficult choices. It is not surprising, then, that our policies have lacked vitality and that public discussion has focused on symptoms, not causes. But it is equally clear that such attitudes doom us to sterility in a revolutionary period.[27]

Kissinger contrasts American attitudes with those of the Soviet bloc. Both sides predicted the eventual success of their system. Communism, however, was committed to activism—committed not only to understanding history but to shaping it. Kissinger observes that "Communism uses its philosophy of history as a *spur* to effort. Faith in evolution provides the conviction for major exertions." In contrast, "many in the West rely on history as a *substitute* for effort." Kissinger sees in this situation "an attitude of resignation, destructive of purpose and values."[28]

> The irony of our period is that the successes of Communism are due less to that ability to forecast events on which it prides itself than to its self-assurance in shaping them. History for Communism is an incentive for action, a guarantee of the meaningfulness of sacrifice. The West, on the other hand, has a tendency to use evolutionary theory as a bromide. Waiting for history to do its work for it, it stands in danger of being engulfed by the currents of our time.[29]

America's passive attitudes produced a foreign policy of negative goals and half measures. Kissinger observes that U.S. policy seemed to exhaust itself in containing Soviet expansion. It could explain what it sought to prevent but not what it sought to promote. More time was spent debating whether we should negotiate with the Soviets than developing goals for those negotiations. As a consequence, America increasingly appeared the more intransigent of the two major powers, i.e., the nation less willing to negotiate. The Soviets provided the initiative for negotiations and selected the issues to be discussed. Hence, America found itself debating issues that had been defined for the world community by the Soviets. Attention was focused on reducing forces in NATO but not the Warsaw Pact; on Soviet arms control proposals but not those of the United States; "on the Congo or Cuba, but not on Hungary, Tibet or East Germany."[30]

America's foreign policy toward the new nations also lacked imagination and vitality. It appeared to be based solely on a desire for popularity—a goal Kissinger thought unattainable given the psychological climate in many of these nations. American policy consisted mainly of economic and military assistance. But the inspiration for this assistance came from the nation's own domestic experience. "Much of our foreign aid program," Kissinger writes, "has been characterized by a kind of nostalgia for the Marshall Plan and the New Deal."[31] America failed to acknowledge the differences between the economic setbacks that the West has periodically experienced and the problems faced by the emerging states. These nations, Kissinger points out, lacked a basic political structure—a void that could not be filled solely by economic programs. American policy would prove fruitless unless it also pursued political construction.

Our policy with respect to Europe was marked by a similar failure. Despite the growth of Soviet power, neither the United States nor the countries of Europe had responded creatively. "Since the creation of the Marshall Plan and of NATO, we have been barren of ideas, evading difficult choices, drawing on capital."[32] The economic vision behind European reconstruction had not been matched by a "comparable political vision."[33] After a decade of economic recovery in most European nations, the Atlantic alliance appeared politically confused and spiritually uncertain.

What accounted for this lack of dynamism? Kissinger offers several reasons for America's policy failures.

THE ROOTS OF FAILURE

Kissinger emphasizes that America was ill-equipped to understand the revolutionary period in which it had assumed world leadership. Most Americans did not even see the "impasse" to which our policy had brought us. Throughout the 1950s, a decade of both relative and absolute decline vis-à-vis the Soviets, there had been no fundamental review of American foreign policy. Instead, the Eisenhower and later the Kennedy administration stressed the bipartisan consensus supporting American policy. Kissinger finds this willingness to rely on unexamined assumptions particularly troubling, for we faced a world of revolutionary upheaval without "yardsticks by which to decide between our alternatives or even to determine what they are."[34]

Nowhere was this more evident than in our relations with the Soviet Union. Kissinger attributes America's defensive reactions to its being a "status quo" power. Similar to other status quo powers throughout history, America did not believe that the Soviet Union's purpose was truly revolutionary, that is, that it truly aimed to overturn the existing order. The status quo nation sees the rules of the international system as the normal basis for interstate relations. Because it believes that the revolutionary power is inside the international system, it tries to resolve that nation's grievances according to these rules. "All the instincts of the status quo power tempt it to gear its policy to the expectation of a fundamental change of heart of its opponent—in the direction of what seems obviously 'natural' to it."[35]

Kissinger believes that this mistaken view of the Soviet Union partly accounted for America's policy of containment. Since the Soviet Union could still be integrated into the existing order, containment was designed to evoke the "change of heart" needed to resolve its differences with the West. Kissinger criticized America for "choos[ing] the interpretation of Soviet motivations which best fits its own preconceptions."[36]

Neither Lenin's writings, nor Stalin's utterances, nor Mao's published works, nor Khrushchev's declaration has availed against the conviction of the West that a basic change in Communist society and aims was imminent and that a problem deferred was a problem solved.[37]

America's response to the anticolonial upheaval in Asia and Africa has been even more inadequate. Kissinger writes that, despite our good will, our culture prevented us from understanding the revolutionary changes in the emerging nations. He discerns in Americans a "tendency to think of man as largely motivated by economic considerations. Nothing seems more natural than to 'get ahead in the world,' by which we generally mean material advancement."[38] Because of this tendency, American officials believed that the new nations should concentrate on economic development. Kissinger stresses that this view ignored the driving force of revolutionary leaders such as Nasser and Castro. These men accepted struggle and deprivation in order to achieve political power, not wealth. Kissinger comments that, for Castro, the goal of facilitating economic reform in Cuba would appear trivial "compared with leading a revolution throughout Latin America."[39]

Kissinger maintains that the West did not fully understand anticolonialism. American leaders, particularly Dulles, regarded anticolonialism and nonalignment as hostile to the West. In contrast, Kissinger views revolution in the emerging nations as the fulfillment of colonialism. "In a real sense it is a continuation of a revolution started by the colonial powers and carried on under their aegis. . . . As the ideals of the British, French and American revolutions became diffused, partly through the very spread of colonialism, the seeds were sown for the destruction of colonialism itself."[40] Because of the western influence on the leaders of many of the new nations, anticolonialism became a means of assuring personal and national identity. Viewed in this light, many revolutionary leaders were not so profoundly anti-western as they might seem. Kissinger writes that "neutralism and anti-colonialism are not so much a policy as a spiritual necessity."[41]

Why did communism appeal to the emerging nations? Kissinger believes that communism filled the spiritual void that many of the revolutionary leaders faced in the first days of independence. It offered a coherent set of social and political values and a dynamic philosophy of history. Ironically, the attraction of communism came more from "the theological quality of Marxism than through the materialistic aspect on which it prides itself."[42] The United States, on the other hand, based its appeal to the emerging nations on its ability to raise their standards of living through industrialization.

Kissinger believes that the roots of U.S. policy failures in Europe are also discernible. To the extent that America offered a political vision for the Atlantic alliance, it linked that vision to schemes of European integration, i.e., of supranational federal institutions controlled by a European parliament. Economic integration would provide the basis for political integration. Although the Kennedy administration pursued this policy most aggressively, all postwar American presidents supported the idea. Kissinger notes that this emphasis on supranational institutions resulted from "the conviction that the American experience was directly applicable to Europe."[43] Further, "the incentive to urge the American model was especially great because the nation-state, according to American spokesmen, had become obsolete."[44]

Kissinger maintains that the American outlook prevented the development of a true Atlantic community. None of the factors that led to a federal structure in America applied to Europe. Kissinger observes that "an attempt to abolish the European nation-states, or to reduce their role drastically, represents a much more profound wrench with the past than the establishment of the United States of America did two centuries earlier."[45] Unlike the American colonies, the nations of Europe do not share a common history, culture, and language. European states developed in unique ways. Nations pride themselves on the original contributions of their cultures. They identify sovereignty with a self-reliant foreign policy and national defense. Kissinger believes that these obstacles could not be overcome by economic cooperation.

All of these factors accounted for the failure of American leadership and policy. Each contributed to the passivity and resignation that characterized the American approach. In analyzing the roots of America's foreign policy failures, however, Kissinger identifies one additional source of misunderstanding—a source that had important implications for American policy in general. He rejects the view of political evolution held by most American intellectuals and government leaders. "All too frequently we have relied for the solution of our problems on an evolutionary theory in which the assumed forces of history have replaced purpose and action. The notion of an inevitable development toward a more desirable and enlightened political structure has been applied equally to the two great revolutions of our time: Communism and the emergence of new nations in formerly colonial areas."[46] The predominant American idea of political evolution and its relationship to foreign policy is the subject we must now address.

Political Evolution and Foreign Policy

Why does Kissinger emphasize the American view of political evolution? Many of his works criticizing American foreign policy refer to this theme. He devotes an entire chapter of *The Necessity of Choice* to this subject.

Kissinger regards America's beliefs on this matter as the intellectual basis for much of its postwar foreign policy. Containment was the umbrella term applied to American policy from the time of the Truman Doctrine in 1947 to the post–Vietnam War era in the 1970s. Kissinger seeks to clarify the relationship between containment and America's concept of political evolution.

The policy of containment rested on two assumptions. The first concerned the need for a vigilant U.S. policy of counterforce against Soviet aggression at shifting geographical locations. The intellectual architect of containment, George Kennan, expressed the core of this policy in the now famous "X" article published in the July 1947 issue of *Foreign Affairs:* "it is clear that the main element of any United States policy toward the Soviet Union must be that of long-term patient but firm and vigilant containment of Russian expansive tendencies."[47] Kennan stated that communist ideology postulated an innate antagonism between the capitalist and socialist worlds. Furthermore, Soviet aggressive behavior was not likely to change "until the internal nature of Soviet power is changed."[48]

The second assumption of containment was more speculative. It rested on the proposition that, if the Soviets were successfully contained, Soviet society itself would undergo a transformation that would end its expansionist policies. Vigilant counterforce would lead to a "mellowing" of Soviet conduct. American foreign policy could significantly alter the political evolution of the Soviet Union:

> It is entirely possible for the United States to influence by its actions the internal development, both within Russia and throughout the international Communist movement, by which Russian policy is largely determined. . . . the United States has it in its power to increase enormously the strains under which the Soviet policy must operate, to force upon the Kremlin a far greater degree of moderation and circumspection than it has had to observe in recent years, and in this way to promote tendencies which must eventually find their outlet in either the break-up or the gradual mellowing of Soviet power.[49]

Considerable debate has surrounded the doctrine of containment; critics dispute whether Kennan intended it to be mainly a political or a military doctrine. Far less criticism has been directed to the process of "mellowing" that Kennan believed containment would cause. In predicting this "mellowing," the architects of containment relied on theories of political evolution that Kissinger finds questionable at best. American policymakers applied these theories not only to the impending transformation of the Soviet Union, but to the political development of the emerging nations and Europe.

The theories of political evolution that were applied to the Soviet Union, the Third World, and Europe have several elements in common. First, the driving force in political evolution is defined as change in the economic structure of the nation or group of nations. Political values are associated with different economic structures; structural changes in a nation's economy would inevitably alter its political institutions. Second, evolution is regarded as a linear process. It occurs in a straightforward, cumulative fashion; each stage provides the basis for the next. Third, political evolution is almost always progressive. For Americans, this means that economic and political evolution will lead to more liberal and democratic institutions.[50] Finally, this theory of evolution is said to have relevance for different cultures and different historical periods.

These elements are true of the theory of "convergence" with respect to the Soviet Union; of the "stages of growth" approach toward the emerging nations; and of "functionalism" and "integration theory" as applied to Europe. Each of these terms will be discussed fully in the pages that follow.

CONVERGENCE

If containment were to create the conditions that would bring about the transformation of Soviet society, the convergence theory explains how this transformation would occur. The adherents of the convergence theory believed that the political and economic institutions of the United States and Soviet Union were growing more alike.[51] For example, the Soviets were said to be moving toward more western values. Concomitantly, American economists and social scientists such as John Kenneth Galbraith and Robert Heilbroner argued that centralized economic planning and control like that found in communist countries would eventually replace the loosely coordinated capitalist economic system.[52]

According to convergence theorists, industrialization and urbanization will lead to increased social diversity in the Soviet Union. This growing pluralism will produce interest groups, such as scientists, engineers, and medical experts, who cannot be controlled by the Communist party.[53] The role of communist ideology as a determinant of political behavior will decline accordingly.[54] Industrialization will also lead to increased affluence and a greater concern for consumer goods. This result will cause the Soviets to change their system of rigid economic planning and their emphasis on producer goods and military equipment.

Over time, according to this theory, convergence of the Soviet Union with the West will lead to the political and military "mellowing" that Kennan described. Hence economic change will transform Soviet society and produce a less expansionist foreign policy. An unstated corollary of this theory, however, was that until convergence had run its course, negotiations with the Soviets were not likely to prove fruitful.[55]

A similar theory of economic and cultural evolution was offered for the emerging nations. Its major proponent, W. W. Rostow, is also regarded as a leading advocate of convergence. Known as the "stages of growth theory," this theory attempts to explain political development in the new states.

THE STAGES OF GROWTH

Rostow characterized his book *The Stages of Economic Growth* as a noncommunist manifesto.[56] His purpose was to offer "a theory about economic growth and a more general, if still highly partial, theory about modern history"[57] that would serve as an alternative to Marxism. Rostow had outlined his theory in an earlier book, *A Proposal: Key to an Effective Foreign Policy*,[58] which he wrote with Max F. Millikan. Both works shaped American policy toward "nation-building" in the emerging countries.[59]

Rostow maintained that all nations pass through five stages. These stages are progressive; they lead from a pastoral stage of existence in which the concept of the nation scarcely exists, to the final stage that involves a highly complex, highly interdependent social entity, as represented by the modern nation-state. Political institutions and values are shaped by the economic structure associated with each stage of growth.[60] Rostow's five stages include: the traditional society, largely an agricultural stage; the stage in which the preconditions for economic take-off are formed; the take-off stage, in which the society rapidly industrializes; the stage of high mass consumption characteristic of mature economies; and the post–mass consumption stage.

A description of each stage is beyond the scope of this study. The significance of this theory in the present context lies in Rostow's argument that societies are vulnerable to communism only in the early stages of industrialization. Communism is a "disease of transition."[61] As societies pass from the early stages of growth to modern economies, communism loses its appeal. "Communism is likely to wither in the age of high mass-consumption."[62] For this reason, Marxism attracts the emerging nations, but is considered moribund in the modernized societies of Western Europe and North America.[63]

On the basis of this analysis, Rostow prescribed an expanded foreign assistance program to combat communism in the Third World. Such a program would speed the evolution of nations in Africa and Asia up to the stages in which communism would lose its appeal. The unstated corollary of this theory was that political values and institutions do not matter much in the early stages of growth. New nations are primarily concerned with improving their economic conditions. A foreign policy that addresses political distinctions—such as the moral superiority of democratic institutions—is likely to prove counterproductive. Kissinger's description of this theory and its implications for foreign policy deserves to be quoted in full:

> [The emerging nations] are said to be in the phase of industrial development where the requirements of economic growth inevitably take precedence over those of political organization. The ability to promote industrialization and a rising standard of living is for them the chief test of political leadership, much more meaningful than terms like "freedom" and "human dignity." Means will necessarily be subordinated to ends. In the early stages of development some form of dictatorship is therefore extremely likely. The West, according to this school of thought, would make a great mistake were it to seek to promote in the new nations its own political forms or values, since these are either not understood at all or else interpreted as a new and subtler form of foreign intervention. The hope for the West in the underdeveloped areas, it is said, is to identify itself with the striving for economic growth. Competition with the Communists should take place above all in the realm of industrialization. Our task should be to prove our ability to raise the standard of living more efficiently than our Communist opponents without resorting to their methods of regimentation. In the long run the satisfaction of wants will promote a more liberal political system as well. In our approach to the new nations and to Communism we should expect political results not from the impact of our ideas but from the indirect influence of a transformation of the economy.[64]

Kissinger argues vehemently against defining our competition with the Soviet Union in the emerging nations solely in economic terms. Nor does he think it wise to regard the political evolution of the emerging nations as governed by an autonomous economic process such as the "stages of growth" theory espoused. I will return to a full treatment of Kissinger's criticism in a later section of this chapter.

The American view of political development in postwar Europe also emphasized economic factors. The theory of European integration shaped American foreign policy from the Truman to the Kennedy-Johnson years.

EUROPEAN INTEGRATION

European integration was not an American invention. The goal of European unity has existed since the fall of Rome. The most prominent advocates of European integration in the postwar period were themselves Europeans—men such as Jean Monnet, Robert Schuman, and Walter Hallstein. However, this theory can be characterized as American in the sense that it received consistent support from American officials and frequent elaboration in American academic circles.[65]

The theory of European integration depends on what Ernst Haas referred to as "spillover"[66] or what David Mitrany terms "ramification."[67] These men believed that economic integration possesses an inner dynamic that will lead to political unity. This "spillover" results from the alleged fact that the principal tasks facing modern governments involve nonpolitical, technical functions. Because problems transcend national borders, governing is the work of specialists rather than political leaders. David Calleo summarizes this theory: "The federalizing tendencies of economic union will spill over into politics until national governments finally will have ceded so much of their power that European unity will have occurred in fact before it is conceded in principle. 'Political integration is not a condition of economic integration but its consequence.' "[68]

The theory of European integration supported America's postwar policy of a united Europe.[69] This idea of a "United States of Europe" received its most forceful articulation in Kennedy's "Grand Design" or the so-called "dumbbell" theory.[70] The United States and a united Europe would be the two sides of an Atlantic dumbbell. "A politically and economically integrated Europe would become an equal partner with the United States and share . . . the burdens and obligations of world leadership."[71]

Americans stressed European unification because they believed that European nationalism needed to be checked. Twice in one century, the excesses of that nationalism had engulfed the world in war. In his *Memoirs*, de Gaulle observes that President Roosevelt was not "in the least eager that the Europeans should revive as great powers."[72] A fragmented quarreling Europe would never be an equal partner to the United States; a Europe of small states would be unable to share the burdens and responsibilities of world leadership. Kissinger writes that:

> As the years went by one particular form of European organization came to be identified with the substantive policy which a united Europe was likely to carry out. In the American view, an "integrated" Europe would be "outward-looking"; a less cohesive Europe would be parochial. A supranational Europe would become a partner to the United States; a Europe organized differently would remain a burden or perhaps turn into a rival. In short, an integrated Europe was essential to complete the Grand Design.[73]

Kissinger rejects each of these theories of political evolution. He holds them in contempt because they allowed the American people to believe that, in the postwar struggle for legitimacy, history would hand us victory without exertion. He seriously questions the historical validity of both convergence theory and the stages of growth theory. Yet in his most damning criticism, Kissinger refers to these evolutionary theories as a "purer version of Marxism."[74] By emphasizing the primacy of economic forces, these theories blur the distinction between Marxist philosophy and the philosophy of the West.

> The interesting question then presents itself: are these interpretations, often hailed as alternatives to Marxism, not in fact a purer version of Marxism than that practiced in Communist countries? The notion that economic structure inevitably has certain associated political forms is surely acceptable to Marxists. The proposition that values are altered by changing the economy is also one of the keystones of Marxism. Indeed, the Communist interpretation of history differs from many of the evolutionary theories of the West not so much in its assumptions as in the conclusions drawn from them. The dispute is not between two different philosophies but instead concerns the interpretation of a very similar orthodoxy: Communism maintains that industrialization inevitably produces the dictatorship of the proletariat. The evolutionary theories described above hold that economic development involves an automatic trend toward liberal institutions.[75]

The next section will deal with Kissinger's own ideas about political evolution. I will trace the implications his views have for American foreign policy.

Political Evolution Reconsidered

THE VIEWS OF THE HISTORIAN

Anyone familiar with Kissinger's early scholarship would understand his antipathy to these American theories of political evolution. His historical and philosophical studies led him to reject all forms of determinism. We have seen that, although he was attracted to the historical patterns that Spengler and Toynbee described, he dismissed the deterministic element of their thought. It is little wonder that he would oppose theories that attribute political change to autonomous economic forces.

The role of choice is central to Kissinger's view of history. Choice is also at the center of his view of political evolution. The political institutions of any society result from countless choices, not from a process of economic change.

A historian of evolution examines an array of forms which have lived and passed on. To such an observer the whole train of evolution has a foreordained appearance. . . . But it is only to posterity that evolution appears inevitable. The historian of evolution . . . has no way of knowing what was most significant to the participants: the element of choice which determined success or failure.[76]

Kissinger believes that a nation's political development is a major part of its distinctiveness. Political institutions embody the nation's traditions and values and the choices it has made in pivotal eras. Kissinger describes the nature of these choices:

Historians fond of evolutionary interpretations tend to overlook the fact that what animated even the successful adaptations was not a theory of evolution but some purpose expressing their inner nature. By the same token, societies have collapsed not because their leaders did not understand what the environment demanded of them but because they understood it only too well. The Austro-Hungarian Empire failed to survive because to adapt to the forces of nationalism and liberalism seemed to its rulers inconsistent with the reason for its existence. It could have participated in the evolutionary process only by giving up its distinctive qualities—the qualities which made life seem worthwhile.[77]

Kissinger's view of political evolution differs from that of most American theorists. He disputes their contention that political development always leads to western-type institutions. Such institutions may be adopted in the emerging nations when their political structures are still malleable. But Kissinger stresses that this possibility does not justify the "expectation of a more or less automatic transformation of societies in the direction of forms familiar to the West."[78] Furthermore, once societies such as the Soviet Union develop their own political structures, change usually occurs within these structures—not toward western forms. Kissinger maintains that there is nothing inherent in the process of political development that ensures the emergence of democracy.

American theorists, however, allege that industrialization automatically leads to democratic institutions. Kissinger argues against the historical validity of this view. In fact, the relationship he stresses is exactly the opposite: "there is no country in which democratic institutions developed after industrialization and as a result of economic development. Where the rudiments of democratic institutions did not exist at the beginning of the industrial revolution, they did not receive impetus from industrial growth."[79] Throughout the nineteenth century, western political theorists considered democracy the most progressive form of government, in part because they believed that political freedom fostered economic growth.

American theorists also link industrialization with liberal values. They argue that industrialization requires a higher level of education and that education fosters a "questioning spirit." This spirit in turn leads to the liberalization of social institutions. Kissinger doubts that this relationship is automatic. Increased education has rarely resulted in fundamental changes to a society. Historically, violence has been the mechanism for introducing greater political freedom—even in western societies. Furthermore, "education does not necessarily produce a critical attitude relevant to political action."[80] Kissinger observes that studying Kant or Hegel may lead to reflection about authority and freedom, but studying physics and chemistry need not do so. Nor does education in industrial societies necessarily promote independent political judgment.

Democratic theory of the eighteenth and nineteenth centuries was the product of many factors: the secularization of the concept of the uniqueness of the individual soul which originated in Christian theology, the scientific revolution, a rationalistic philosophy asserting the pre-eminence of reason. All these together led to the notion of the "universal man" capable by the exercise of his reason of judging all facets of human experience. The pre-eminent field of study was philosophy—the effort to give significance to life itself. Such an education tended to produce independent political judgment. It is much less clear, however, whether the same is true in the twentieth century. Education is or can be made largely vocational. It can be made to repeat the specialization of an industrial society. And specialization in day-to-day life is purchased at the price of considerable ignorance of most other fields.[81]

Kissinger also rejects the universal applicability that American theorists claim for their views of political evolution. Proponents of theories such as the "stages of growth" believe that all societies are subject to the same patterns of economic and political development. The nations of Europe and North America provide the models for these theories; few question the relevance of these models to fundamentally different cultures.

In contrast, Kissinger stresses that political evolution is a highly individualized process. Nations might exhibit similar patterns in their development, but nothing about their history is foreordained. There are no causal laws that explain the political evolution of states. Drawing on the philosophical themes he addressed in his undergraduate thesis, Kissinger acknowledges the role of both freedom and necessity in political development. Freedom here means the choices that a nation makes—the decisions that define the type of political structure it develops, the role of the state vis-à-vis society, the nature of its constitution, and so forth. Yet each choice a nation makes narrows the range of its future choices. This is why, as Kissinger points out, only young societies are usually in a position to make radical changes in their social structures. In older societies where values, traditions, and social institutions have developed over a long period of time, changes in the social structure are much more difficult to accommodate.

Kissinger concludes that no theory can predict the course of political evolution. Instead, he offers a more historical approach: "The evolutionary process . . . depends on three factors: its starting point, the values animating the participant (expressed as criteria of choice), and the pressures of the environment."[82] Kissinger defines a nation's starting point as its present political structure and the influence of its history. The nation's traditions and culture provide the values that shape its future direction, its historical choices. Finally, both its physical and social environment affect its evolution—but almost never, in Kissinger's view, to the extent argued by determinists.

This historical approach raises serious questions regarding the dominant American theories. It is from this basis that Kissinger challenges the American view of political evolution and the foreign policy that it supported.

THE SOVIET UNION

Kissinger considers political evolution in the Soviet Union not only possible, but inevitable. "No system of government is immune to change."[83] But, he argues, the nature of the transformation cannot be guaranteed.

It can move towards liberalization; but it can also produce the gray nightmare of 1984. It can lead to the enhancement of freedom; it may also refine the tools of slavery. Moreover, the mere fact of a transformation is not the only concern of our generation. Equally important is the time scale by which it occurs. It was, after all, no consolation for Carthage that 150 years after its destruction Rome was transformed into a peaceful status quo power.[84]

Kissinger emphasizes that the starting point of political evolution in the Soviet Union was fundamentally different from that of the West. In Europe, political pluralism developed over centuries. Democracy emerged from several unique factors. These included a church outside the control of the state; the Greco-Roman heritage; a rising middle class; the industrial revolution; and the existence of several states. Kissinger observes that industrialization was by no means the most important element in fostering democracy; moreover, if any of the other elements had been missing, industrialization alone would not have produced democratic values.[85]

Significantly, most of the elements that fostered the development of democratic societies in the West were absent in the Soviet Union. Because of its different history and culture, Russia had always appeared enigmatic to the West. The journalist Hedrick Smith points out that Russia, even apart from the influence of communism, is an alien culture. Russian society did not experience the historical changes that shaped the West—the Renaissance, the Reformation, the era of constitutional liberalism. Smith writes that "here is a culture that absorbed Eastern Orthodox Christianity from Byzantium, endured Mongol conquest and rule, and then developed through centuries of Czarist absolutism with intermittent periods of opening towards the West followed by withdrawal into continental isolation."[86]

The second element of political evolution concerns the nation's values. In the Soviet Union, communist ideology provides these values. Kissinger believed that ideology would continue to play an important role in Soviet society even if its revolutionary fervor declined. Communist ideology would be perpetuated in the very institutions it had created. "Now that Communism has been established for over a generation, the evolutionary process, if anything, works in its favor."[87] Thus, evolutionary change in the Soviet Union will confirm communist values. Kissinger observes that the establishment of a western-type democracy (as posited by American theorists) would not be the result of evolution, but rather of revolutionary upheaval.

> After nearly two generations of Communist rule, marked by a dramatic economic development, the possibilities of drastic change are much fewer. There may be a degree of liberalization—indeed there has been—but it will be a liberalization of a *Communist* regime, not an evolution toward a democratic one. The direction and nature of any transformation will be determined by the structure built up over forty years of Communist rule. We could make no worse mistake than to apply to it the criteria of our own evolution.[88]

Kissinger also believes that the Soviet Union had mastered the third element of political evolution, the pressures of the environment. The Soviet Union has systematically integrated its ablest individuals into the Communist party. Opposition in the Soviet Union therefore has lacked political leadership. Furthermore, Kissinger believes that through propaganda, incentives, and the destruction of all alternatives, the Soviets have gained the support of most of their people. Such support made the Soviet Union and other modern totalitarian states caricatures of democracy. "Classical democratic theory assumed that the tyranny to be resisted was that of a minority conscious of serving its own ends. . . . The essence of modern totalitarianism is that it justifies itself, not as government by a minority but as the most direct expression of the popular will."[89]

All of these factors led Kissinger to reject American theories of convergence. No amount of industrialization and consumerism would transform the Soviet Union into a western society.

THE EMERGING NATIONS

The starting point for political evolution in the emerging nations also differs from that of the West. Kissinger observes that most of these nations lack a national identity. "The problem of political organization thus confronts the new nations at the very beginning of the process of development in an even more acute form than it ever did the West."[90] He thought it naive that American leaders would suggest economic remedies for this problem—remedies such as a Marshall Plan for the nations of Asia and Africa. The success of the Marshall Plan lay in the fact that it "revitalized an existing political framework."[91] No comparable framework exists in the emerging nations.

> Many of the new countries are the product neither of a common history nor of a common culture nor even of a common language—the unifying forces of European nationalism. The primary factor of cohesion very frequently is the common experience of colonial rule. Frontiers—particularly in Africa—reflect the administrative convenience of the former colonial powers or the outcome of imperial struggles. Most of the new states therefore are in quest not only of independence but of identity.[92]

To the extent that the new nations exhibited political values, they emphasized the central role of the state. "All the new nations," Kissinger writes, "see in the state a chief instrument for social and economic progress. Above all, it is the primary unifying force."[93] The idea that government has only limited functions seemed meaningless in the context of the emerging nations. Moreover, the traditions and legal institutions that limit the authority of government in more advanced nations are not present in the new states.

Finally, the new nations face enormous physical and social challenges that affect their political development. Economic deprivation, overpopulation, and the lack of education are among these challenges. In addition, most of the new states lack social cohesiveness; tribal and regional schisms threaten their very existence.

The economic theorists justified authoritarianism in the new states as a necessary transitional phase of economic and political development. Only a strong central figure they say can unify the nation during its "take-off" stage. These theorists believed that economic development would ameliorate authoritarianism. Kissinger disputes this conclusion. "Authoritarianism is likely to become more rather than less well established as time goes on. As it develops its own structure and its own values, the scope for affecting it will constantly diminish."[94]

On the basis of these factors, Kissinger rejects the "stages of growth" theories. The central problem in the new states is political—not economic. These states have to develop political structures that can ensure economic growth without becoming totalitarian pro-Soviet countries in the process. Hence, relying on an economic process to produce enlightened political institutions was, for Kissinger, "to reverse the real priorities."[95] He believed that whatever political system brought about economic development in the new nations would become more firmly established as a result of its success.

EUROPE

The starting point of political evolution in postwar Europe was for Kissinger, as for de Gaulle, the individual European nations. Although World War II left much of Europe in ruins, Kissinger believed that the political dynamism of the individual nations would return. The future course of Europe, even its unity, would be based "on the vitality of the traditional European states."[96] This "Gaullist" outlook was in sharp contrast to the views of American leaders and European integrationists who held that the nation-state was an antiquated concept—especially in the European context—and that it was the source of the continent's traditional and all-too-destructive rivalries.

Kissinger thought it contradictory that many of the American proponents of "nation-building" in the new countries and of nationalism in Eastern Europe decried any resurgence of nationalism in Western Europe.[97] He thought this view especially ironic, because Europe had been the birthplace of the modern nation-state.

Kissinger's historical perspective, which emphasizes the distinctiveness of the great states, leads him to reject any theory that belittles national distinctions. According to the integrationists, European political life would come to depend on the functional interdependence of national economies; political issues would become largely technical in nature. These developments would support political unification.

Kissinger contrasts the "analytical truth" of the integrationists with the "historical truth" of de Gaulle.[98] The unique cultures and separate historical development of the European nations argue against an automatic process of integration. Political will and leadership still take precedence over technical problem-solving. Like de Gaulle, Kissinger believes that "the states are the only legitimate source of power; only they can act responsibly."[99] He quotes de Gaulle:

> it is true that the nation is a human and sentimental element, whereas Europe can be built on the basis of active, authoritative and responsible elements. What elements? The States, of course; for, in this respect, it is only the States that are valid, legitimate and capable of achievement. I have already said, and I repeat, that at the present time there cannot be any other Europe than a Europe of States, apart, of course, from myths, stories and parodies.

> The States are, in truth, certainly very different from one another, each of which has its own spirit, its own history, its own language, its own misfortunes, glories, and ambitions; but these States are the only entities that have the right to order and the authority to act.[100]

Kissinger believes that national interests will provide the basis for political decisions in Europe in the future as in the past. Again, he echoes de Gaulle. He believes that de Gaulle—more than American leaders cared to admit—represented the political outlook of most Europeans. He finds merit in de Gaulle's contention that "a political unit must mean something to itself before it can have meaning to others."[101]

This point had particular significance for political development in Europe. The basis of national identity differed in each of the great states. De Gaulle believed that the grandeur of France could only be restored by political action that overshadowed the reality of its defeat in two world wars and the political chaos of the Third and Fourth Republics.[102] This kind of action was inconsistent with the view of the state held by the integrationists. De Gaulle believed that European integration would destroy the "moral substance" of the integrated nations.

> Thus de Gaulle's proposal for European unity invariably envisages a confederation of states rather than supranational institutions. . . . He has opposed supranational institutions for Europe because he told a press conference in 1965 such a Europe would be "governed in appearance by anonymous technocratic, and stateless committees; in other words, a Europe without political reality, without economic drive, without a capacity for defense, and therefore doomed, in the face of the Soviet bloc, to being nothing more than a dependent of the great Western power, which itself had a policy, an economy, and a defense—the United States of America.[103]

For Britain, the issue of national identity was linked to its future political association, i.e., whether it would seek its primary role in a

European confederation or in an Atlantic community with the United States. Germany too had its own choices to make. Kissinger believes that Chancellor Adenauer was correct in suggesting that Germany must achieve stability by linking its identity to something greater than itself. "The German nightmare is a reappearance of the historical isolation that for almost its entire history has forced Germany to confront hostility on all its borders, east and west."[104] But how should it prevent this isolation—in a "Europe of the Fatherlands" (built on a Franco-German *entente*) or in a wider Atlantic community? And how could it end its isolation and still achieve German reunification? Kissinger believes that no economic process could override these questions involving national interests.

Finally, Kissinger maintains that the external challenges that would influence European political development in the postwar era would be largely confined to Europe. American spokesmen complained that Europeans had become "inward-looking." They believed that economic revitalization should lead Europe to assume a role as a world power. But Kissinger disagrees. Nations assume roles in the international arena based on their political aspirations and national identity—not their economic vitality. "As a result of decolonization," Kissinger writes, "our European Allies have ceased to think of themselves as world powers."[105] He notes that decolonization had itself contributed to Europe's revival. "Freed from overseas commitments, many European countries for the first time in a generation are able to develop a specifically European role for themselves."[106]

Kissinger's assertions regarding political evolution in the Soviet Union, the emerging nations, and Europe suggested a different course for American foreign policy. His views on the content of this policy are discussed in the next section.

The Prospects of American Foreign Policy

THE SOVIET UNION

America's foreign policy toward the Soviet Union, Kissinger stresses, should be directed at its behavior in the international community, not at its domestic society. Our concern with the transformation of Soviet society made us forget "that we have to deal in the first instance with Soviet foreign and not with its domestic policy."[107] Our actions could have little effect on the internal development of the Soviet Union. It was precisely because American and Soviet societies were likely to remain hostile that a more activist American foreign policy was required.

What would this foreign policy entail? First, it requires the recognition that military power will always be an essential element of our relationship with the Soviet Union. It was for this reason that Kissinger placed such importance on developing a capacity for limited war. He stresses that Soviet leaders would never give up an opportunity to fill a vacuum in order to build good will in the West. It is naive to assume that the "spirit" of a summit or a periodic relaxation of tensions would override the Soviet way of thinking. Hence, military power would always be needed to demonstrate to the Soviets that the relationship of forces had not tilted in their favor.

Yet, Kissinger stresses that the cold war also demanded diplomatic creativity. In contrast, advocates of containment considered diplomatic contact with the Soviet Union meaningless until that society had changed. Kissinger believes that an activist American foreign policy would serve two purposes: first, to negotiate genuine agreements with the Soviets; and second, to demonstrate Soviet intransigence when negotiations failed.

Kissinger emphasizes that taking an active role in defining the issues for negotiation would give a positive content to our foreign policy. He also believes that although the Soviet Union was a revolutionary power, nuclear weapons have created a negative community of interests between the two nations. This was not the same as saying that both major powers accepted the international order. Their mutual fear of destruction, however, did provide a basis for genuine negotiations.

"If serious negotiations are possible between the free world and the Communist states," Kissinger writes, "arms control would seem the obvious subject."[108] If our military strategy was properly conceived, arms control agreements could enhance our overall security. Yet we should not seek a unilateral advantage from these agreements, because they would only be accepted if they increased the relative security of both powers. Furthermore, the different force structures of the Soviet Union and the United States and the rapidly changing nature of technology made arms control agreements exceedingly complex. Kissinger, however, thinks that agreements could be reached in such areas as force reductions; the prevention of surprise attack or accidental war; nuclear proliferation (often called the "Nth country" problem); and the control of hostilities in world trouble spots.

Kissinger suggests other potential agreements that would reduce tensions and contribute to world order. He proposes negotiations on the future of Germany, which he regards as the key to European stability. He outlines a two-stage plan that could be enacted over a fifteen-year period. The first stage would focus on an "Austrian" type solution in East Germany, i.e., the western nations would acknowledge the existence of an East German state, provided that its government was militarily neutral and freely elected. The second stage would allow for German unification; the Federal Republic would accept the existing frontier of the Oder-Neisse and renounce nuclear weapons.

American diplomacy could seize the initiative in other areas. The important thing was that the nation stop being a status quo power, seemingly fearful of diplomatic contact with the Soviets. Failure here would leave the Soviets free to define the issues on the international agenda and make the United States appear intransigent to the world community. Creative diplomacy could embolden the West vis-à-vis the Soviets and capture the imagination of the other nations in the international system.

THE EMERGING NATIONS

Kissinger insists that the United States cannot dictate the political development of the emerging nations. This fact should be the starting point for American foreign policy toward these countries. It was true that the emerging nations were at the beginning of the evolutionary process. Their situation offered the greatest opportunities for shaping social and political institutions. It was also true that the emerging nations would probably resist U.S. solutions—whatever their merits—because they would "interpret any attempt by the West to assist political development as simply another form of colonialism."[109]

Kissinger acknowledges this constraint on American foreign policy. Yet he argues that we should not limit our involvement in Asia and Africa to economic assistance, or trust the political evolution of the new nations to an autonomous economic process. Instead, we need to make such values as personal freedom and respect for human dignity meaningful to the new nations, while remembering that the political institutions that develop will reflect the unique conditions of these countries. Unless our policy addresses the importance of political values and demonstrates the moral superiority of the West, "the much-vaunted economic competition between us and Communism in the uncommitted areas will be without meaning. . . . The challenge of the new nations is that they cannot live by bread alone; to offer nothing but bread is to leave the arena to those who are sufficiently dynamic to define their purpose."[110]

Despite the failures of American policy, Kissinger remained optimistic about American prospects in the new nations. He speaks of a "spiritual kinship" between these nations and the West because of their colonial past.[111] This bond offered foreign policy opportunities for the United States. But it was important to understand that these opportunities could only be realized by the exercise of leadership—not by a quest for popularity. The idea that American policy should be determined by "world opinion" was an excuse for inaction. As the strongest power, America should shape world opinion, not react to it. "The price of our power is leadership. For what else is leadership except the willingness to stand alone if the situation requires?"[112]

Kissinger emphasizes that because of our history, the United States should be sympathetic to the new nations' stance of nonalignment. He criticizes Dulles's policy of opposing nonalignment.[113] Yet he also points out that the new nations do not understand the realities of power in world politics. American policy had to address this gap. Nonalignment was acceptable as long as the new nations appreciated America's responsibility to maintain the balance of power. In fact, this very balance permitted the new nations their stance of nonalignment.

> The importance of United States leadership is all the greater because many of the newly independent nations have so little understanding of international relations and the nature of power. Although they distinguished themselves in the struggle with the former colonial powers, the independence movements, almost without exception, provided a poor preparation for an understanding of power in international relations. Based on the dogmas of late nineteenth-century liberalism, especially its pacifism, the independence movements relied more on ideological agreement than on an evaluation of power factors. . . . Condescending as it may seem to say so, the United States has an important educational task to perform in the uncommitted third of the world. By word and by deed we must demonstrate that the inexorable element of international relations resides in the necessity to combine principle with power, that an exclusive reliance on moral pronouncements may be as irresponsible as the attempt to conduct policy on the basis of considerations of power alone.[114]

According to Kissinger, the United States must couple its compassion for the problems of the emerging nations with a "greater majesty."[115] America needed to act decisively, making our military power tangible if need be in the emerging nations of the Third World. We needed to display a political firmness that would show the world that our foreign policy had purpose and direction.

Kissinger recommends several specific policies that would demonstrate American leadership. He argues that military alliances such as SEATO and CENTO, constructed during the Eisenhower presidency, added little to overall security. The security concerns of the nations in the Middle East and Southeast Asia were primarily local rather than global. More importantly, our alliances included regional actors, such as Pakistan, whose major security threat was another country (in this case, India) with whom the United States also had ties. Kissinger suggests that the United States should safeguard security unilaterally in these regions through its ability to fight limited wars.

> The military contribution of SEATO and the Baghdad Pact (to which we belong in all but name) does not compensate for the decision of India and Egypt to stand apart and for the domestic pressures these instruments generated in some of the signatory countries. The primary function of these pacts is to draw a line across which the U.S.S.R. cannot move without the risk of war and to legitimize intervention by the United States should war break out. But the line could have been better drawn by a unilateral declaration, as in the Truman Doctrine for Greece and Turkey, and the Middle East doctrine of President Eisenhower.[116]

Behind this unilateral shield, American policy should aim at developing shared objectives. Kissinger believes, for example, that SEATO should have emphasized nonmilitary functions. Such an emphasis might have paved the way for other nations, such as Indonesia and India, to join the alliance.

Kissinger stresses that our policy in the emerging nations should foster regionalism. The United States should be responsive to the national aspirations of these countries, but "it should also encourage larger groupings, particularly on a regional basis."[117] America could foster such groupings by supporting the development of one powerful nation within each region. "The best method of having a major impact on many countries will be to make a going concern of *one* country. India in Asia, Brazil in Latin America, Nigeria in Africa could become magnets and examples for their regions if we acted with the boldness and on the comparative scale of the Marshall Plan."[118] As these regional groupings developed, their own common interests would result in a common defense. Such groupings around the Soviet periphery would restrain the Soviets politically. Even if these regional associations did not always support American policies, they would be in America's interest in the long term.

EUROPE

American foreign policy toward Europe also needed new direction. America's emphasis on supranational institutions stymied more creative approaches. Furthermore, American foreign policy had failed to keep pace with the "structural" changes that influenced the Atlantic alliance. The economic recovery in Europe, decolonization, and the growth of the Soviet nuclear arsenal had not been taken into account. The stalemate in NATO over the merits of nuclear deterrence versus conventional defense and over the issue of separate European nuclear forces had deepened.

For these reasons, Kissinger characterized our relations with Europe as a "troubled partnership."

As we have seen, Kissinger adopts a Gaullist outlook, stressing that American policy must gear itself to the continued existence of the separate nations of Europe. We should not base our planning on the expected emergence of a United States on the other side of the Atlantic. De Gaulle's rejection of English membership in the Common Market in 1963 indicated that political interests still took precedence over economic integration.

Kissinger criticizes schemes for European defense such as the Multilateral Nuclear Force (MLF). He disparages it as a "hardware" solution, for although it called for naval forces composed of European and American crews, it failed to address the central problems of European defense. NATO strategy was still at an impasse because control of the MLF essentially remained in American hands. Kissinger suggests that the Europeans should be allowed to develop their own nuclear forces. Such a move would be in accord with their sovereignty and would complement the changing U.S.-Soviet strategic balance. Kissinger also believes that the European nations need to contribute more conventional forces to NATO.

Although Kissinger rejects the concept of a supranational Europe, he maintains that the Atlantic alliance should not be built merely on a policy of consultation. The interests of the United States and Europe do not always coincide. The United States' concerns are global; Europe's are regional. Moreover, their relative power and resources are unequal. European nations were often put in the position of being "advisors in an American decision-making process."[119] A process of consultation could work if a prior political consensus existed, but consultations could not create this consensus.

American leaders needed to recognize that their interests were not always the same as those of their European partners. The United States must be prepared to act alone in regions where Europe no longer has a stake. Although a common U.S.–European foreign policy on many issues is unlikely, Kissinger believed that it was essential to narrow the range of divergence. The central question that governed the future of the Atlantic alliance was: "How much unity do we want? How much pluralism can we stand? Too formalistic a conception of unity risks destroying the sense of responsibility of our Allies. Too absolute an insistence on national particularity must lead to a fragmentation of any common effort."[120]

Kissinger suggests that institutional approaches could be used to avoid this kind of fragmentation. For example, he praises the Fouchet Plan,[121] which called for institutionalized meetings of foreign ministers and subcabinet officials to coordinate common policies and reconcile differences. Over time such a forum could develop into a mechanism for policy formulation. In addition, it would permit more flexibility in U.S.–European relations than is suggested by the "twin pillars" theory. "A confederal Europe would enable the United States to maintain an influence at many centers of decision rather than be forced to stake everything on affecting the views of a single supranational body."[122]

Kissinger also urges the establishment of a political arm of NATO. An executive committee would formulate a common NATO foreign policy as well as define the limits of autonomous action. It would also develop a common strategic doctrine to support NATO's political functions.

Despite his advocacy of such institutions, Kissinger stresses that "organizational devices should never be confused with substantive solutions."[123] The West needed a broader vision of an Atlantic commonwealth.[124] Kissinger seems to base this broader vision on common values and to rely on creative leadership to demonstrate how such a commonwealth could be realized. "The leap forward in the next decade is the creation of a political framework that will go beyond the nationalism which has dominated the past century and a half. Detailed institutional arrangements are less urgent at this stage than a commitment to a bold program of political construction."[125]

Kissinger clearly attached great importance to debunking the theories of political evolution that had become intellectually fashionable in America. The ready acceptance of these theories troubled him; as a historian, he knew that national development was far more complex. These theories helped to shape American foreign policy; Kissinger held their influence responsible for many of our setbacks in the postwar era. The belief that autonomous economic forces would work to America's advantage led to an absence of activist leadership in critical areas. The emphasis on economics as the primary element of political change blurred the distinctions between the communist system and our own.

America's power in the period after 1945 involved responsibilities unprecedented in the nation's history. Our power placed us at the center of the world community where we could exercise profound influence. Never was the need for this influence greater. Kissinger believed that our ability to exercise this influence in the face of the communist challenge would test more than our ability to survive; "it will be the measure of our worthiness to survive."[126]

Kissinger's criticism of American foreign and defense policies and his ideas on statecraft and leadership, which I have discussed in parts 1 and 2, provide the only suitable background for considering his actions as a statesman. Rarely has there been an American leader whose thought was so much a part of the public record before entering office. The relationship between Kissinger's thought and his statecraft and the nature of his legacy are examined in the conclusion of this study.

PART 3
Years of Leadership

The Historian as Statesman: Kissinger's Legacy

The Kissinger Cycle

Writing in the first years of the Carter administration, the theorist Stanley Hoffman sought to explain the changes that had occurred in contemporary international politics and the challenges that confronted American foreign policy.[1] Hoffmann argued that not only had the world become more complex, but that America itself was seeking a new consensus to deal with this complexity. For most of the period since 1945, American foreign policy had focused on the policy of containment. Beginning in 1969, Hoffmann observed, American policy embarked on a different course—a course he called the "Kissinger cycle."[2] The unity of the containment cycle rested on one central concept; the unity of the latter period depended on the personality of one central figure.

I offer Hoffmann's views not because they describe American foreign policy today. In fact, he argued that the Kissinger cycle had ended with Kissinger's departure from office—even though elements of continuity might be found in later administrations. More than a decade has passed since Hoffmann presented his ideas. During this time, the Carter and Reagan presidencies have borrowed from both of the preceding cycles rather than beginning a new era of their own.[3]

Hoffmann's ideas are important because they indicate the extent to which Kissinger's direction of American foreign policy represented a fundamental break with the past. Hoffmann traces the source of these policy changes to Kissinger's early ideas on statecraft and international politics. Understanding the innovations of the period "consists of taking the intellectual side of Dr. Kissinger more seriously and of believing that he came to power, if not with a full-fledged doctrine, at least with a definite set of dogmas."[4]

In truth, Kissinger always sought a wider audience for his views than was provided by the academy. As Stephen Graubard observes, his commentaries on the policy failures of successive administrations were never merely scholarly works. His major concern was to influence the direction of American foreign policy.[5] It should not be surprising that, when given the chance to shape American statecraft, he drew on the ideas he had formed in over two decades of study and writing.

To a greater extent than any other contemporary public figure, Kissinger's leadership represents the application of thought to action. In previous chapters, I have explored Kissinger's historical philosophy and related it to his critique of American foreign policy. Yet if Kissinger's ideas are important in themselves, they derive added importance from the fact that they shaped his actions as statesman during a pivotal period in American history.

In the following pages, I will examine the relationship between Kissinger's early ideas and his later policies. Apart from demonstrating the continuity of his views, a study of Kissinger's statecraft provides a basis for assessing the relevance of his ideas to the practice of foreign policy. Kissinger's policies and the opposition they inspired illustrate the contrast between his European worldview and the traditional American approach to foreign affairs. In conclusion, I will attempt to evaluate Kissinger's legacy to American statecraft—to determine whether his ideas and diplomatic achievements will have a lasting impact on American foreign policy.

Kissinger in Perspective: Thought and Values

Before examining Kissinger's actions as a statesman, I wish to offer some observations about his thought and values. This discussion will provide the bridge between his efforts as a scholar and the specific policies that he promoted during his years in public office.

Some writers have challenged the very idea that there is a bridge, an inner continuity, between Kissinger's thought and his statecraft.[6] They maintain that Kissinger's actions as a statesman constitute an implicit renunciation of the convictions that he held as a scholar. Specifically, they contrast the policies of détente and the opening to China with the hard-line anticommunist position he expressed in his writings.

To an extent, Kissinger is responsible for this criticism. As a scholar, he pays insufficient attention to the question of change in the international system—specifically as it relates to a revolutionary power, such as Napoleonic France or the Soviet Union. What factors other than a military defeat cause a revolutionary power to accept the legitimacy of the international system? Although Kissinger emphasizes that changes have occurred in the Soviet Union, the fact that he never explicitly characterizes it as a legitimate state led many to question the basic premises of détente.

Kissinger's critics offer several explanations for the alleged differences between his early and later views. Some characterize him as a pragmatic statesman.[7] We can understand his policies not by referring to concepts that he formed before holding office, but by treating them solely as solutions to the immediate problems that he confronted as a statesman. Other writers portray Kissinger as an opportunist.[8] They see his own desire for accomplishment as the motivation behind his celebrated diplomatic efforts—efforts that were frequently undertaken in conditions of which Kissinger the scholar would disapprove.[9] Like Nixon, Kissinger's turnaround is explained as Disraeli-like.[10] His very stature as a hard-line anticommunist gave him the credibility needed to carry off a rapprochement with the Soviet Union.

Another group of critics attributes Kissinger's departure from his earlier views to his belief that America's power was waning.[11] Thus, even though Kissinger remained opposed to the Soviet Union, his actions as a statesman were based on the belief that America had lost its spirit. These writers claim that the policies of détente are essentially defeatist—they represent an attempt on the part of the declining West to accommodate the political and military ascendancy of the Soviet Union.

I believe that these criticisms are fundamentally mistaken. Not only do they err in asserting that Kissinger's thought and statecraft lack continuity, they also misread the deeper elements of his historical philosophy and beliefs. I will consider each of these points in turn.

The view that Kissinger's policies depart from the main lines of his scholarship can only be maintained by ignoring the complexity of both. Unquestionably, Kissinger as a scholar argued vigorously for the continuation and enhancement of our military strength vis-à-vis the Soviets. His advocacy of limited war was designed to make our power more viable in the face of Soviet aggression. He urged the nation to recognize and combat the ideological dimension of the Soviet challenge. The views that he held on these subjects parallel those of other cold warriors.

But Kissinger the anticommunist was simultaneously an advocate of negotiating with the Soviet Union and a severe critic of containment. Even in the fifties, we find in his writings an emphasis on structuring patterns of conduct with the communist world. Kissinger was philosophically at odds with the American realists—many of whom were among the leading proponents of containment. He believed that they ignored the creative possibilities of an activist statecraft, encouraging instead the type of sterile diplomacy that characterized John Foster Dulles's State Department. He faulted the realist school for its reliance on military power divorced from diplomacy and its belief that we could not negotiate with the Soviet Union until Soviet society had changed.

Kissinger's policies are characterized by this same complexity. He believed that we must both confront and negotiate with the Soviets. Kissinger the détentist statesman is simultaneously the advocate of new weapon systems and defenses; of a continued military presence in Vietnam; of contesting the Soviets in the Middle East; and of other actions that demonstrate America's resolve to oppose the Soviets militarily. Once out of office, Kissinger criticized the Carter administration for its failure to maintain the global military balance and for its weak response to such actions as the Soviet invasion of Afghanistan.

Those who depict Kissinger's policies as a pragmatic or opportunistic reversal of his earlier writings choose to ignore essential aspects of both his statecraft and scholarship. This is particularly true with respect to the policies of détente with the Soviet Union. Kissinger had long argued that the nuclear age imposed an imperative on both superpowers to restrain their differences. Those who portray his policies as defeatist, however, present a far more troubling argument. This critique goes beyond contesting the policies of détente; it raises questions about Kissinger's philosophical approach and his qualification to hold high public office in America.

Many Americans perceive Kissinger as extremely pessimistic in temperament. His writings are said to reveal a Spenglerian fatalism, a belief in the inevitable decline of American power. Tragedy has been a constant theme in Kissinger's thought since his undergraduate writings, and many commentators have called attention to his "tragic vision."[12] Against this background, it is not surprising that some would challenge his ability to provide the West with inspiration and leadership. The emphasis on Kissinger's pessimism and tragic outlook represents an incomplete understanding of his historical philosophy. It also obscures the deeper designs of his statecraft.

To fully understand Kissinger is to grasp that his most fundamental perceptions—of history, of statecraft, of life itself—are based on a reconciliation of·opposites. Freedom and necessity; inspiration and organization; creativity and decline—these are the dualities that are found throughout his writings. His effort to find some common ground on which to reconcile these opposites has been the source of his deepest insights. What specifically does this kind of reconciliation involve?

In his earliest work, "The Meaning of History," Kissinger indicates that historical understanding can be attained by confronting the seeming paradox of freedom and necessity. Each of us lives with the belief that our individual actions are freely chosen. Yet each choice that we make narrows the range of our future choices. In retrospect, one's life appears to have followed a set course—after a certain point its outcome appears determined. Similarly, Kissinger observes, the great figures of history have confronted momentous choices at critical periods in the lives of their nations. Yet, in retrospect, historical events appear to have occurred inevitably. A scholarship of determinism reduces history to a series of causes and effects.

Kissinger struggles, or more appropriately, continues to struggle with this paradox. His thought is still marked by the inner tension caused by these opposites. In Spengler and Toynbee, Kissinger discovered a historical erudition that deeply impressed him. But their thought was also troubling, because they maintained that there are recurring patterns in history that are independent of human choice. On the basis of Spengler and Toynbee's historical knowledge, one cannot but conclude that a fatedness governs history. Every civilization that ever existed—particularly those such as Greece and Rome whose military power and culture held sway throughout the known world—ultimately has lost its inner unity, has receded in territorial expanse, and has declined culturally and militarily. Spengler and Toynbee pointed Kissinger in the direction of determinism.

However, in their quest to understand the grand sweep of history, Spengler and Toynbee failed to grasp the importance of its inner dimension—choice. Kissinger finds this dimension in Kant. Man the subject is at the center of history—not the inexorable movement of impersonal forces. Through his actions and choices, man gives meaning to history. Unfolding events may narrow the range of choices, but it is the attitude that man adopts toward these events that provides the shaping force of history. True historical understanding, according to Kissinger, consists in a reconciliation of the knowledge of history's fatedness with a feel for the past as willed occurrence—as alive with choice.

Kissinger suggests that life itself involves a similar paradox. We live with the knowledge that our lives have taken a certain course and that future events are somewhat determined. More importantly, we know we must die. Despite the fatedness of our existence, we live with a sense of permanence. Through innumerable acts of choice we give meaning to life.

Unlike individuals, however, nations do not physically die. Aging in a culture, Kissinger indicates, is not an organic but a spiritual decline—a loss of inspiration. Because the decline of nations is caused by a failure of creativity, Kissinger believes that it can be prevented.

How does Kissinger's historical philosophy influence his actions as a statesman? The knowledge that nations decline (and that this is true of America also) does not lead Kissinger to attitudes of resignation and fatalism. To the contrary, this knowledge explains his emphasis on activist statecraft, on perpetual striving. Kissinger identifies profound policy with continuous creativity.[13] Through ceaseless efforts, the statesman can inspire his society to meet and master challenges that nurture

its spirit and growth. This commitment to activism also helps us understand Kissinger the man. Each stage of his adult life has been characterized by almost Faustian efforts to achieve. His peripatetic mode of
statecraft was aptly described by Hans Morgenthau as the "diplomacy of
movement."[14]

Against this background, why do Americans perceive Kissinger solely
as pessimistic? I believe that his historical philosophy represented such a
departure from the ideas traditionally expressed by American leaders
that it caused most Americans to overlook the inner tension in his
thought. American leaders have usually conveyed a sense of optimism,
particularly in their public statements; they believe that all problems can
be solved. Moreover, most have accepted the idea that America is a
special country with a role that transcends the historical fate of other
nations. In contrast, Kissinger emphasized that the nation's accomplishments would be transitory unless they were maintained by constant
effort. He stressed that America was similar to other nations in that it too
could decline. Its power was finite. Its values were not shared by all
societies, and they were vehemently opposed by some. It could neither
escape from nor dominate history. America, Kissinger believed, had to
learn to accept its limits—a theme I will discuss at length later in this
chapter.

Against the background of his historical knowledge, Kissinger makes
his own commitment to activism. His emphasis on creativity, however,
raises a fundamental question—creativity for what? What values warrant
the dedication and constant effort to which he calls the statesman?

Remembering Kissinger's attraction to German historical thought can
help us answer this question. A key element of German historicism is
the importance it attaches to the uniqueness of different cultures.
Spengler and Toynbee also emphasize individual civilizations and
cultures. Kissinger displays a similar sensitivity to the inner spirit of
civilizations. When he visited other nations as a statesman, his public
speeches frequently referred to the original contribution of different
cultures.

Kissinger, however, values no civilization more than that of the West.
He believes that western political and social institutions and western
intellectual and artistic accomplishments represent an unparalleled record of human achievement. Kissinger himself is quintessentially a man
of the West. As we have seen, he drew deeply from the classical education he received at Harvard and from his study of European thought.

Kissinger's criticism of American foreign policy was inspired by a
desire to see the values of the West prevail. America emerged as the
leader of the West at a time when its values were being challenged by the

Soviet Union. As I have tried to show, Kissinger believed that American leadership and American policies were failing to meet this challenge.

How do we r concile Kissinger's own belief in the value of western society with his policies of détente—policies that many saw as compromising western values? Specifically, how do we reconcile such values as the freedom and integrity of every individual with a rapprochement with the Soviet Union—a nation that denies basic freedoms to its own citizens, as well as to the nations of Eastern Europe? Kissinger's understanding of international life and the importance he attaches to world order provide the basis for this reconciliation. As he states in *A World Restored*, nations subconsciously rebel from involvement in foreign affairs. International life requires every nation to recognize that its power is limited and that its values are not absolute. Nations have attempted to overcome the insecurity that thus characterizes their existence in the state system, and war has usually resulted.

In the nuclear age, Kissinger believes that the statesman must be mindful of a hierarchy of goals. Although he places great importance on western values, détente is rooted in the recognition that no values can be realized unless we survive. Détente was intended to stabilize the relationship between the United States and the Soviet Union in the nuclear age. For Kissinger, it represented a "recognition of the necessity of peace—not moral callousness."[15]

This hierarchy of values confused many Americans. They criticized Kissinger for what they saw as his survivalist philosophy and the moral "hollowness" of his policies—particularly toward the Soviets. The fact that détente dampened our ideological rivalry with the Soviet Union, that it required official silence regarding Soviet dissidents and human rights, deeply offended many who believed that our policies should have a moral content.

The questions raised by Kissinger's approach are central to a consideration of contemporary American foreign policy. Largely in reaction to the alleged moral insensitivity of Kissinger's policies, the Carter administration made human rights the centerpiece of its foreign policy. Yet its attempt to influence the domestic policies of the Soviet Union not only failed, it also detracted from policies designed to ensure Soviet cooperation in the international arena. The Reagan administration has emphasized military assertiveness, although its policies have also been characterized by a moral and ideological appeal. Both presidencies have subordinated any design for world order to a moral contest with the Soviet Union—a contest that has at times been reminiscent of the early years of the cold war.

These issues will continue to influence foreign policy discussions in

America. During the years of Kissinger's stewardship of American foreign policy, the nature of U.S.–Soviet relations was portrayed in stark contrast. For the most part, postwar American foreign policy had been based on a claim of moral primacy vis-à-vis the Soviet Union. Détente signified the attempt to subordinate America's traditional claim of moral primacy to a particular conception of world order in order to decrease the risk of nuclear war. It is far from certain that the American people will be able to accept the hierarchy of values implicit in the policies that Kissinger espoused.

In the following sections, I wish to address Kissinger's policies and the ideas behind them more directly. I will begin by discussing a concept that can be traced back to Kissinger's opposition to the insular nature of American foreign policy.

The Historian as Statesman

LINKAGE: A CENTRAL CONCEPT

In writing about American foreign policy in the Nixon-Kissinger years,[16] most commentators treat "linkage" as a subordinate element of détente—a process that is designed to give détente concrete form. Linkage meant that progress in one area of U.S.–Soviet relations would necessarily be related to developments in other areas. Kissinger indicates that linkage is a function of both the natural interrelationship of global issues and the spirit of cooperation between the two powers. It was intended to foster a durable pattern of conduct based on mutual restraint. "Our approach," Kissinger explained, "proceeds from the conviction that, in moving forward across a wide spectrum of negotiations, progress in one area adds momentum to progress in other areas. . . . We have looked for progress in a series of agreements settling specific political issues, and we have sought to relate these to a new standard of international conduct appropriate to the dangers of the nuclear age."[17] Hence, the Soviet Union could not expect to benefit from expanded trade with the West unless it demonstrated restraint in the Third World. Similarly, progress in strategic arms negotiations was linked to Soviet assistance in ending the Vietnam War.

Linkage has generally been interpreted as a process aimed at moderating the behavior of the Soviet Union. Linkage involved the Soviet Union in a cross-cutting pattern of agreements from which it supposedly could not free itself. As Hoffmann writes, "Linkage suggested a process. The net was to be the outcome. The Russian bear had to be caught in a dense web of agreements it would have neither the interest nor the possibility

of breaking out of."[18] Officially, Kissinger provides the same justification: "By acquiring a stake in the network of relationships with the West,
the Soviet Union may become more conscious of what it would lose by a
return to confrontation. Indeed, it is our hope that it will develop a self-
interest in fostering the entire process of relaxation of tensions."[19]

I believe that this interpretation represents only a partial understanding of linkage. From the beginning of his career as a scholar, Kissinger
worked to change America's traditional approach to foreign policy. The
nation needed to break with its past, with its tendency to conduct
foreign policy as if events were unrelated and problems could be solved
permanently.

I have used the term "insularity" to describe the traditional patterns of
American foreign policy. Against this background, I believe that linkage
served a dual purpose in Kissinger's grand design.[20] It was as much an
attempt to transform American attitudes toward foreign affairs as it was
to discipline the Soviets. The same dense web of agreements that would
foster Soviet restraint would also serve to control America's characteristic impetuosity. The nation would learn that its relations with the
Soviets consisted of interrelated elements that placed limits on its own
behavior. The reverse side of linkage—a side that received little attention
until President Carter's human rights policies renewed Soviet-American
hostility[21]—was that America, too, would be enmeshed in a web of
relations from which it could not free itself without being blamed for
destroying détente, and with détente the basis for world order. The
nation would have to subordinate its penchant for moral appeals to a
standard appropriate to the nuclear age.

Linkage became a central part of America's foreign policy in the
Nixon-Kissinger years. It represented a break with the nation's traditional cycles of involvement and isolation.

> Perception of linkage is, in short, synonymous with an overall strate-
> gic view. We ignore it at our peril. It is inherent in the real world. The
> interrelationship of our interests, across issues and boundaries, exists
> regardless of the accidents of time or personality; it is not a matter of
> decision or will but of reality. And it cannot be ended by an act of
> policy. If we are to have a permanent conception of American foreign
> policy there must be an appreciation of the fact that merits of individ-
> ual actions can be judged only on a wider canvas.[22]

This wider canvas and strategic view provide a principal justification
for the Nixon administration's activist foreign policy and its grand design. A cohesive worldview that recognized the interrelationship of
events became the starting point for American policy. We could not
divorce our policies toward the Soviets from our relations with China.

Similarly, China measured the value of its relations with us by our ability to maintain the overall geopolitical balance. Impotence in one area of the world (such as Southeast Asia) affected our influence in other areas (such as the Middle East). Accepting these interrelationships also meant that there could be no end to our exertions in foreign affairs. Such a commitment to international involvement was especially significant in the aftermath of Vietnam—a time when many Americans favored retrenchment.

Kissinger was mindful that this strategic view represented a major departure from America's traditional outlook. Such a departure entailed changes in attitudes as well as policies. In his early writings on statecraft, Kissinger describes a similarly demanding departure from insularity. He praises Castlereagh for conducting England's foreign policy from a "European" perspective that linked the nation to the affairs of the continent. So, too, Kissinger shaped an American foreign policy that linked the nation to global affairs. Explaining the difficulty that Americans had accepting linkage, Kissinger draws on ideas he had formed years before.

> So strong is the pragmatic tradition of American political thought that linkage was widely debated as if it were an idiosyncrasy of a particular group of policymakers who chose this approach by an act of will. . . . Linkage is not a natural concept for Americans, who have traditionally perceived foreign policy as an episodic enterprise. Our bureaucratic organization, divided into regional and functional bureaus, and indeed our academic tradition of specialization compound this tendency to compartmentalization. And American pragmatism produces a penchant for examining issues separately: to deal with issues individually, as if they existed as abstractions, without the patience, timing, or sense of political complexity which are so often vital to their achievement; to display our morality in the proclamation of objectives rather than in a commitment to the operational consequences of our actions in an inherently ambiguous environment.[23]

In addition to linkage, the major innovations of the Nixon-Kissinger era rested on a recognition that the world had entered a period of transition—a period that demanded new approaches. America needed policies suited to the changing conditions of global politics.

A WORLD IN TRANSITION

A study of *A World Restored* shows that Kissinger regards the leader's understanding of his historical period as an essential element of statecraft. Leaders such as Metternich and Bismarck exhibited this quality or intuition. The great statesman grasps the "structure of the age," that is, the alignment of power relations and the presence of other forces that give the age its particular form. No foreign policy can be meaningful unless it takes these factors into consideration.

For this reason, Kissinger and Nixon took great pains to explain that their policies addressed a world in transition. In the first of the so-called "State of the World" messages, Nixon spoke of an end of an era.[24] He expands on this theme in the second of these messages.

> The postwar order of international relations—the configuration of power that emerged from the Second World War—is gone. With it are gone the assumptions and practices of United States foreign policy since 1945. No single sudden upheaval marked the end of the postwar era in the way the World Wars of this century shattered the prewar orders of international relations. But the cumulative change since 1945 is profound nonetheless.[25]

What were the main outlines of this new period? First, the presidential message indicated that the cold war era of rigid blocs had given way to a more fluid alignment of nations. "It is an increasingly heterogeneous and complex world, and the dangers of local conflict are magnified. But so, too, are the opportunities for creative diplomacy."[26] Europe, Japan, and China represented centers of power that could act autonomously and that had to be accommodated. Emphasis would be placed on multi-lateral diplomacy. Second, the administration acknowledged that the Soviet Union possessed military power that equaled that of the United States. This fact had significant implications for U.S. defense doctrine and diplomacy. Third, the new nations of the Third World were develop-ing their own identities. Increasingly, they would emerge as the major actors in different regions of the world. Finally, the report recognized that a range of issues, such as environmental concerns, now existed that showed nations to be more interdependent than they had been seen as before.

Such changes demanded a "New American Role."[27] In the future, relations with our allies would be based on partnership. As Nixon and Kissinger explained, partnership represented a definite change in the postwar pattern of our relations with Western Europe and Japan. These nations now possessed the power to act more autonomously. Henceforth they should expect that we too would act with greater autonomy when it was in our interest. "We are not involved in the world," stated Nixon, "because we have commitments; we have commitments because we are involved. Our interests must shape our commitments, rather than the other way around."[28]

Regarding the Soviet Union, the administration spoke of an "era of negotiation" replacing the cold war "era of confrontation."[29] The basis of this new era was twofold: the official acceptance by the United States of strategic parity with the Soviet Union, and the Sino-Soviet rift. Strategic parity suggested that the Soviet Union would become more of a status quo power. Its conflict with China gave it a major incentive for stabilizing relations with the United States. U.S.–Soviet negotiations were designed to provide a durable "structure of peace" that both powers would have a vital stake in preserving.

The final element of the new American role—military strength— supported both partnership and negotiations. The administration stressed that military power would be integrated with its foreign policy objectives. The Nixon Doctrine reflected the increasing pluralism of the international system. Henceforth, the United States would no longer take military responsibility for local conflicts such as Vietnam, but would depend on the nations primarily involved or on major regional allies. Additionally, the administration emphasized that meaningful negotiations with the Soviets depended on our maintaining the overall geostrategic balance.[30]

There are several parallels between the new American role outlined by the Nixon administration and Kissinger's ideas as a scholar and critic of American foreign policy.

The new American role signified the end of containment. As we have seen, Kissinger criticized containment, because it made negotiations with the USSR contingent on a fundamental change in Soviet domestic society. From the mid-1950s, Kissinger had argued that it was naive to expect such changes; moreover, there was little America could do to produce a transformation of the Soviet system.

In contrast, Kissinger believed that it was because Soviet and American societies are so fundamentally different that agreements are necessary to govern their relationship. Détente was based on an acknowledgement of these differences, not on the convergence of the two systems. Furthermore, he stressed that a stable international order depends primarily on U.S.–Soviet relations.

The question of dealing with Communist governments has troubled the American people and the Congress since 1917. There has always been a fear that by working with a government whose internal policies differ so sharply from our own, we are in some manner condoning these policies or encouraging their continuation. Some argue that until there is a genuine "liberalization"—or signs of serious progress in this direction—all elements of conciliation in Soviet policy must be regarded as temporary and tactical. In that view, demands for internal changes must be the precondition for the pursuit of a relaxation of tensions with the Soviet Union. Our view is different. We shall insist on responsible international behavior by the Soviet Union and use it as the primary index of our relationship. . . . We have profound differences with the Soviet Union—in our values, our methods, our vision of the future. But it is these very differences which compel any responsible administration to make a major effort to create a more constructive relationship.[31]

Kissinger also emphasized that diplomatic flexibility is an essential element of creative foreign policy. He admired this aspect of Bismarck's policies.[32] Bismarck's great success as a statesman was that he was able to spin a web of relationships with other European powers that placed Prussia at the center. Prussia's "equidistance" from all of the other powers gave it the maximum scope for its own diplomacy.

Similarly, Kissinger attempted to place the United States at the center of a web involving both its allies and adversaries. He used the pluralism of the new order to justify these policies, but the need for greater flexibility in U.S.–European relations, for example, had been a key point in his writings for some years. The United States, Kissinger emphasized, was a global power with global interests, whereas Europe's interests were primarily regional. This relationship demanded that America neither seek nor expect European support for many of its policies outside Europe. Furthermore, he stressed that a resurgent Europe (and Japan) would likely take different positions on issues affecting allied relations. Although our interests were largely congruent, they were far from identical.

Both Nixon and Kissinger recognized that the Sino-Soviet rift offered creative opportunities for U.S. diplomacy.[33] Ironically, both had maintained a monolithic view of the communist world well into the 1960s, portraying China as a revolutionary actor.[34] Once in power, however, Nixon and Kissinger fostered both détente with the Soviet Union and the normalization of political relations with China. They used the Sino-Soviet rift to create a new political alignment in international politics situated on a Moscow-Peking-Washington axis. The Nixon administration, because it developed more constructive relations with both the Soviet Union and China than either had with the other, used its position in the Moscow-Peking-Washington triangle to gain maximum diplomatic advantage vis-à-vis the two communist powers. In essence, both the Soviet Union and China competed to keep the United States from establishing a rapprochement with the other power.

The final element of continuity with Kissinger's early writings concerns the administration's attitude toward military power. As a scholar, Kissinger had stressed two principal ideas about power. First, power is a major element in world politics, but its effectiveness is derived from the strategy that governs it. Second, power and political purpose are inseparable. The most important element of any military strategy is the political role that it is designed to serve.

These attitudes toward power account for many of the innovations of the Nixon-Kissinger period. The acceptance of strategic sufficiency[35] vis-à-vis the Soviets, and the adjustment of force levels from those needed to fight two-and-a-half wars to those needed to fight one-and-a-half wars represent efforts to base defense planning on informed strategies. The Nixon Doctrine was an attempt to make American power usable in local situations. As the late Robert Osgood suggests, Nixon and Kissinger wanted to alter our military role in order to preserve our political role.[36] The administration consistently took the view that military power derived its significance from its political uses. To a greater extent than in any previous administration, national security planning was linked to arms control efforts.

The new American role was related to a conception of order that Nixon and Kissinger shared regarding world politics. This conception influenced the assumptions they made about changes in the contemporary period and the policies they promoted.

THE CONCEPT OF ORDER

In defining the purposes of American foreign policy in the Nixon years, Kissinger emphasized one theme over others—the need for world order. The changes in international politics demanded the creation of a new international system. Kissinger thought it inconceivable that a new system could emerge without a significant American contribution. The nation's interests were inseparable from global stability.

Kissinger believed that the starting point for constructing a new international order lay in forming an adequate conception of it.[37] What were the fundamental conditions of world order? How could they be achieved given the new conditions of the contemporary period?

In his study of the nineteenth-century state system, Kissinger had identified two conditions of order: first, a balance of power sufficient to deter aggression; and second, the legitimacy of the overall system, that is, its acceptance by the major powers. The Nixon-Kissinger approach sought to ensure both balance and legitimacy. I will examine each of these goals in turn.

A rigid, bipolar conception of world politics characterized the cold war period. The international system was split into two hostile blocs. A gain for one side was automatically seen as a loss for the other. This situation made the global equilibrium particularly unstable. Although the military forces of each superpower served to deter aggression, diplomatic relations lacked the flexibility inherent in a traditional balance of power system.

The Nixon-Kissinger approach addressed a more fluid world. A multi-tiered balance of power became the primary condition for order. The administration sought to create conditions of military equilibrium at several levels of the state system. Nixon and Kissinger believed that this approach conformed to the changes that had occurred in the international system and to the way in which it would continue to evolve.

U.S.–Soviet relations represented the top tier in this multitiered balance. Military parity provided the key to equilibrium at this level. The administration emphasized the acceptance by both sides of a strategic balance and sought to establish this concept as the basis for U.S.–Soviet relations in the Strategic Arms Limitation Talks (SALT). Nixon explained this policy in an early statement:

> Our purpose, reflected both in our strategic programs and in our SALT proposals, is to maintain a balance, and thereby reduce the likelihood of nuclear war. . . . The United States and the Soviet Union have now reached a point where small numerical advantages in strategic forces have little military relevance. The attempt to obtain large advantages would spark an arms race which would, in the end, prove pointless. For both sides would almost surely commit the necessary resources to maintain a balance.[38]

The military relationship between the two superpowers also recognized spheres of influence. The Western Hemisphere was seen to constitute such a sphere of influence of the United States. But the administration also maintained that, militarily, Eastern Europe was in the Soviet sphere. The so-called Kissinger-Sonnenfeldt Doctrine acknowledged that the development of an "organic" link between Eastern Europe and the Soviet Union—and western acceptance of this link—was in the interest of world order. Principally, the Kissinger-Sonnenfeldt Doctrine envisioned a process of "Finlandization" in Eastern Europe—that is, a process whereby the nations of Eastern Europe would practice foreign and defense policies acceptable to the Soviet Union (characteristic of Finland) in exchange for relative autonomy in terms of domestic political, cultural, and economic affairs. The Helsinki Accords of 1975 accepted the status quo in Eastern Europe, including Soviet geopolitical influence.[39]

No other nation possessed the military power of the United States or the Soviet Union. In a strictly military sense, the world would remain bipolar. Yet immediately below the top tier of the international system, the Nixon administration saw a five-power world emerging—a world that included Western Europe, China, and Japan in addition to the United States and the Soviet Union. A pentagonal balance among these powers would encompass political and economic elements as well as military factors. Describing this emerging global structure of power, Nixon stated:

> as we look ahead 5, 10, and perhaps 15 years, we see five great economic superpowers: the United States, Western Europe, the Soviet Union, mainland China, and, of course, Japan. . . . These are the five that will determine the economic future and, because economic power will be the key to other kinds of power, the future of the world in other ways in the last third of the century.[40]

The administration—particularly Kissinger—was not unmindful that the classical European balance of power system had included five major powers. This arrangement provided the greatest amount of political and military interplay. The Nixon-Kissinger policies encouraged the development of such a balance in the modern world through America's opening to China and more evenhanded relations with its allies. Nixon explained the importance of this goal in a 1972 interview:

> We must remember the only time in the history of the world that we have had any extended period of peace is when there has been a balance of power. It is when one nation becomes infinitely more powerful in relation to its potential competitor that the danger of war arises. So I believe in a world in which the United States is powerful: I think it will be a safer world and a better if we have a strong healthy United States, Europe, Soviet Union, China, Japan, each balancing the other, not playing one against the other, an even balance.[41]

Below the level of the major powers, the administration encouraged regional powers to take responsibility for their security. Within this third tier, nations such as Brazil and Iran were identified as major regional powers. Where conflicting sources of power existed (particularly in the Middle East), the Nixon-Kissinger policies fostered local balances through arms sales. The need to support regional powers and local balances provided the principal justification for the Nixon Doctrine.[42]

This concept of a multitiered global equilibrium was significantly more complex than the traditional conception of the balance of power. But Kissinger did not regard even this simpler European balance as a satisfactory basis for order. The major powers had to establish a political foundation for order built on the acceptance of the international system. Such acceptance or legitimacy was also a major aim of the Nixon-Kissinger policies. As Kissinger indicated in a major speech on détente, this goal was at the heart of U.S.–Soviet relations.

We must strive for an equilibrium of power, but we must move beyond it to promote the habits of mutual restraint, coexistence, and, ultimately, cooperation. We must stabilize a new international order in a vastly dangerous environment, but our ultimate goal must be to transform ideological conflict into constructive participation in building a better world. This is what is meant by the process called "détente."[43]

Nixon and Kissinger regarded U.S.–Soviet relations as central to the stability of the state system. Order in other regions of the world would be a derivative from this relationship. Ensuring workable arrangements between the two major powers provided the key to the legitimacy of the international system.

These political arrangements (i.e., détente) centered on arms control. The SALT negotiations aimed at reducing the strategic military competition between the superpowers. Trade and cultural exchanges provided other important building blocks. Finally, détente was based on the exercise of mutual restraint by both the United States and the Soviets in various areas of the globe. The "Basic Principles of U.S.–Soviet Relations," which were agreed to at the May 1972 Moscow summit, sought to clarify rules of international conduct between the two nations.

The administration intended détente to give the Soviets a stake in preserving the international order. John Stoessinger indicates how central this idea was to Kissinger's design for order:

> For Henry Kissinger, America's relationship with Russia was absolutely basic to any policy that sought stability. Détente would depend, at least to some extent, on the ability of the United States to convert the Soviet Union from a "revolutionary" power with unlimited ambition, to a "legitimate" state with more circumspect objectives. A "legitimate" state, in Kissinger's view, could still remain a dictatorship vis-á-vis its own people. This was not his main concern. What mattered enormously to him was that the *external* goals of Soviet Russia would have to be adjusted to the overall imperatives of a stable world order. If he succeeded in this task, all else, he hoped, would fall into place.[44]

The Nixon-Kissinger approach to world order provoked intense controversy. Some regarded it as an antiquated world view. Scholars such as Richard Falk criticized Kissinger for adhering to the Westphalian system of autonomous states grouped around an inherently unstable balance of power.[45] Falk suggested that contemporary international society was closer to the pre-Westphalian system, which featured transnational forces (such as the Catholic Church) similar to those affecting the modern world.[46] To an extent, this criticism is valid. Kissinger believed that the world would never become so interdependent that economic and social issues would replace political and military ones. As a result, he often overlooked the fact that such interdependencies existed, particularly with respect to trade and monetary questions.

The Trilateralists[47] also presented an alternative approach. They believed that the Nixon-Kissinger emphasis on U.S.–Soviet relations had damaged relations with our European and Japanese allies. The Trilateralists emphasized relations among the industrial democracies as the key to global stability. These relations would also support economic policies designed to integrate the Third World into the international system. It is ironic that U.S.–European ties were strained during the Nixon years, despite the fact that both Nixon and Kissinger considered themselves European specialists. Their policies were relatively devoid of creative departures toward the Third World. Yet Trilateralism—because it did not address U.S.–Soviet relations in a fundamental way—remained primarily an "Atlantic concept" rather than a world vision. In the Carter years, Trilateralism contributed little to global stability.

I believe, however, that a more serious criticism can be made of the Nixon-Kissinger concept of order. Despite speeches to the contrary, Kissinger never fully grasped the extreme heterogeneity of the postwar state system.[48] His concept of legitimacy was derived from the example of nineteenth-century Europe, which for the most part consisted of a community of nations with shared political values. As Edward Vose Gulick points out, a distinguishing feature of the classical European state system was that the European nations exhibited a conscious sense of their political homogeneity.[49] But how could legitimacy be made a central element of order in a world that lacked a sense of community? On what basis would nations accept the international system?

Kissinger wrestled with this question as both a scholar and a statesman, but he never fully resolved it.[50] As a result, he was unable to articulate a legitimizing principle that addressed the concerns of the major powers and that accommodated the new forces emerging in the Third World. Kissinger's concept of order remained hierarchical in an age of growing egalitarianism. He believed that U.S.–Soviet acceptance of the international system by means of détente was sufficient to ensure its legitimacy. Stability between the superpowers would supposedly reverberate throughout the international system—moderating conflicts wherever they occurred.

The nations of the Third World, however, questioned the hierarchical structure of the present system, introducing a new element of instability. Instead of working with the United States to control this instability, the Soviet Union sought to take advantage of it. All of the major Soviet challenges to détente—e.g., the Yom Kippur War of 1973, and the use of

Cuban proxy troops in support of the pro-Soviet faction in Angola in 1975–76—occurred in the Third World. Although Kissinger had to deal with each of these challenges in the Third World, his concept of order only addressed the fundamental sources of instability in these regions relatively late in his tenure. Given his worldview and its emphasis on the great states, it is unlikely that he could have done so sooner. Even his sensitivity to Third World issues came about largely because of the ability of these issues to impact the global power alignment. The OPEC oil embargo illustrates this point. Likewise, the precipitous fall of the remaining Portuguese regimes in Africa, rather than issues of racial justice, was a main factor in Kissinger's celebrated speech in Lusaka, Zambia in April 1976 in which he proclaimed U.S. support for majority rule in Southern Africa.

ACTIVIST STATECRAFT

Nixon and Kissinger gave American foreign policy new goals; they also introduced a new approach to policy formulation, one that depended on their own vision and activism as leaders. As I indicated in chapter 4, Nixon and Kissinger shared the same view of the role of the statesman. Nixon's description of the statesman as the "man in the arena,"[51] i.e., the man at the center of events, typifies their neoromantic conception of leadership. In no other area did Nixon and Kissinger's actions so closely conform to their thought.

Both Nixon and Kissinger regarded the bureaucracy with contempt. It was unimaginative; it could at best perform routine functions. Policy creation depended on the leader's vision—particularly his conception of the state system and the elements of order. These views made it inevitable that Nixon and Kissinger would control foreign policy formulation in the White House.

The National Security Council (NSC) system that Kissinger set up provided the mechanism for control. The NSC system imposed a hierarchical structure on the agencies involved in foreign affairs. In the past, the president had acted as an honest broker, resolving conflicts among the various departments. American foreign policy often represented as much a bureaucratic compromise as a response to external problems. Now, however, policy would emanate from the president and his staff, and it would be based on a consideration of genuine alternatives.

Kissinger's NSC system used the bureaucracy to gather information. Policy papers known as National Security Study Memoranda (NSSMs) were prepared in the individual agencies. The NSSMs were refined by the NSC in order to pose issues and present policy choices to Nixon.

Some 138 NSSMs relating to key aspects of American foreign policy were prepared in the first three years of the Nixon administration. They provided the basis for major policy innovations.[52]

Kissinger's NSC system gave American policy formulation a new coherence. In the past, the autonomy of individual agencies had resulted in the fragmentation of policymaking into discrete areas such as trade and arms control. Now there was a more effective means for weaving the different threads of policy into a whole cloth.

Yet the real significance of this system was that it became the vehicle that Nixon and Kissinger used to elaborate their own views of world politics. Although the NSC system sharpened the focus of policy debates, the alternatives that Nixon and Kissinger chose were those consistent with their own outlook. As Roger Morris points out, Kissinger reversed the traditional process of policy formulation—now the president provided the departments with an ostensible hearing just as they had once ostensibly deferred to the White House.[53] Morris notes further that, in the end, the NSC system mattered "much less for its abstract merits in decisionmaking" than as a technique for concentrating power in the hands of two men.[54] Nixon and Kissinger's foreign policy was derived from their own vision of global order rather than from an inductive process.

In the field of diplomacy, Nixon and Kissinger frequently employed the so-called "back channel." U.S.–Soviet relations, SALT, and the Vietnam peace talks all involved secret discussions that paralleled those being conducted in official channels. Using this approach gave them greater flexibility. They were able to resolve issues privately and to make these agreements the basis for dramatic breakthroughs in the public discussions. Nixon and Kissinger also used the element of drama and surprise to develop support for their policies. The opening to China provides an example of this element of their statecraft.

No American president has devoted more effort to foreign policy in a period of relative peace than Richard Nixon. Yet the Nixon-Kissinger style of statecraft raised deep concerns in the Congress and in the nation. The centralization of power in the White House, the secret talks, and the dramatic reversal of policies seemed to place foreign policy beyond the control necessary to a democratic state. How could the American people—through their legislators—judge the wisdom of a foreign policy if they possessed little insight into its formulation? George Ball voiced this criticism of the Nixon-Kissinger policies, and, specifically, of Kissinger in his role as "Master Player":

But if a policy of maneuver is the only game for the Master Player, is it an appropriate policy for a democracy fully in charge of itself? Just as a

policy of alliances cannot be administered without diffusion of information and a delegation of authority, so a policy of maneuver cannot
be institutionalized. Its administration cannot be delegated. Secrecy is
essential. The Master Player must not only keep foreign nations in the
dark, awaiting surprising moves, but he must also conceal his tactics
from the State Department bureaucracy, the American Congress, and,
of course, the American people. A democratic system will tolerate
such practices for only a limited period of time. To secure the consent
of the governed, major shifts and alterations of policy must be dis-
closed and their rationale publicly explained.[55]

Both Nixon and Kissinger objected to the excesses of majoritarian
democracy. The detailed examination of public officials by congressional
committees and the press made other governments concerned that sensitive talks—which often involved compromises that would affect them
domestically—would be revealed in the worst possible light. Creative
policies depended on proper timing, timing that did not always allow for
public debate. As Kissinger points out, opportunities cannot be
hoarded; once past, they are irretrievable. Finally, innovative policies, by
their very nature, tend to arouse partisan political debate that can destroy the basis for innovation. Could the U.S. have achieved its opening
to China if Congress had debated our China policy as a precondition for
Washington-Peking talks?

To be sure, there is a deep antipopulist strain in Kissinger's thought.
His European intellectual influences portray genuine leadership as the
reserve of a select few. Nixon's ideas on leadership, however, resemble
those of Edmund Burke. The elected leader was more than a representative—he owed his constituents his judgment as well as his vote. Leadership, for both Nixon and Kissinger, was synonymous with acting
alone—particularly in foreign affairs. It was unthinkable that the great
leader would build policies by searching for a democratic consensus. His
role was to create such a consensus on the basis of his policies. As
Kissinger writes, this role entailed bridging the gap between the people's experience and the leader's vision, between the nation's foreign
policy tradition and its future role in world affairs.

How did Nixon and Kissinger reconcile these views with the need for
informed public debate? They emphasized the educative role of leadership—a role that Kissinger regards as one of the leader's major functions. Although policy was made less openly during the Nixon-Kissinger
years than before, the rationales for policies received greater articulation
than in any other presidency. The "State of the World" messages that
Nixon sent to the Congress each year of his first term discussed the
major foreign policy themes of the Nixon presidency. Similarly,
Kissinger's briefings as NSC adviser, as well as his later press con-

ferences and congressional testimony as secretary of state, cannot be viewed as mere political justifications for policies. Instead, Kissinger attempted to explain the underlying philosophy that had led to a particular policy choice.

In *A World Restored*, Kissinger makes the leader's ability to obtain domestic support for his policies the ultimate test of leadership. Castlereagh—whom Kissinger praises for departing from England's insular approach—ultimately failed to obtain this support. He failed because his policies outran the experience of the British people. In this vein, how are we to regard Kissinger's leadership? What permanent value will his ideas and his policies have for American foreign policy?

The Kissinger Legacy

It is understandable that many regard Henry Kissinger's impact on American foreign policy as short-lived. Détente is scarcely mentioned today. All of its major elements—SALT, trade, and principles of mutual restraint between the United States and the Soviets—have either frayed or unraveled completely. The United States has maintained relations with China, but has allowed Kissinger's triangular Moscow-Peking-Washington arrangement of power to erode. His efforts to bring about an Egyptian-Israeli disengagement in the Middle East failed to provide a basis for a comprehensive peace in that region.

Critics have attacked Kissinger's approach for its lack of moral purpose. Some argue that the evenhandedness of the Nixon-Kissinger policies with respect to our adversaries and allies served to demoralize America in the face of the Soviet challenge as well as to weaken our alliances. In different ways, both the Carter and Reagan presidencies have characterized U.S.–Soviet relations in the more familiar terms of a moral contest. Over the last ten years, we find few references to a pentagonal world order in which Europe and Japan play major roles in maintaining the global balance of power. The Nixon-Kissinger policies have also been criticized for neglecting problems involving the international economy and the Third World—problems that many believe present challenges to global order as fundamental as that entailed in the U.S.–Soviet rivalry.

America also seems to have rejected Kissinger's style, his public persona. As a nation, we never became comfortable with his neoromantic pronouncements. His tragic vision was sharply at odds with our native optimism and lightheartedness. Critics faulted Kissinger's direction of American statecraft for creating a reliance on one man, and for emphasizing form over substance.[56] Both of the administrations that followed have taken a more collegial approach to foreign policy leadership.

Yet it would be wrong to dismiss Kissinger's significance on this basis. The grand design was only partly in place when Watergate over-shadowed Nixon's second term. It is not unthinkable that, given a strong president no longer constrained by the war in Vietnam, the main elements of détente could have been developed fully. In addition, a large part of the reaction to the Nixon-Kissinger approach was aimed not at the specifics of the policies themselves, but at their departure from the American tradition. The Nixon-Kissinger approach represented a transition in America's role in global politics that many viewed with great ambivalence.

Therein, however, lies Kissinger's significance. I believe that he will come to be regarded as a transitional figure—a figure bridging two eras in American foreign policy. In the first of these eras—the period after World War II—America possessed strategic military supremacy and economic hegemony. It was an era in which the world reckoned with America's vast power. The second era, which began in the mid-1960s, centered on the Vietnam War, although factors such as the relative economic decline of the United States and the growth of Soviet strategic power also played an important part. The second era was an era in which America reckoned with its own limits.

To a large extent, the adjustment of American foreign policy to the changed physical circumstances that distinguish these two eras has already taken place. The United States is no longer the sole engine of the world economy. The early 1970s marked the end of the postwar Bretton Woods system, which had been built on American economic liberalism and the hegemonic role of the dollar. This period also witnessed a realignment of America's conventional military power. With the Vietnam War, we relinquished the role of "world policeman" we had assumed throughout the cold war period. American influence in the developing nations also declined significantly. The Soviet Union, which had been in a position of strategic inferiority with respect to the United States as late as the 1962 Cuban missile crisis, now possessed military power equal to our own.

These changes are reflected in the quantitative comparisons that Americans make between their own nation and others. Although we do not yet regard ourselves as the "ordinary" country that Richard Rose-crance claims we have become,[57] we are clearly aware that our status and influence have been reduced. The idea of a Pax Americana, which many authors referred to in the early postwar years, had a short life.

Yet if Americans have accepted these changes, it is less clear that we have absorbed their significance in terms of our outlook on foreign policy. A corresponding change in our attitudes and approach to the world has yet to occur fully, although I believe that such a change represents the direction in which American foreign policy should move. I believe that it is in this area that Kissinger's legacy will ultimately be established.

To achieve this change of approach, America must recognize its limits—a theme that Kissinger repeated in many of his major addresses. Several authors have pointed out that the doctrine of limits is the starting point of Kissinger's political philosophy.[58] What does Kissinger mean by a recognition of limits?

On one level, Kissinger's emphasis on limits refers to the physical restraints on America's freedom of action and the implications that these restraints have for foreign policy. We can no longer overwhelm problems with resources. Instead we must practice diplomacy with creativity and skill. Kissinger sees Vietnam as a turning point in this regard.

> It was . . . a rude awakening when in the 1960s and 1970s the United States became conscious of the limits of even *its* resources. . . . Vietnam was the trauma and the catharsis, but the recognition was bound to come in any event. Starting in the 1970s, for the first time, the United States has had to conduct a foreign policy in the sense with which Europeans have always been familiar: as one country among many, unable either to dominate the world or escape from it, with the necessity of accommodation, maneuver, a sensitivity to marginal shifts in the balance of power, an awareness of continuity and of the interconnections between events.[59]

Yet Kissinger's emphasis on limits has a deeper meaning. From the time of his undergraduate thesis, Kissinger has linked the concept of limits to maturity and spiritual growth. The acceptance of limits is synonymous with self-awareness. Kissinger expresses this connection in "The Meaning of History":

> Yet out of this seeming inevitability, there appears to emerge a feeling of humility, a recognition by man of his limits. "Know thyself"—was the motto of the oracle of Delphi. This was not meant psychoanalytically but implied: "Know that you are a man and not God." From the acceptance of limits derives the feeling of reverence which sees history not merely as an ordeal, or mankind as a tool but a deep fulfillment.[60]

Thus, Kissinger's emphasis on limits is an emphasis on self-awareness. Out of the tragedy of Vietnam and other changes of the present era, the nation could achieve a new level of maturity.

In psychological literature, maturity is associated with an understanding of the self, i.e., an understanding that one has developed into a unique person and that there are limits inherent in the human condition. From such self-awareness develops an acceptance of others. Kissinger discusses the connection between limits and the national character in similar terms. Maturity is acceptance of the fact that, while our nation is unique and our power great, both are finite. Like other nations, America can decline; like other nations, America is not free from tragedy. Kissinger believes that the acceptance of finitude and tragedy would deepen our national character. The acceptance of our limits also implies an acceptance of other nations—even those whose domestic values and culture differ markedly from our own.

Kissinger considers the recognition of limits not only as a sign of maturity, but as one of the principal lessons that history offers. As Toynbee suggested, civilizations begin to break down when they lose a sense of their own limits.

In the postwar period, America's overwhelming power allowed it to retain the elements of its insular approach to foreign policy. A sense of omnipotence; the belief that problems could be deferred until they became clear-cut; the emphasis on the morally desirable over the politically possible; the quest for final solutions—all continued to shape our response to world events.

Now, however, our foreign policy should reflect our acceptance of limits. Kissinger, however, does not equate our recognition of limits with a reduced role in world affairs. Rather, this recognition means that although our physical role might be reduced, our political role would become more prominent. This new role actually represents an even greater involvement in world affairs.

Kissinger describes several elements of this new role. Activist statecraft, creativity, and the continuity of our policies figure prominently. America can no longer offer remedies for world problems, but instead must create the conditions in which solutions can be found.

> The United States is no longer in a position to operate programs globally; it has to encourage them. It can no longer impose its preferred solution; it must seek to evoke it. In the forties and fifties, we offered remedies; in the late sixties and in the seventies our role will have to be to contribute to a structure that will foster the initiative of others.[61]

The interconnection of events and the limits placed on our actions would also have to play a part in our policies. Diplomacy cannot be episodic—our involvement in foreign affairs is permanent. These ideas are longstanding themes in Kissinger's writings; he makes them the test of future administrations as well as the one in which he served.

Yet no element of the nation's new role is more important than America's responsibility for world order. Therein lies the major test of our recognition of limits. Kissinger regards our acceptance of this responsibility as the central theme of détente.

Before examining the importance of Kissinger's approach to world order, we should first consider two alternative views—views that preceded and followed his tenure as the steward of American statecraft. The postwar period of containment was also said to have its basis in world order. Order, however, was identified with military resistance to communist expansion. Unless the Soviet system changed, diplomatic contact was pointless. Diplomatic agreements with the communist bloc represented a moral compromise, for such agreements would be tantamount to recognizing the legitimacy of these tyrannical societies.

As we have seen, Nixon and Kissinger rejected this approach to world order, even though U.S.–Soviet relations remained the key to global stability. In the years immediately following the Nixon administration, however, a significant revision occurred in the intellectual premises of American foreign policy—a revision that occurred partially in response to the Nixon-Kissinger policies. The theorists of interdependence[62] argued that henceforth the major problems of international stability would involve economic and technical concerns. The East-West orientation of our policies no longer addressed the major issues of world order.

I have identified these alternative approaches to world order, because they can help us to assess Kissinger's future significance. The events of the last ten years have already validated Kissinger's rejection of the claims made by the theorists of interdependence. The erosion of U.S.–Soviet relations during the Reagan presidency and the resulting threat to world stability have made it clear that relations with Moscow will continue to provide the central focus for our policies in the decades ahead.

In retrospect, I believe that the moderation of U.S.–Soviet relations achieved by détente allowed many prominent Americans—particularly those directing foreign policy during the Carter administration—to assume that these relations had moved into the background. Although it is true that global stability involves other factors besides U.S.–Soviet relations, it is equally true, as Kissinger states, that "there can be no peaceful international order without a constructive relationship between the United States and the Soviet Union."[63]

However salient economic and technical issues have become in the day-to-day workings of foreign policy, it is doubtful that they will ever overshadow the importance of political and military matters. The Soviet invasion of Afghanistan, the Iranian crisis, and the erosion of the strategic balance of power during the Carter presidency were the foreign policy issues that dominated the 1980 election. The Reagan administration has made the reassertion of America's strategic power vis-à-vis the Soviets the centerpiece of its foreign policy.

The primary importance of U.S.–Soviet relations forces us to confront the nature of these relations. Throughout the period of containment, Kissinger continually stressed that negotiations, particularly on arms control, were essential. It was unrealistic to await a change in Soviet society before these negotiations could take place. Because our societies are fundamentally different, we need rules of international behavior to govern our respective actions. Détente attempted to establish these rules.

Behind the opposition to détente—particularly the charge that the Soviets benefited from it more than the West—lies the belief that the nature of Soviet society prevents genuine political cooperation. The isolation of dissidents and the repression of political liberties in Eastern Europe create in Americans a deep moral antagonism to the Soviet system.

Yet can we continue to make these concerns the basis for our policies toward the Soviet Union? How do we weigh the requirements for international order against our moral antagonism to the Soviet system? What limits do we face in confronting these questions?

These are the concerns that Kissinger raised when he responded to the critics of détente:

> What is the alternative they propose? What precise policies do they want us to change? Are they prepared for a prolonged situation of dramatically increased international danger? Do they wish to return to the constant crises and arms budgets of the Cold War? Does detente encourage repression—or is it detente that has generated the ferment and the demands for openness that we are now witnessing? Can we ask our people to support confrontation unless they know that every reasonable alternative has been explored?[64]

I believe that Kissinger defined the essential elements of U.S.–Soviet relations—and thus of world order—so clearly that the questions he posed will be central to American policy in the years ahead. I offer this observation despite the rejection of Kissinger's policies by the last two administrations. And because these questions will remain central to American policy, I believe that we must reexamine the approach to world affairs taken during the Nixon-Kissinger years. The direction in which the policies of this period point appears to me the only promising direction for the future—the only direction that accommodates both our role as a great power and the recognition of our limits.

Finally, I believe that a reconsideration of Kissinger's contribution as a statesman would be incomplete unless we begin with his writings as a scholar. I have tried to show that, for almost every role that he played as a statesman, Kissinger had developed strong ideas before stepping onto the world stage. His historical philosophy and world view were, by his own admission, the intellectual capital on which he drew during his years in office. Kissinger's legacy to American foreign policy will be that of a transitional figure bridging two eras. Yet a careful study of his earlier writings—particularly his critique of American insularity—shows that Kissinger urged such a transition long before events made it inevitable.

Thus, Kissinger's principal contribution is one of thought, not action. He once observed that the irony of America's rivalry with de Gaulle was that the French leader had conceptions greater than his power and we power greater than our conceptions.[65] Kissinger offers Americans a philosophy of world politics and an approach to foreign policy designed to give us conceptions worthy of our power.

Notes

Introduction

1. Stephen R. Graubard, *Kissinger: Portrait of a Mind* (New York: W. W. Norton, 1973), p. xvi.

2. For examples, see Seyom Brown, *The Crisis of Power: Foreign Policy in the Kissinger Years* (New York: Columbia University Press, 1979), pp. 1–18; Peter W. Dickson, *Kissinger and the Meaning of History* (Cambridge: Cambridge University Press, 1978), p. 17; and Stanley Hoffmann, *Primacy or World Order: American Foreign Policy since the Cold War* (New York: McGraw-Hill, 1978), p. 38.

3. The "State of the World" messages are actually a series of foreign policy reports that President Nixon sent to the Congress. They are unusual for their concern to elaborate fully the conceptual framework of the Nixon administration's approach to foreign policy. They show the heavy influence of Kissinger's thinking. These texts passed through numerous drafts under Kissinger's supervision. Titles in this series include: *U.S. Foreign Policy for the 1970's: A New Strategy for Peace* (Washington, D.C.: U.S. Government Printing Office, 1970); *U.S. Foreign Policy for the 1970's: Building for Peace* (Washington, D.C.: U.S. Government Printing Office, 1971); *U.S. Foreign Policy for the 1970's: The Emerging Structure of Peace* (Washington, D.C.: U.S. Government Printing Office, 1972); and *U.S. Foreign Policy for the 1970's: Shaping a Durable Peace* (Washington, D.C.: U.S. Government Printing Office, 1973).

4. Robert E. Osgood, et al., *Retreat from Empire: The First Nixon Administration* (Baltimore: The Johns Hopkins University Press, 1973), p. 2.

5. Even at this date, the Dickson text is the sole work that thoroughly treats Kissinger's earliest historical and philosophical studies.

6. See John Stoessinger, *Henry Kissinger: The Anguish of Power* (New York: W. W. Norton, 1976).

7. See Thomas J. Noer, "Henry Kissinger's Philosophy of History," *Modern Age* 19 (Spring 1975): 180–89; and William T. Weber, "Kissinger as Historian: A Historiographical Approach to Statesmanship," *International Affairs* 141, no. 1 (Summer 1978): 40–56.

8. Graubard, *Kissinger: Portrait of a Mind*, p. xii.

9. See Bruce Mazlish, *Kissinger: The European Mind in American Policy* (New York: Basic Books, 1976).

10. The "operational code" analysis is linked primarily with Alexander L. George. See Alexander L. George, "The Operational Code: A Neglected Approach to the Study of Political Leaders and Decision-Making," *International Studies Quarterly* 13 (June 1969): 190–222. See also, O. R. Holsti, "The Operational Code Approach to the Study of Political Leaders: John Foster Dulles' Philosophical and Instrumental Beliefs," *Canadian Journal of Political Science* 3 (March 1970): 123–57; and D. McLellan, "The Operational Code Approach to the Study of

Political Leaders: Dean Acheson's Philosophical and Instrumental Beliefs," *Canadian Journal of Political Science* 4 (March 1971): 52–75.

11. Hoffmann, *Primacy or World Order*, p. 3.

Chapter 1.   The Historicism of Henry Kissinger

1. Peter Dickson, *Kissinger and the Meaning of History* (Cambridge: Cambridge University Press, 1978), p. 22. Dickson discusses this relationship as well as other aspects of Kissinger's historical and philosophical beliefs. Alone among scholars who have written about Kissinger, Dickson provides a learned treatment of Kissinger's undergraduate thesis on Spengler, Toynbee, and Kant. Although I disagree with Dickson's central point that Kant is the most prominent influence on Kissinger's thought almost to the exclusion of Spengler, Toynbee, and others, I make repeated reference to his book because of its importance and its scholarly contribution.

2. Henry Kissinger, "The Footsteps of History," Remarks made at the 1980 Davos Symposium of the European Management Forum, 31 January 1980, in *For the Record: Selected Statements 1977–1980* (Boston: Little, Brown, 1981), p. 261.

3. See "Partial Transcript of an Interview with Kissinger on the State of the Western World," *The New York Times*, 13 October 1974. Kissinger makes this point to James Reston in an interview that provides some of the most revealing insights regarding the historical and philosophical principles that support his statecraft.

4. Henry Kissinger, *White House Years* (Boston: Little, Brown, 1979), p. 54.

5. Henry Kissinger, *A World Restored: Metternich, Castlereagh and the Problems of Peace, 1812–1822* (Boston: Houghton Mifflin, 1957), p. 331.

6. The Dickson text has been mentioned previously. See also Thomas J. Noer, "Henry Kissinger's Philosophy of History," *Modern Age* 19 (Spring 1975): 180–89; John G. Stoessinger, *Henry Kissinger: The Anguish of Power* (New York: W. W. Norton, 1976); and William T. Weber, "Kissinger as Historian: A Historiographical Approach to Statesmanship," *International Affairs* 141, no. 1 (Summer 1978): 40–56.

7. See Harvey Starr, *Henry Kissinger: Perceptions of International Politics* (Lexington, Kentucky: University of Kentucky Press, 1984), pp. 44–75; and Stephen G. Walker, "The Interface Between Beliefs and Behavior: Henry Kissinger's Operational Code and the Vietnam War," *Journal of Conflict Resolution* 21 (March 1979): 129–68.

8. See Albert F. Eldrige, "Pondering Intangibles: A Value Analysis of Henry Kissinger," in *Henry Kissinger: His Personality and Policy*, ed. Dan Caldwell (Durham, North Carolina: Duke University Press, 1983), pp. 64–86.

9. Bruce Mazlish, *Kissinger: The European Mind in American Policy* (New York: Basic Books, 1976).

10. Stanley Hoffmann, *Primacy or World Order: American Foreign Policy Since the Cold War* (New York: McGraw-Hill, 1978), p. 37.

11. Ibid.

12. Noer, "Kissinger's Philosophy of History," p. 181.

13. William T. Weber makes the point that Kissinger should be understood as a historian rather than as a diplomat in "Kissinger as Historian."

14. Marvin and Bernard Kalb, *Kissinger* (New York: Dell Books, 1975), p. 56.

15. Dickson, *Kissinger and the Meaning of History*, pp. 42–43.

16. Kalb, *Kissinger,* p. 57.

17. Kissinger, *A World Restored,* p. v, Acknowledgments.

18. Kalb, *Kissinger,* p. 57.

19. Dickson, *Kissinger and the Meaning of History,* p. 43.

20. Ibid., p. 42.

21. Mazlish, *Kissinger: The European Mind,* p. 64.

22. Stephen R. Graubard, *Kissinger: Portrait of a Mind* (New York: W. W. Norton, 1973), pp. 6 and 16.

23. See Dickson, *Kissinger and the Meaning of History,* p. 28; Mazlish, *Kissinger: The European Mind,* pp. 171–86; and Stoessinger, *Kissinger: The Anguish of Power,* pp. 8–9.

24. See Michael Reskin, "An American Metternich: Henry A. Kissinger and the Global Balance of Power," in *Makers of American Diplomacy,* ed. Frank J. Merli and Theodore A. Wilson (New York: Charles Scribner's Sons, 1974), pp. 373–96; and James Chace, "Bismarck and Kissinger," *Encounter* 42 (June 1974): 44–47.

25. See particularly Graubard, *Portrait of a Mind,* p. 14.

26. Henry A. Kissinger, "The Meaning of History: Reflections on Spengler, Toynbee and Kant," unpublished undergraduate honors thesis (Harvard University, 1950), p. i.

27. Ibid., p. 1.

28. Ibid.

29. Ibid., pp. 5–6.

30. Ibid., p. 22.

31. Ibid., pp. 9–10.

32. Ibid., p. 4.

33. Ibid., p. 10.

34. Toynbee's philosophy of history actually combines both a linear and a circular view of history. Unlike Spengler, Toynbee postulates a teleology in history in the form of divine purpose.

35. Kissinger, "The Meaning of History," p. 64.

36. Oswald Spengler, *The Decline of the West,* abridged edition, ed. Helmut Werner and Arthur Helps (New York: Alfred A. Knopf, 1962), p. 20. Spengler characterizes this feel for history's becoming as a Copernican revolution of historical thought. This aspect of his thought as well as the influence of Goethe are discussed in a passage entitled "The Historical Eye."

37. Kissinger, "The Meaning of History," p. 115.

38. Arnold Toynbee, *A Study of History,* 2 vol. abridgment by D. C. Somervell (New York: Dell Books, 1965). In chapter 4, Toynbee discusses the various causes of the breakdown of civilizations and the processes involved in the loss of vitality and self-determination.

39. Kissinger, "The Meaning of History," p. 244.

40. Dickson, *Kissinger and the Meaning of History,* p. 6.

41. In his *Idea for a Universal History from a Cosmopolitan Point of View,* Kant refers to the mechanism by which history accomplishes this objective as the "unsocial sociability." Through competitiveness in artistic, economic, and political endeavors, men enrich a nation's culture and elevate its social life. Hence, unsociability leads obliquely to greater sociability. Similarly, the competition of nations leads to greater international cooperation. The moral norm of the categorical imperative—to treat other persons as ends in themselves—is fostered by the cooperative institutions that the "unsocial sociability" produces.

42. Kissinger, "The Meaning of History," pp. 321–22.

43. Georg G. Iggers, *The German Conception of History: The National Tradition of Historical Thought from Herder to the Present*, rev. ed. (Middletown, Connecticut: Wesleyan University Press, 1983), pp. 32–33.

44. Friedrich Engel-Janosi, *The Growth of German Historicism* (Baltimore: The Johns Hopkins University Press, 1944), p. 12.

45. Iggers, *The German Conception of History*, p. 5.

46. Ibid., p. 6.

47. Kissinger, *A World Restored*, p. 331.

48. Henry Kissinger, "The Lessons of the Past: A Conversation with Walter Laqueur," in *For the Record*, p. 124.

49. Kissinger, "The Meaning of History," p. 323.

50. Ibid., p. 325.

51. The concept of understanding history from the "inside," which is central to Collingwood's historical idealism, is discussed in R. G. Collingwood, *The Idea of History* (New York: Oxford University Press, 1956).

52. Kissinger, "The Meaning of History," p. 326.

53. In the final chapter of "The Meaning of History," Kissinger devotes considerable attention to the reconciliation that occurs between freedom and necessity, particularly as it is exhibited in poetry.

54. Mazlish, *Kissinger: The European Mind*, p. 64.

55. Kissinger, "The Meaning of History," p. 330.

56. Ibid., p. 12.

57. Ibid., pp. 331–32.

58. Ibid., p. 333.

59. Reston, "Partial Transcript of an Interview," p. 34.

60. Kissinger, "Constancy and Change in American Foreign Policy," a speech before the Atlanta Chamber of Commerce, 23 June 1975, Department of State Press Release No. 342 (23 June 1975), p. 2.

61. Spengler, *Decline of the West*, p. 20.

62. Kissinger, "The Meaning of History," p. 24.

63. Kissinger, *A World Restored*, pp. 324–25.

64. Dickson, *Kissinger and the Meaning of History*, pp. 18–19.

65. Ibid., p. 20.

66. I consciously use this term to link Kissinger's own views of history to the nineteenth-century German historian Leopold von Ranke. This link emerges in greater detail in chapter 2. An excellent treatment of Ranke's historicism is provided in chapter 4 of Iggers, *The German Conception of History*. See also Theodore Von Laue, *Leopold Ranke: The Formative Years* (Princeton: Princeton University Press, 1950).

67. See Iggers, *The German Conception of History*, pp. 81–82.

68. See F. W. Coker, *Organismic Theories of the State* (New York: Longmans, Green and Co., 1910); and L. T. Hobhouse, *The Metaphysical Theory of the State*, 6th ed. (London: Georg Allen and Unwin, 1960).

69. Iggers, *The German Conception of History*, p. 82.

70. Ibid., pp. 81–82.

71. Kissinger, *A World Restored*, p. 331.

72. Ibid., p. 19.

73. Noer, "Kissinger's Philosophy of History," p. 185.

74. Kissinger, *A World Restored*, p. 331.

75. Noer, "Kissinger's Philosophy of History," p. 182.

76. Toynbee, *A Study of History*, p. 253.

77. Spengler, *Decline of the West*, p. 384.

78. Kissinger, *A World Restored*, p. 317.

79. Henry Kissinger, "Domestic Structure and Foreign Policy," in *American Foreign Policy*, 3d ed. (New York: W. W. Norton, 1977), p. 45.

80. Kissinger, *A World Restored*, p. 322.

81. Hoffmann, *Primacy or World Order*, p. 41.

Chapter 2.   The Outlook of the Continental Statesman

1. Eytan Gilboa, "Intellectuals in the White House and American Foreign Policy," *The Yale Review* 65, no. 4 (June 1976): 481–97. Gilboa characterizes men as "action-intellectuals" based on "their willingness to take an active part in politics and policymaking rather than merely talking about the actions of others."

2. Traditionally, England had conceptualized its role as the "holder of the balance." Edward Vose Gulick in *Europe's Classical Balance of Power* (New York: W. W. Norton, 1955), pp. 65–66, observes that "the phrase is used to describe the role of a third party interested in preserving a simple balance between two other powers." England's island location made it ideally suited for this role. Similarly, its aloofness and flexibility were enhanced by its naval power, which made it "a kind of immediate neighbor to all" other European powers. Often overlooked is that while England's island geography made it suited for the role of "balancer," the role itself mandated that it remain an insular nation—both politically and philosophically. For to the extent that England became enmeshed in continental affairs, it no longer would hold the balance as such, but instead would be a part of it.

3. Quoted in Stephen R. Graubard, *Kissinger: Portrait of a Mind* (New York: W. W. Norton, 1973), p. 10.

4. Henry Kissinger, "The Lessons of the Past: A Conversation with Walter Laqueur," in *For The Record: Selected Statements 1977–1980* (Boston: Little, Brown, 1981), p. 118.

5. Stanley Hoffmann, *Primacy or World Order: American Foreign Policy Since the Cold War* (New York: McGraw-Hill, 1978), p. 35.

6. Henry Kissinger, "Reflections on a Partnership: British and American Attitudes to Postwar Foreign Policy," in *Observations: Selected Speeches and Essays, 1982–1984* (Boston: Little, Brown, 1985), p. 7.

7. Henry Kissinger, *A World Restored: Metternich, Castlereagh and the Problems of Peace, 1812–1822* (Boston: Houghton Mifflin, 1957), p. 163. Kissinger states that it is precisely because an insular nation's policies are not "precautionary" but defensive that it "will make the cause of war depend on an overt act that 'demonstrates' the danger. But the danger to the equilibrium is never demonstrated until it is already overturned. . . ."

8. Ibid., pp. 5–6.

9. Other authors who refer to the insular-continental typology include Ludwig Dehio, *The Precarious Balance: Four Centuries of the European Power Struggle* (New York: Vintage Books, 1965) and Arnold Wolfers and Laurence W. Martin, eds., *The Anglo-American Tradition in Foreign Affairs* (New Haven: Yale University Press, 1956).

10. It is clear from Kissinger's writings that in using the terms insular and continental he means something more fundamental than a nation's foreign policy approach. Stephen Graubard observes that "Kissinger saw two distinct

mentalities; each perceived foreign policy in a different way" (*Portrait of a Mind*, p. 19). Graubard links Kissinger's view of a nation's mentality to its domestic social structure and internal politics. Based on his undergraduate thesis, Kissinger was familiar with several authors who believed that a nation or civilization is definable by a distinct character. The sources of a nation's character include its history, its geography, and the challenges it confronts. Its character can be discerned in its social institutions. The national character can also be found in the nation's dominant intellectual traditions, e.g., American pragmatism, French Cartesianism, English empiricism, German idealism, and so forth. I believe that Kissinger refers to a nation's mentality in the most comprehensive sense, i.e., as a spirit that pervades both the outward life of the society as well as its intangible traditions.

11. See James E. Dougherty and Robert L. Pfaltzgraff, Jr., *Contending Theories of International Relations* (Philadelphia: J. B. Lippincott, 1971).

12. See Zbigniew Brzezinski, "U.S. Foreign Policy: The Search for Focus," *Foreign Affairs* 51, no. 4 (July 1973): 708–27, and Seyom Brown, *The Crises of Power: An Interpretation of United States Foreign Policy in the Kissinger Years* (New York: Columbia University Press, 1979).

13. I am mindful that foreign policy realism is not an American phenomenon. Furthermore, many American realists themselves emigrated from Europe. Morgenthau is a prime example. I use the term American realists primarily to describe the tradition of realism or *realpolitik* as it was absorbed into American academic and political circles. For many, realism represented a much-needed palliative to American idealism, which traditionally emphasized legal and moral approaches to international politics. It is against this background that I contrast Kissinger's views.

14. Henry Kissinger, *The Necessity for Choice: Prospects of American Foreign Policy* (New York: Harper and Row, 1961), p. 357.

15. Henry Kissinger, "Strains on the Alliance," *Foreign Affairs* 41, no. 2 (January 1962): 285.

16. Ibid.

17. Henry Kissinger, *The Troubled Partnership: A Re-appraisal of the Atlantic Alliance* (New York: McGraw-Hill, 1965), p. 251.

18. Stanley Hoffmann, *The State of War: Essays on the Theory and Practice of International Politics* (New York: Praeger, 1965), p. 14.

19. Hedley Bull, *The Anarchical Society: A Study of Order in World Politics* (New York: Columbia University Press, 1977), p. 48.

20. Brown, *The Crises of Power*, p. 2.

21. Hans J. Morgenthau, *Scientific Man Versus Power Politics*, 6th ed. (Chicago: University of Chicago Press, 1967), p. 71.

22. Quoted in Georg G. Iggers, *The German Conception of History: The National Tradition of Historical Thought from Herder to the Present*, rev. ed. (Middletown, Connecticut: Wesleyan University Press, 1983), p. 81.

23. Ibid., p. 39. In this regard, German historicist thinkers contrasted their own political theory with English utilitarianism, which they believed represented a superficial view of man and the purpose of human society.

24. Henry Kissinger, "The Next Summit Meeting," *Harper's Magazine*, December 1960.

25. Kissinger, *A World Restored*, p. 2. Kissinger actually states that limited wars "will be fought in the name of the existing structure and the peace which follows will be justified as a better expression of the . . . general consensus."

26. Kenneth Waltz, *Man, the State and War: A Theoretical Analysis* (New York: Columbia University Press, 1954), pp. 16–41.

27. Ibid., pp. 80–123.

28. Kissinger, *A World Restored*, p. 144.

29. Ibid.

30. Ibid.

31. Ibid., pp. 328–29.

32. Ibid., pp. 1–2.

33. Lee Cameron MacDonald, *Western Political Theory, Part 2: From Machiavelli to Burke* (New York: Harcourt, Brace, Jovanovich, 1968), p. 297. This point is supported by Hajo Halborn, *Germany and Europe* (Garden City, New York: Doubleday, 1979); and Friedrich Meinecke, *Cosmopolitanism and the Nation State* (Princeton: Princeton University Press, 1970) (first published in 1908).

34. Kissinger, *A World Restored*, p. 329.

35. Henry Kissinger, "Domestic Structure and Foreign Policy," in *American Foreign Policy*, 3rd ed. (New York: W. W. Norton, 1977), p. 12.

36. Peter Dickson, *Kissinger and the Meaning of History* (Cambridge: Cambridge University Press, 1978), p. 19.

37. Ibid., p. 20.

38. Arnold Wolfers, "The Statesman and Moral Choice," in *Discord and Collaboration: Essays on International Politics* (Baltimore: The Johns Hopkins University Press, 1962), p. 49.

39. Dickson, *Kissinger and the Meaning of History*, p. 12.

40. Wolfers, "The Statesman and Moral Choice," p. 51.

41. Henry Kissinger, "The Process of Détente," in *American Foreign Policy*, p. 145.

42. Henry Kissinger, *Nuclear Weapons and Foreign Policy* (New York: Harper and Row, 1957), p. 264.

43. Henry Kissinger, "Central Issues of American Foreign Policy," in *American Foreign Policy*, p. 57.

44. John G. Stoessinger, *Henry Kissinger: The Anguish of Power* (New York: W. W. Norton, 1976), p. 14.

45. Kissinger, *A World Restored*, p. 326.

46. Ibid.

47. Ibid., p. 2.

48. Ibid.

49. Ibid., p. 1.

50. Ibid., pp. 317–18.

51. Henry Kissinger, "Force and Diplomacy in the Nuclear Age," *Foreign Affairs* 34 (April 1956): 351.

52. Kissinger, *A World Restored*, p. 318.

53. See Vose Gulick, *Europe's Classical Balance of Power*. Note also the parallel to the Nixon-Kissinger foreign policy approach that emphasized a pentagonal balance that included the United States, Soviet Union, Western Europe, China, and Japan as the major powers.

54. Kissinger, "Central Issues of American Foreign Policy," p. 56.

55. Vose Gulick, *Europe's Classical Balance of Power*, p. 83.

56. Metternich was the principal advocate of a generalized right of interference. Kissinger writes that "oppressed by the vulnerability of its domestic structure in an age of nationalism, the polyglot Austro-Hungarian empire insisted on a generalized right of interference to defeat social unrest wherever it

occurred" (*A World Restored,* p. 5). Kissinger's own policy actions in Chile and such initiatives as the Helsinki Accords, which recognized Soviet primacy in Eastern Europe, suggest a "spheres of influence" policy.

57. This point was made in chapter 1. History for Kissinger, as for Ranke, is the history of the great powers. The Latin American author Gabriel García Márquez claims that Kissinger indicated that American policy interests extend on an East-West axis to include Moscow and Peking, and that south of the Pyrenees there were no power interests of major concern.

58. Kissinger, *A World Restored,* pp. 146–47.

59. Oswald Spengler, *The Decline of the West,* abridged edition, ed. Helmut Werner and Arthur Helps (New York: Alfred A. Knopf, 1962), p. 358.

60. Kissinger, "Central Issues in American Foreign Policy," p. 85.

61. See Dickson, *Kissinger and the Meaning of History,* pp. 83–116; and Bruce Mazlish, *Kissinger: The European Mind in American Policy* (New York: Basic Books, 1976), pp. 177–83.

62. Arnold Toynbee, *A Study of History,* 2 vol. abridgement by D. C. Somervell (New York: Dell Books, 1965). See chapter 4 for an extensive treatment of the breakdown of civilizations.

63. Kissinger, *A World Restored,* p. 317.

64. Ibid., pp. 144–45.

65. Ibid., p. 145.

66. Henry Kissinger, "The White Revolutionary: Reflections on Bismarck," *Daedalus* 91, no. 3 (Summer 1968): 909.

67. Ibid., p. 922.

68. Kissinger, "Lessons of the Past," pp. 121–22.

69. Kissinger, *A World Restored,* p. 1.

70. Ibid., p. 146.

71. Ibid., pp. 1–2.

72. Ibid., p. 1.

73. Kissinger, "Force and Diplomacy in the Nuclear Age," p. 355.

74. Kissinger, *A World Restored,* pp. 138–39.

75. See Stephen Garrett, "Nixonian Foreign Policy: A New Balance of Power—or a Revived Concert?" *Polity* 9, no. 3 (Spring 1973): 389–421; and Coral Bell, "Kissinger in Retrospect: The Diplomacy of Power Concert?" *International Affairs* 53 (April 1977): 202–16. Likenesses can be drawn between the European concert system and the process of détente—particularly in regard to the political mechanism of "linkage."

76. Kissinger, *A World Restored,* pp. 25–26.

77. Ibid., p. 3.

78. Ibid., p. 2.

79. Revolutionary nations attempt to universalize their own domestic values so that other nations are forced to accept their "way of life." This is what Kissinger means by Napoleon's attempt "to translate the moral claims of the French Revolution into reality" (*A World Restored,* p. 4). Similarly, Kissinger counters the view that revolutionary states act out of fear that other nations will attempt to crush their domestic revolutions. What distinguishes revolutionary states is not that they are fearful, but that nothing can assuage their fear. Consequently, they seek to "make over" the world order in their own domestic image—to universalize their values. Of course, this amounts to the neutralization of every other state, because in Kissinger's view, a nation without its values or spiritual basis has ceased to function as a state. Kissinger writes: "To be sure,

the motivation of the revolutionary power may well be defensive; it may be sincere in its protestations of feeling threatened. But the distinguishing feature of a revolutionary power is not that it feels threatened—such feeling is inherent in the nature of international relations based on sovereign states—but that nothing can reassure it. Only absolute security—the neutralization of the opponent—is considered a sufficient guarantee, and thus the desire of one power for absolute security means absolute insecurity for all the others" (*A World Restored,* p. 2).

80. Like Ranke, Kissinger emphasizes the primacy of foreign policy. Ranke relates the causes of the French Revolution to France's decline vis-à-vis other European states rather than to its domestic social and economic system. This view is at odds with the economic interpretation offered by most Anglo-American scholars. See Ranke's "The Great Powers," in Theodore Von Laue, *Leopold Ranke: The Formative Years* (Princeton: Princeton University Press, 1950), pp. 181–218. Kissinger's emphasis on the international behavior of revolutionary nations is evident in his description of them. He sees their revolutions beginning with the expressed purpose of transforming the existing world order as much as transforming their own states. In this respect, France and the Soviet Union represent only the starting points of revolutions that are international in nature. See Kissinger, *Nuclear Weapons and Foreign Policy,* pp. 316–21.

81. Kissinger identifies Hitler as a revolutionary conqueror and Lenin as a prophet. He characterizes most Soviet and Chinese leaders as both prophets and conquerors.

82. Kissinger, *A World Restored,* p. 316.

83. Kissinger, *Nuclear Weapons and Foreign Policy,* p. 316.

84. Spengler, *The Decline of the West,* p. 382.

85. Kissinger, *A World Restored,* p. 315.

86. Ibid., p. 316.

87. Ibid., p. 324.

88. Kissinger, "The White Revolutionary: Reflections on Bismarck," p. 894.

89. Kissinger, *A World Restored,* p. 208.

90. Ibid., p. 205.

91. Ibid., p. 322.

92. Ibid.

93. Ibid., p. 324.

94. Ibid., pp. 324–25.

95. Ibid., p. 74. Kissinger writes that "perfect flexibility in diplomacy is the illusion of amateurs. To plan policy on the assumption of the equal possibility of all contingencies is to confuse statesmanship with mathematics. Since it is impossible to be prepared for all eventualities, the assumption of the opponent's perfect flexibility leads to paralysis of action. The individual who understands intangibles realizes, however, that no state can give up its vision of its 'legitimacy' and no individual his raison d'etre, not because it is physically but because it is psychologically impossible."

96. Ibid., p. 325.

97. Kissinger, "Domestic Structure and Foreign Policy," p. 14.

98. Ibid.

99. Kissinger, *A World Restored,* p. 329.

100. Spengler, *The Decline of the West,* p. 383.

101. Ibid.

102. Graubard, *Portrait of a Mind,* p. 12.

103. Kissinger, *A World Restored,* p. 326.

104. Ibid., p. 323.
105. Ibid., p. 326.
106. Ibid.
107. Ibid., p. 329.
108. Spengler, *The Decline of the West*, p. 384.
109. Kissinger, *A World Restored*, p. 329.
110. Ibid., p. 325.
111. Spengler, *The Decline of the West*, p. 386.
112. Henry Kissinger, "Reflections on American Diplomacy," *Foreign Affairs* 33 (October 1956): 54.
113. Kissinger, *A World Restored*, p. 317.
114. Henry Kissinger, "A New National Partnership," in *The Department of State Bulletin* no. 1860 (17 February 1975), p. 197.
115. Kissinger makes this same point in describing Nixon's complex personality in *White House Years* (Boston: Little, Brown, 1979).
116. Kissinger, *A World Restored*, p. 114.
117. Kissinger, "Reflections on American Diplomacy," p. 37. Kissinger specifically states: "It would be a mistake, however, to ascribe our difficulties to this or that error of policy or to a particular administration. . . . What is at issue, therefore, is not a policy but an attitude."

Chapter 3.   The Insular Approach of American Foreign Policy

1. I. F. Stone, *The Haunted Fifties* (New York: Random House, 1963).
2. Eric F. Goldman, *The Crucial Decade and After: America, 1945–1960*, rev. ed. (New York: Vintage Books, 1960), pp. 261–94.
3. Kissinger's criticism was shared by other prominent officials and scholars during this period. See Norman Graebner, *The New Isolationism: A Study in Politics and Foreign Policy Since 1950* (New York: The Ronald Press, 1956). Graebner writes that "for the vast majority of Americans in 1950 the isolationist tradition was no longer relevant. World War II had demonstrated its obsolescence, but had not destroyed the emotions and traditions which underlay it. What remained was significant—a hatred of Europe, a belief in American purity which should not risk corruption by contact with other nations, and a wistful hope that America could live in seclusion while maintaining its traditional virtues. If these emotions were recessive, they continued to have a paralyzing effect on American policy." See also Arthur M. Schlesinger, Jr., "The New Isolationism," *Atlantic* 189 (May 1952): 36. Schlesinger writes that the tendency toward isolationism has "kept America a slumbering giant, unable to export its democratic faith to the peoples of other nations, unable to play a full and affirmative role in the world."
4. Henry Kissinger, *The Necessity for Choice: Prospects of American Foreign Policy* (New York: Harper and Row, 1961), p. 1.
5. For a fairly incisive description of the concept of national character from the perspectives of both historians and social scientists, see David M. Potter, *People of Plenty: Economic Abundance and the American Character* (Chicago: University of Chicago Press, 1954), p. 28.
6. Foremost among the European writers who have addressed the subject of the American character are D. W. Brogan, *The American Character* (New York: Alfred A. Knopf, 1944); Alexis de Tocqueville, *Democracy in America* (New York:

The New American Library, 1956) (first published in 1835 and 1840); and Lord Bryce, *The American Commonwealth* (London: Macmillan, 1899).

7. See Selig Adler, *The Isolationist Impulse: The Twentieth Century Reaction* (New York: Collier Books, 1961).

8. See Henry Kissinger, *The Troubled Partnership: A Re-appraisal of the Atlantic Alliance* (New York: McGraw-Hill, 1965), p. 41. In characterizing the outlook of insular nations, in this case with respect to alliance politics, Kissinger offers the following description of their views:

If an international system could be designed with geometrical symmetry, the primary concern of allies would be the requirements of the common undertaking. Their efforts would be regulated by criteria of over-all efficiency and on the basis of a division of labor. But such a perfect symmetry is the illusion of utopians—or of island powers. Historically aloof and geographically isolated, such nations consider that the main function of foreign policy is to remedy the peril that has caused them to commit themselves to a joint enterprise. Such was the attitude of Great Britain toward the Continent during the Napoleonic wars. This, too, has been the tendency of the United States since it assumed major international responsibilities after World War II.

9. See Henry Kissinger, *A World Restored: Metternich, Castlereagh and the Problems of Peace, 1812–1822* (Boston: Houghton Mifflin, 1957), p. 31; and idem, "Reflections on American Diplomacy," *Foreign Affairs* 53 (April 1955): 40.

10. Kissinger, "Reflections on American Diplomacy," p. 38.

11. Ibid.

12. See Henry Kissinger, "America and the World: Principle and Pragmatism," *Time*, 27 December 1976.

13. Henry Kissinger, *White House Years* (Boston: Little, Brown, 1979), p. 60.

14. Henry Kissinger, "Reflections on a Partnership: British and American Attitudes to Postwar Foreign Policy," in *Observations: Selected Speeches and Essays, 1982–1984* (Boston: Little, Brown, 1985), p. 8.

15. Kissinger, *White House Years*, p. 61.

16. Ibid.

17. For a description of this idea, see Daniel Bell, "The End to American Exceptionalism," in *The American Commonwealth*, ed. Nathan Glazer and Irving Kristol (New York: Basic Books, 1976).

18. Toynbee attributes this passivity to the "failure of self-determination" that often follows a significant advance. This "nemesis of creativity" usually results in the idolization of an ephemeral condition—be it a technique or institution. Toynbee sees it as leading to societal breakdown. See Arnold J. Toynbee, *A Study of History*, 2 vol. abridgement by D. C. Somervell (New York: Dell, 1965), 1: 286–415. Kissinger offers a very explicit Toynbee-like critique in the following passage: "The more effectively the environment is mastered, the greater the temptation to rest on one's oars. The more an organization is elaborated, the easier it becomes to act by rote. Stagnation can then appear as well-being and blandness as wisdom. That is why creativity is usually at its height when society is sufficiently elaborate to keep choices from being random but the structure is not yet so overwhelming that the response verges on the mechanical." See Henry Kissinger, *The Necessity for Choice*, pp. 356–57.

19. Thomas I. Cook and Malcolm Moos, *Power Through Purpose: The Realism of Idealism as a Basis for Foreign Policy* (Baltimore: The Johns Hopkins University Press, 1954), pp. 35–38.

20. Henry Kissinger, "Continuity and Change in American Foreign Policy," in *For the Record: Selected Statements 1977–1980* (Boston: Little, Brown, 1981), p. 74.

21. Kissinger, *A World Restored*, p. 34; and idem, *Nuclear Weapons and Foreign Policy* (New York: Harper and Row, 1957), p. 8.

22. Kissinger, *A World Restored*, p. 34.

23. Ibid., p. 31.

24. Ibid.

25. John H. Herz, *International Politics in the Atomic Age* (New York: Columbia University Press, 1959), pp. 96–108.

26. Kissinger, *Nuclear Weapons and Foreign Policy*, p. 10.

27. Ibid., pp. 8–9.

28. Ibid., pp. 86–131.

29. Kissinger, "Reflections on American Diplomacy," p. 41.

30. Kissinger, "America and the World," p. 41.

31. Kissinger, *The Troubled Partnership*, p. 38.

32. Ibid.

33. Kissinger, *White House Years*, p. 58.

34. Kissinger, "Reflections on American Diplomacy," p. 42.

35. Kissinger, *The Troubled Partnership*, p. 57.

36. Kissinger, *White House Years*, p. 59.

37. Henry Kissinger, "Central Issues of American Foreign Policy," in *American Foreign Policy*, 3rd ed. (New York: W. W. Norton, 1977), pp. 91–92.

38. Kissinger, "Reflections on American Diplomacy," pp. 41–42.

39. Kissinger, "Reflections on a Partnership," p. 6.

40. Henry Kissinger, "American Policy and Preventive War," *Yale Review* 44 (March 1955): 325.

41. Kissinger, *White House Years*, p. 59.

42. Kissinger, "Reflections on a Partnership," p. 5.

43. For a detailed discussion of the "instability of mood" that historically has characterized the American response to foreign policy issues, see Gabriel A. Almond, *The American People and Foreign Policy* (New York: Praeger, 1965).

44. Kissinger, *The Necessity for Choice*, p. 342.

45. Kissinger, "Domestic Structure and Foreign Policy," in *American Foreign Policy*, p. 48.

46. Ibid.

47. Ibid.

48. Ibid., pp. 48–49. Kissinger writes:

Cultures which escaped the early impact of Newtonian thinking have retained the essentially pre-Newtonian view that the real world is almost completely *internal* to the observer. Although this attitude was a liability for centuries—because it prevented the development of the technology and consumer goods which the West enjoyed—it offers great flexibility with respect to the contemporary revolutionary turmoil. It enables the societies which do not share our cultural mode to alter reality by influencing the perspective of the observer—a process which we are largely unprepared to handle or even to perceive.

49. Kissinger, *The Necessity for Choice*, p. 343.

50. Kissinger, "Domestic Structure and Foreign Policy," p. 29.

51. Henry Kissinger, "The Meaning of History: Reflections on Spengler, Toynbee and Kant," unpublished undergraduate honors thesis (Harvard University, 1950), p. 22.

52. Kissinger, *The Necessity for Choice*, p. 342.
53. Kissinger, "Reflections on American Diplomacy," p. 56.
54. Kissinger, "The Meaning of History," p. 333.
55. Kissinger, "Domestic Structure and Foreign Policy," p. 32.
56. Kissinger, *A World Restored*, p. 199. Kissinger writes that in Anglo-Saxon countries the relationship between society and state is juridic. In states such as Metternich's Austria, the state rests on an ethical foundation.
57. Kissinger, "Domestic Structure and Foreign Policy," p. 29.
58. Kissinger, *The Necessity for Choice*, p. 343.
59. Ibid., p. 356.
60. Kissinger, "Reflections on American Diplomacy," p. 39.
61. Kissinger, *A World Restored*, pp. 326–27.
62. Kissinger, *The Necessity for Choice*, p. 340.
63. Zbigniew Brzezinski, "America in a Hostile World," *Foreign Policy* 23 (Summer 1976): 65–96 and in *A Decade of Foreign Policy* (Washington, D.C.: Carnegie Endowment for Peace, 1980), pp. 27–30.
64. Kissinger, *The Necessity for Choice*, p. 3.
65. Ibid.
66. Ibid., pp. 356–57.
67. Ibid., p. 2.
68. Ibid.
69. Ibid.
70. Ibid.
71. Ibid., p. 6.

Chapter 4.   Reflections on American Leadership

1. Richard Nixon, *Leaders* (New York: Warner Books, Inc., 1983), p. 1.
2. Roger Morris, *Uncertain Greatness: Henry Kissinger and American Foreign Policy* (New York: Harper and Row, 1971), pp. 62, 92. Chapter 2 contains an excellent description of the National Security Council as it functioned under Kissinger.
3. Stephen Graubard, *Kissinger: Portrait of a Mind* (New York: W. W. Norton, 1973), p. 54.
4. Ibid., pp. 7–8.
5. Sidney Hook, *The Hero in History: A Study in Limitation and Possibility* (Boston: Beacon Press, 1943), p. 154.
6. Henry Kissinger, *A World Restored: Metternich, Castlereagh and the Problems of Peace, 1812–1822* (Boston: Houghton Mifflin, 1957), p. 322.
7. Nixon, *Leaders*, p. 337. De Gaulle's ideas on leadership, which are highly romantic, are similar to those of Nixon and Kissinger. See Charles de Gaulle, *The Edge of the Sword* (Westport, Connecticut: Greenwood Press, 1975).
8. This phrase is attributed to Fritz Kraemer, an early friend of Kissinger, and it was used to describe Kissinger himself. See Peter Dickson, *Kissinger and the Meaning of History* (Cambridge: Cambridge University Press, 1978), p. 43.
9. See Oswald Spengler, *The Decline of the West*, abridged edition, ed. Helmut Werner and Arthur Helps (New York: Alfred A. Knopf, 1962); and Jose Ortega y Gasset, *The Revolt of the Masses* (New York: W. W. Norton, 1932). Criticism of the egalitarian strain of democratic thought provides a fairly com-

mon theme in European writing about America. De Tocqueville illustrates this point.

10. Kissinger, *A World Restored*, pp. 326–27.

11. Kissinger's criticism of the American leadership style is longstanding and exhibits little change between the 1950s and 1970s. For example, he voices roughly the same criticism in "Reflections on American Diplomacy," *Foreign Affairs* 35 (October 1956): 37–56 as he offers in "The Policymaker and the Intellectual," *The Reporter*, 5 March 1959 and repeats it in "Domestic Structure and Foreign Policy," *Daedalus* 95 (Spring 1966): 503–29 and "Bureaucracy and Policymaking: The Effects of Insiders and Outsiders on the Policy Process," *Bureaucracy, Politics and Strategy*, Security Studies Paper, no. 17 (Los Angeles and Berkeley: University of California Press, 1968).

12. Henry Kissinger, "The Policymaker and the Intellectual," *The Reporter*, 5 March 1959. This article is repeated almost verbatim as the last chapter of *The Necessity for Choice: Prospects of American Foreign Policy* (New York: Harper and Row, 1961). My citations are from the latter publication. The present quotation is found on p. 352.

13. See Henry Kissinger, *Nuclear Weapons and Foreign Policy* (New York: Harper and Row, 1957) for criticism of Dulles and Wilson. Representative criticism of Rusk and McNamara is contained in *The Troubled Partnership: A Reappraisal of the Atlantic Alliance* (New York: McGraw-Hill, 1965). Articles written by Kissinger during both periods and on both subjects largely conform to the arguments he offers in these texts.

14. Henry Kissinger, "Reflections on American Diplomacy," p. 54.

15. Kissinger, *The Necessity for Choice*, p. 355.

16. Henry Kissinger, *American Foreign Policy*, 3d ed. (New York: W. W. Norton, 1977), p. 33.

17. Ibid.

18. Kissinger, *The Necessity for Choice*, pp. 342–43.

19. Ibid., p. 343.

20. Kissinger, "Reflections on American Diplomacy," pp. 54–55.

21. William H. Whyte, Jr., *The Organization Man* (New York: Simon and Schuster, 1956). White's text is regarded as a classic work of American sociology. He identified the nature of modern organizations, both in business and government, and the demands that commitment to the organization places on the individual. These demands were especially significant in light of the value given to individualism in American culture. See David Reisman, *Individualism Reconsidered* (New York: Doubleday, 1954).

22. Kissinger, "Reflections on American Diplomacy," p. 55.

23. Ibid.

24. Kissinger regards the belief that active American involvement in foreign affairs ends with the success of a particular policy as a continuing manifestation of the nation's insularity. In part, this belief accounts for the American quest for total solutions. Kissinger regards this quest as one source of the nation's disillusionment with world affairs, because in international politics all solutions are imperfect and no problem is ever finally resolved. In an interview as secretary of state, Kissinger offered the view that "there is undoubtedly a profound disillusionment in America with foreign policy in general. We have carried the burden for a generation. In fact, if you go back to the beginning of World War II, it doesn't seem to end. Most programs have been sold to Americans with the argument that they would mean the end of exertion. Now we have to convince

Americans that there will never be an end to exertion." It is also significant that in this same interview Kissinger defines part of his own legacy as that of the educator—part of his efforts have involved "a rather self-conscious attempt to try to educate myself, my generation, and my associates, insofar as I can, to living with the world as it is now emerging." See "Partial Transcript of an Interview with Kissinger on the State of the Western World," *The New York Times*, 13 October 1974.

25. A significant body of revisionist literature exists regarding Eisenhower. Current scholarship tends to portray him as a skillful behind-the-scenes operator rather than as an inarticulate military figure. This is decidedly not how he is characterized by Kissinger, although in *White House Years* (Boston: Little, Brown, 1979) Kissinger suggests that he held Eisenhower in high esteem. For an excellent book concerning Eisenhower's approach to national security decision making, see Douglas Kinnard, *President Eisenhower and Strategy Management: A Study in Defense Politics* (Lexington: The University of Kentucky Press, 1977).

26. Quoted in Kissinger, *The Necessity for Choice*, p. 181.

27. Ibid., p. 187.

28. Kissinger first presents a theory of negotiations based on his distinction between legitimate and revolutionary international systems in *A World Restored*, pp. 73–74. He explores this theory in greater detail a few years later in "Reflections on American Diplomacy." The following passage appears on p. 46:

> Nothing is more futile, than to attempt to deal with a revolutionary power by ordinary diplomatic methods. In a legitimate order, demands once made are negotiable; they are put forward with an intention of being compromised. But in a revolutionary order, they are programmatic; they represent a claim for allegiance. In a legitimate order, it is good negotiating tactics to formulate maximum demands because this facilitates compromise without loss of essential objectives. In a revolutionary order, it is good negotiating tactics to formulate minimum demands in order to gain the advantage of advocating moderation. In a legitimate order, proposals are addressed to the opposite number at the conference table. They must, therefore, be drafted with great attention to their substantive content and with sufficient ambiguity so that they do not appear as invitations to surrender. But in a revolutionary order, the protagonists at the conference table address not so much one another as the world at large. Proposals here must be framed with a maximum of clarity and even simplicity, for their major utility is their symbolic content. In short, in a legitimate order, a conference represents a struggle to find formulae to achieve agreement; in a revolutionary order, it is a struggle to capture the symbols which move humanity.

Kissinger regards American diplomacy as a failure because it does not recognize the revolutionary nature of the Soviet challenge and disregards the symbolic aspects of diplomacy. Kissinger argues that American purposes would have been best served by formulating "minimum" proposals during the 1950s. Soviet rejection of such proposals (and this was to be expected of a revolutionary state) would demonstrate its unlimited objectives and intransigence to the rest of the world.

29. Kissinger, *Nuclear Weapons and Foreign Policy*, p. 337.

30. Ibid., p. 338.

31. Kissinger, *The Necessity for Choice*, p. 341. Spengler also characterized America as a commercial nation and deprecated its values. Spengler attributed the absence of a great tradition of statecraft in America to the dominance of commercialism. See Oswald Spengler, *The Decline of the West*, p. 402.

32. Kissinger, *The Necessity for Choice*, p. 341.

33. See Kinnard, *President Eisenhower and Strategy Management*.

34. John C. Donovan, *The Cold Warriors: A Policy-Making Elite* (Lexington, Massachusetts: D. C. Heath, 1974).

35. Nitze's career typifies this pattern. His formative influences came as a member of Dillon-Reed, investment bankers. His government career includes the following positions: 1944–46, Vice-Chairman of the U.S. Strategic Bombing Survey; 1946, Deputy Director for International Trade Policy; 1948–49, Deputy Assistant Secretary of State for Economic Affairs; 1950–53, Department of State Policy and Planning Staff; 1950s, Director of the Foreign Service Educational Foundation; 1961–63, Assistant Secretary of Defense for International Security Affairs; 1963–67, Secretary of the Navy; 1967–69, Deputy Secretary of Defense. During the 1950s, Nitze helped prepare the Gaither Committee study of national defense policy. He is considered the principal author of NSC–68. Nitze is currently presidential adviser to the U.S.–Soviet Strategic Arms Reduction Talks (START).

36. Kissinger, *The Necessity for Choice*, p. 341.

37. Ibid.

38. Ibid.

39. See Charles E. Bohlen, *The Transformation of American Foreign Policy* (New York: W. W. Norton, 1969); and David Halberstam, *The Best and the Brightest* (Greenwich, Connecticut: Fawcett Books, 1973).

40. Kissinger, *The Necessity for Choice*, p. 350.

41. Ibid., pp. 349–51.

42. Ibid., p. 348.

43. Ibid., p. 349.

44. Ibid.

45. Ibid., p. 353.

46. Henry Kissinger, "Domestic Structure and Foreign Policy," *Daedalus* 95 (Spring 1966): 503–29. Included in *American Foreign Policy*, pp. 9–50. All quotes are from *American Foreign Policy*.

47. Ibid., p. 27. In this passage, Kissinger also observes that

> the hysterical cast of the policy of Imperial Germany was given impetus by a domestic structure in which political parties were deprived of responsibility while ministers were obliged to balance a monarch by divine right against a Parliament composed of representatives without any prospect of ever holding office. Consensus could be achieved more easily through fits of national passion which in turn disquieted all of Germany's neighbors. Germany's foreign policy grew unstable because its domestic structure did little to discourage capricious improvisations; it may even have put a premium on them. Ibid., pp. 27–28.

48. Kissinger's emphasis on the ideological nature of Soviet thinking is important in light of the criticism of his policies of détente. Normally, détente is associated with a conscious attempt to "de-ideologize" foreign policy.

49. The following works are representative of, or deal at length with, the bureaucratic basis of American foreign policymaking: Graham T. Allison, *Essence of Decision: Explaining the Cuban Missile Crisis* (Boston: Little, Brown, 1971); Morton H. Halperin, *Bureaucratic Politics and Foreign Policy* (Washington, D.C.: The Brookings Institute, 1974); I. M. Destler, *Presidents, Bureaucrats, and Foreign Policy: The Politics of Organizational Reform* (Princeton: Princeton University Press, 1972); Roger Hilsman, *The Politics of Policy Making in Defense and Foreign Affairs*

(New York: Harper & Row, 1971); John Spanier and Eric M. Ulsaner, *How American Foreign Policy Is Made* (New York: Holt, Rinehart and Winston, 1978); and Lincoln P. Bloomfield, *The Foreign Policy Process: A Modern Primer* (Englewood Cliffs, New Jersey: Prentice-Hall, 1982).

50. The bureaucratic politics model is one of the three models for understanding foreign policy outlined by Graham Allison. The others are the rational actor and organizational process models. Kissinger views the nation primarily as a unitary—albeit not always rational—actor.

51. For this contrast, see Samuel Huntington, *The Common Defense* as cited in Allison, *The Essence of Decision*, p. 156.

52. Richard E. Neustadt, *Presidential Power: The Politics of Leadership* (New York: John Wiley, 1960), p. 10; and Richard E. Neustadt, "Whitehouse and Whitehall," *The Public Interest* 2 (Winter 1966): 64.

53. Morris, *Uncertain Greatness*, p. 63.

54. Marion D. Irish, "The Organization Man in the Presidency," *Journal of Politics* 20 (May 1958): 259–77.

55. Whyte, *The Organization Man*.

56. Irish, "The Organization Man in the Presidency," p. 268.

57. Henry Kissinger, "Bureaucracy and Policy Making: The Effects of Insiders and Outsiders on the Policy Process," in Henry Kissinger and Bernard Brodie, *Bureaucracy, Politics and Strategy*, Security Study Paper Number 17 (Los Angeles and Berkeley: University of California, 1968), p. 8.

58. Ibid., p. 6.

59. Ibid., pp. 3–4.

60. Ibid., p. 9.

61. See *Prospect for America: The Rockefeller Panel Reports* (Garden City, New York: Doubleday, 1961).

62. Kissinger, *The Necessity for Choice*, p. 346.

63. See George F. Kennan, "America's Administrative Response to Its World Problems," *Daedalus* 87 (Spring 1958): 5–24.

64. Ibid., pp. 17–18.

65. Hans Morgenthau, "Can We Entrust Defense to a Committee?," *The New York Times Magazine*, 7 June 1959.

66. See Dean Acheson, "Thoughts about Thought in High Places," *New York Times Magazine*, 11 October 1959; W. W. Rostow, "The Fallacy of the Fertile Gondolas," *Harvard Alumni Bulletin*, 25 May 1957; and Paul H. Nitze, "Organization for National Policy Planning in the United States," Paper presented to the American Political Science Association, September 1959.

67. Hilsman, *The Politics of Policy Making in Defense and Foreign Affairs*, p. 162.

68. See Hans Morgenthau, "Can We Entrust Defense to a Committee?" Morgenthau's proposal in this article is significant in light of Kissinger's later domination of the National Security Council (NSC) machinery and American foreign policymaking in the Nixon-Ford years. Morgenthau suggests that what is needed is a "First Secretary of the Government" for foreign policy who would superintend the NSC process. Morgenthau writes that such a first secretary would impose his will on an "Executive Branch fragmented into semi-autonomous fiefdoms." As with Kissinger, substantive knowledge of foreign policy issues would be a requirement for such a figure.

69. Kissinger, "Bureaucracy and Policymaking," p. 8.

70. Stephen Graubard substantiates this point in *Kissinger: Portrait of a Mind*, pp. 223–27.

71. See Hilsman, *The Politics of Policy Making in Defense and Foreign Affairs*, p. 162.

72. See John Franklin Campbell, *The Foreign Affairs Fudge Factory* (New York: Basic Books, 1971).

73. Hilsman, *The Politics of Policy Making in Defense and Foreign Affairs*, p. 46.

74. I. M. Destler, *Presidents, Bureaucrats and Foreign Policy,* p. 107.

75. Quoted in Destler, p. 115.

76. Kissinger, "Bureaucracy and Policy Making," p. 9.

77. Henry Kissinger, "Reflections on Cuba," *The Reporter,* 22 November 1962.

78. Kissinger, "Bureaucracy and Policy Making," p. 7.

79. Kissinger's views on the controversy are found in "The Skybolt Affair," *The Reporter,* 17 January 1963.

Chapter 5.   The Need for Doctrine in the Nuclear Age

1. See Henry Kissinger, *The Troubled Partnership: A Re-appraisal of the Atlantic Alliance* (New York: McGraw-Hill, 1965).

2. Even an abbreviated list of the group's members conveys its prominence. Kissinger's study group included: Hamilton Fish Armstrong of the Council on Foreign Relations; Hanson Baldwin, military editor of *The New York Times;* Robert Bowie, most recently of the State Department and soon to be appointed director of Harvard's Center for International Affairs; McGeorge Bundy, dean of the Faculty of Arts and Sciences at Harvard; Thomas K. Finletter, formerly secretary of the air force; General James Gavin, famed commander of the 82d Airborne Division, later ambassador to France; Roswell Gilpatric, later deputy secretary of defense; Caryl Haskins, president of the Carnegie Institution of Washington; Paul Nitze; Frank Pace, Jr., formerly secretary of the army, chairman of General Dynamics Corporation; James Perkins, later president of Cornell University; Don K. Price, Jr., vice-president of the Ford Foundation; I. I. Rabi, Nobel Prize–winning physicist; David Rockefeller of the Chase Manhattan Bank; Oscar Ruebhausen, associate of Nelson Rockefeller; General Walter Bedell Smith, former under secretary of state, ambassador to Russia, and director of the Central Intelligence Agency; Carroll Wilson of the Massachusetts Institute of Technology, formerly general manager of the Atomic Energy Commission; and Arnold Wolfers, historian and professor of international relations at Yale. For a detailed discussion of Kissinger's work with the Council on Foreign Relations, see Stephen R. Graubard, *Kissinger: Portrait of a Mind* (New York: W. W. Norton, 1973), pp. 54–64. The above list was taken from p. 63 of Graubard's study.

3. Graubard, *Portrait of a Mind*, pp. 106–07.

4. Ibid., p. 105.

5. Kissinger repeatedly demonstrated a capacity to translate his own intellectual interests into institutional structures. He was also able to link his work in the academy to a wider arena of power and ideas. While a graduate student at Harvard, he helped organize the International Seminar. Men and women from foreign countries who were destined for prominence in politics, journalism, the civil service, and so forth, were invited to Harvard for a summer of study. Kissinger also helped establish and became editor of a Harvard journal entitled *Confluence*. Over time, this journal published articles by Reinhold Niebuhr, Karl Jaspers, André Malraux, Alberto Moravia, and Bertrand de Jouvenel, among others.

6. Graubard, *Portrait of a Mind*, p. 115. Schelling's works have become classics in the field. Their focus includes the application of game theory and bargaining techniques to strategic conflict. See Thomas C. Schelling, *The Strategy of Conflict* (Cambridge: Harvard University Press, 1960); and idem, *Arms and Influence* (New Haven: Yale University Press, 1966).

7. Robert A. Levine, *The Arms Debate* (Cambridge: Harvard University Press, 1963).

8. Thomas C. Schelling and Morton Halperin, *Strategy and Arms Control* (New York: Twentieth Century Fund, 1961).

9. "As I look back," Kissinger said, "at the area of strategic arms limitation, most of the creative thought with which I am familiar dates back to the late fifties and was then introduced into Government in the Kennedy Administration and then, I hope, in ours." See "Partial Transcript of an Interview with Kissinger on the State of the Western World," *The New York Times*, 13 October 1974.

10. Kahn is usually given precedence because of the seminal nature of his works. See, for example, Herman Kahn, *On Thermonuclear War* (Princeton: Princeton University Press, 1960); and *Thinking About the Unthinkable* (New York: Horizon Press, 1962). See also Albert Wohlstetter, "The Delicate Balance of Terror," *Foreign Affairs* 37, no. 2 (January 1959): 211–34; Donald Brennan, ed., *Arms Control, Disarmament and National Security* (New York: George Braziller, 1961); William Kaufmann, *The Requirements of Deterrence*, Center of International Studies Memorandum No. 7 (Princeton: Princeton University Press, 1954); and Glen Snyder, *Deterrence and Defense: Toward a Theory of National Security* (Princeton: Princeton University Press, 1961).

11. Bernard Brodie, *Strategy in the Missile Age* (Princeton: Princeton University Press, 1959).

12. Robert E. Osgood, *Limited War: The Challenge to American Security* (Chicago: The University of Chicago Press, 1957). See also Robert E. Osgood, *Limited War Revisited* (Boulder, Colorado: Westview Press, 1979).

13. Morton H. Halperin, *Limited War: An Essay on the Development of the Theory and an Annotated Bibliography* (Cambridge: Harvard University Center for International Affairs, 1962). See also Morton H. Halperin, *Limited War in the Nuclear Age* (New York: John Wiley and Sons, 1963).

14. The Gaither Committee was an ad hoc committee organized in 1957 to investigate America's defense preparedness. In the face of a significant Soviet defense effort, the committee recommended a build-up of both our strategic and conventional forces. See Morton Halperin, "The Gaither Committee and the Policy Process," *World Politics* 13 (April 1961): 360–84.

15. Maxwell D. Taylor, *The Uncertain Trumpet* (New York: Harpers, 1959).

16. Henry Kissinger, *Nuclear Weapons and Foreign Policy* (New York: Harper and Row, 1957), p. 1.

17. See Bruce Mazlish, *Kissinger: The European Mind in American Policy* (New York: Basic Books, 1976), p. 108; and John G. Stoessinger, *Henry Kissinger: The Anguish of Power* (New York: W. W. Norton, 1976), pp. 26–29.

18. Graubard, *Portrait of a Mind*, p. 64.

19. Kissinger met regularly at Harvard and on various discussion panels with scientists who were writing in the field of nuclear weapons. Through his work with the Rockefeller Brothers Fund, he had been introduced to Edward Teller, one of America's foremost physicists. Similarly, he became involved with the Pugwash movement in 1957. This movement traced its origin to the call by Bertrand Russell for closer cooperation between Soviet and western scientists to

avoid nuclear war. Kissinger followed the Pugwash meetings with great attention, and through his involvement met many European and Soviet scientists. See Graubard, *Portrait of a Mind*, pp. 116–17.

20. Ibid., p. 117.

21. Ibid., p. 103.

22. Henry Kissinger, "Strategy and Organization," *Foreign Affairs* 35, no. 3 (April 1957): 394.

23. These terms are used by George E. Lowe in *The Age of Deterrence* (Boston: Little, Brown, 1964).

24. See Henry Kissinger, "Limited War: Nuclear or Conventional?—A Reappraisal," *Daedalus* 89, no. 4 (Fall 1960): 800–17.

25. For the Halle quotation, see Chalmers M. Roberts, "How Containment Worked," *Foreign Policy* no. 7 (Summer 1972): 42.

26. Ibid.

27. For an in-depth discussion of these "forms" of containment, see John Lewis Gaddis, *Strategies of Containment: A Critical Appraisal of Postwar American National Security Policy* (New York: Oxford University Press, 1982); and Charles Gati, *Caging the Bear: Containment and the Cold War* (Indianapolis: Bobbs-Merrill, 1974).

28. Henry Kissinger, *A World Restored: Metternich, Castlereagh and the Problems of Peace, 1812–1822* (Boston: Houghton Mifflin, 1957), p. 39.

29. Ibid.

30. Walter Lippmann, *The Cold War: A Study in U.S. Foreign Policy* (New York: Harper and Brothers, 1947), p. 12.

31. Henry Kissinger, *The Necessity for Choice* (New York: Harper and Row, 1961), pp. 176–77. This quotation and Kissinger's entire discussion of containment appear almost verbatim in *White House Years* (Boston: Little, Brown, 1979).

32. Henry Kissinger, "American Policy and Preventive War," *Yale Review* 44 (March 1955): 325.

33. Kissinger, *The Necessity for Choice*, p. 178.

34. Churchill pushed for a "spheres of influence" policy, particularly in Europe. This was to form the basis of the negotiations that Churchill stressed.

35. Kissinger, *The Necessity for Choice*, p. 179 and passim.

36. Kissinger, "American Policy and Preventive War," p. 325.

37. Kissinger, *The Necessity for Choice*, p. 179.

38. Ibid., p. 6.

39. Kissinger, *A World Restored*, p. 2.

40. Henry Kissinger, "Central Issues of American Foreign Policy," in *American Foreign Policy*, 3d ed. (New York: W. W. Norton, 1977), pp. 60–61.

41. Kissinger, *Nuclear Weapons and Foreign Policy*, p. 7. For an expanded discussion of this point, see Henry Kissinger, "Force and Diplomacy in the Nuclear Age," *Foreign Affairs* 34, no. 3 (April 1956): 349–66.

42. Kissinger, *Nuclear Weapons and Foreign Policy*, p. 5.

43. Ibid., p. 16.

44. Henry Kissinger, "Military Policy and Defense of the 'Grey Areas,'" *Foreign Affairs* 33 (April 1955): 419.

45. Kissinger, "American Policy and Preventive War," p. 322.

46. Kissinger, "Military Policy and Defense of the 'Grey Areas,'" p. 416.

47. Ibid., pp. 418–19.

48. See Albert Wohlstetter, "The Delicate Balance of Terror," in *Problems of National Strategy*, ed. Henry Kissinger (New York: Praeger, 1965), pp. 34–58.

49. Counterforce is associated with targeting the opponent's military power. Hence, a counterforce strategy requires a retaliatory force large enough to survive a first strike and still devastate the enemy's remaining strategic forces. Finite deterrence is associated with the minimum retaliatory force necessary to survive a first strike and still destroy the enemy's population centers and industry. Proponents of finite deterrence believed that this level of destruction would be sufficient to deter an enemy attack.

50. See Kissinger, *The Necessity for Choice*, pp. 56 and 210–86.

51. Kissinger's geopolitical ideas are similar to those associated with Halford Mackinder. Mackinder's famous dictum was that the Eurasian land mass was the "heartland" of the "world island." Surrounding the "heartland" was an outer circle of island and peninsular nations known as the "rimlands." Mackinder also viewed the struggle between the landpower and seapower nations as a recurring historical theme. See James Dougherty and Robert L. Pfaltzgraff, Jr., *Contending Theories of International Relations* (Philadelphia: J. B. Lippincott, 1971), pp. 52–54.

52. Kissinger, "Military Policy and Defense of the 'Grey Areas,' " p. 423.

53. Kissinger, *Nuclear Weapons and Foreign Policy*, p. 320.

54. Ibid., p. 151.

55. Kissinger, "Military Policy and Defense of the 'Grey Areas,' " p. 421.

56. Kissinger, *Nuclear Weapons and Foreign Policy*, pp. 43–80.

57. Kissinger, "Military Policy and Defense of the 'Grey Areas,' " p. 418.

58. Kissinger, *Nuclear Weapons and Foreign Policy*, p. 331.

59. Henry Kissinger, "Reflections on American Diplomacy," *Foreign Affairs* 34 (October 1956): 42.

60. Kissinger, *Nuclear Weapons and Foreign Policy*, p. 321.

61. Ibid., p. 340.

62. See Samuel P. Huntington, *The Common Defense: Strategic Programs in National Politics* (New York: Columbia University Press, 1961), pp. 14–20.

63. Kissinger, "Military Policy and Defense of the 'Grey Areas,' " p. 416.

64. Ibid.

65. Ibid.

66. Huntington, *The Common Defense*, pp. 78–79.

67. Ibid., pp. 65–66.

68. Ibid., p. 66.

69. Kissinger, "Force and Diplomacy in the Nuclear Age," p. 353.

70. See Raymond Aron, *The Century of Total War* (Boston: Beacon Press, 1954).

71. Kissinger, *Nuclear Weapons and Foreign Policy*, pp. 87–88.

72. Ibid., p. 87. Kissinger characterizes the American Civil War as a "revolutionary" struggle.

73. Osgood, *Limited War*, p. 29.

74. Kissinger, *Nuclear Weapons and Foreign Policy*, p. 87.

75. Ibid., p. 91.

76. Ibid., p. 359.

77. Ibid., pp. 28–29. Kissinger quotes congressional testimony by Army General McLain in 1948: "In case of another major war, the pattern would probably take the following form: First the blitz, using all modern means. If this should succeed, the war would be over. . . . If the blitz, however, is stopped, the second phase would be a softening-up phase in which bases, industries, and

ports would be bombarded. The final phase would be a struggle between complete teams, air, sea, and ground, in which the accompanying attrition would finally point to the victor."

78. Ibid., pp. 30–31.
79. Ibid., p. 60.
80. Ibid., pp. 19–20.
81. Kissinger, "Military Policy and Defense of the 'Grey Areas,' " p. 418.
82. Kissinger, *Nuclear Weapons and Foreign Policy*, p. 240.
83. Ibid.
84. Ibid., p. 238.
85. Ibid., p. 43.
86. Ibid.
87. Ibid.
88. Ibid., p. 44.
89. Ibid., p. 22.
90. Ibid., pp. 7–8.
91. See Edward Luttwak, *The Pentagon and the Art of War* (New York: Simon and Schuster, 1985).
92. Kissinger refers to a similar concept in characterizing our idea of power as "literal." He writes that "the literalness of our notion of power made it impossible to conceive of an effective relationship between force and diplomacy." *Nuclear Weapons and Foreign Policy*, p. 40.
93. Ibid., p. 12.
94. Ibid., p. 1.
95. Ibid., p. 22.
96. Ibid., p. 18.
97. Ibid., pp. 146–47.
98. Ibid., pp. 143–44.
99. Ibid., p. 143.
100. Kissinger, "Force and Diplomacy in the Nuclear Age," p. 357.
101. Kissinger, *Nuclear Weapons and Foreign Policy*, p. 136.
102. Ibid., p. 140.
103. Kissinger, "Strategy and Organization," pp. 390–91.
104. Kissinger, *Nuclear Weapons and Foreign Policy*, pp. 191–92.
105. Kissinger, "Military Policy and Defense of the 'Grey Areas,' " p. 420.
106. It should be noted how similar the main lines of this strategy are to the Nixon Doctrine, implemented some fifteen years later.
107. Kissinger, "Military Policy and Defense of the 'Grey Areas,' " p. 422.
108. Kissinger, "American Policy and Preventive War," p. 336.
109. Kissinger believes that Tito's break with the Soviet bloc was caused in part by Stalin's lack of support for Yugoslavia in its claims regarding Trieste. He believes that the correct use of force and diplomacy could create situations that would erode the Soviet bloc. Kissinger writes that "while it is impossible to predict the precise circumstances of a possible split within the Soviet orbit, its general framework can be discerned. . . . It is not clear how much China would risk to rescue the U.S.S.R. from embarrassments in Europe or in the Middle East, or to what lengths the U.S.S.R. is prepared to go to increase the power of China in Asia. A test of our strategy is, therefore, its ability to bring about situations which accentuate differences within the Soviet bloc." See *Nuclear Weapons and Foreign Policy*, p. 148.
110. Kissinger, "Force and Diplomacy in the Nuclear Age," pp. 365–66.

Chapter 6.   American Foreign Policy: Themes of Political Evolution

1. Henry Kissinger, *White House Years* (Boston: Little, Brown, 1979), p. 116.
2. Henry Kissinger, *The Necessity for Choice: Prospects of American Foreign Policy* (New York: Harper and Row, 1961), p. 99.
3. Kissinger, *White House Years,* p. 118.
4. Ibid.
5. Ibid., p. 117.
6. Henry Kissinger, "America and the World: Principle and Pragmatism," *Time,* 27 December 1976.
7. See Kissinger, *The Necessity for Choice,* p. 300.
8. Ibid.
9. For a detailed explanation of the major elements of communist philosophy, see Charles J. McFadden, *The Philosophy of Communism* (New York: Benzinger Brothers, 1963).
10. Kissinger, *The Necessity for Choice,* p. 303.
11. Specifically, Kissinger writes: "From the Soviet point of view, relations between the Soviet and non-Soviet world, therefore, reflect an equilibrium of forces in flux, in which the task of the Communist leadership is to tilt the scale by constant if imperceptible pressure in the direction predetermined by the forces of history." See Henry A. Kissinger, *Nuclear Weapons and Foreign Policy* (New York: Harper and Row, 1957), p. 333. For elaboration of concepts such as the "correlation of forces," see Arthur P. Mendel, ed., *Essential Works of Marxism* (New York: Bantam Books, 1961).
12. Several writers, for example, point out that today a majority of nations call for greater political and economic equality in the state system. "The idea of equality," writes Zbigniew Brzezinski, "is increasingly the underlying mood and the felt aspiration in an increasingly congested world." Hence, for many nations—particularly but not exclusively in the Third World—egalitarianism has become the legitimizing principle of the world community. See Zbigniew Brzezinski, "America in a Hostile World," in *A Decade of Foreign Policy* (Washington, D.C.: Carnegie Endowment for International Peace, 1980), p. 28. See also Robert W. Tucker, *The Inequality of Nations* (New York: Basic Books, 1977).
13. Kissinger, *The Necessity for Choice,* p. 6.
14. Dean Acheson, *Power and Diplomacy* (New York: Atheneum, 1966), p. 69.
15. Ibid.
16. Specifically, Kissinger writes that:

The formalism of the Western approach to negotiations raises the question whether the real obstacle to a flexible and purposeful Western diplomacy is not the absence of moral assurance. The impression is sometimes strong that too many in the West consider conviction incompatible with negotiation. Too often the laudable tendency to see the other point of view is carried to the extreme of refusing to make any moral distinctions. In 1948 Henry Wallace professed to be able to discern no difference between the policies of the West and those of the U.S.S.R.—if anything, he was much more charitable towards the latter. . . . The tendency to equate our moral shortcomings with those of the Soviet bloc deprives the West of the inward assurance to negotiate effectively. See *The Necessity for Choice,* pp. 206–8.

17. Ibid., p. 5.
18. Henry Kissinger, "Reflections on American Diplomacy," *Foreign Affairs* 34 (October 1956): 37.

19. Ibid.

20. Ibid.

21. Kissinger, *The Necessity for Choice*, p. 5.

22. Henry Kissinger, "American Policy and Preventive War," *Yale Review* 34 (March 1955): 322.

23. Ibid., p. 323.

24. Kissinger, *The Necessity for Choice*, pp. 6–7.

25. See Walter Lippmann, *The Cold War: A Study in U.S. Foreign Policy* (New York: Harper and Brothers, 1947), p. 12.

26. Kissinger, *The Necessity for Choice*, p. 308.

27. Ibid., pp. 5–6.

28. Ibid., p. 289.

29. Ibid.

30. Ibid., p. 206.

31. Ibid., p. 5.

32. Ibid., p. 100.

33. Ibid.

34. Ibid., p. 3.

35. Ibid., p. 174.

36. Ibid.

37. Ibid.

38. Ibid., p. 326.

39. Ibid.

40. Kissinger, *Nuclear Weapons and Foreign Policy*, pp. 255–56.

41. Ibid., p. 215.

42. Kissinger, *The Necessity for Choice*, p. 328.

43. Henry Kissinger, *The Troubled Partnership: A Re-appraisal of the Atlantic Alliance* (New York: McGraw-Hill, 1965), p. 34.

44. Ibid., p. 35.

45. Ibid., p. 38.

46. Kissinger, *The Necessity for Choice*, p. 287.

47. George F. Kennan, "The Sources of Soviet Conduct," *Foreign Affairs* 25 (July 1947): 566–82 in *Caging the Bear: Containment and the Cold War*, ed. Charles Gati (Indianapolis, Indiana: Bobbs-Merrill, 1974), pp. 17–18.

48. Ibid., p. 15.

49. Ibid., pp. 22–23.

50. Kissinger uses this term without definition. In general, the context in which he uses the term signifies the idea of social pluralism, i.e., the existence of institutions outside of the control of the state. These institutions exist prior to the state and, therefore, limit its sphere of authority.

51. For a description of convergence, see Zbigniew Brzezinski and Samuel P. Huntington, *Political Power: USA/USSR* (New York: Viking Press, 1963), p. 9–14.

52. See John Kenneth Galbraith, *The New Industrial State*, 4th ed. (Boston: Houghton Mifflin, 1985); and Robert L. Heilbroner, *Business Civilization in Decline* (New York: W. W. Norton, 1976).

53. For a discussion of interest group theory applied to the Soviet Union, see Fredrick C. Barghoorn, *Politics USSR* (Boston: Little, Brown, 1972).

54. For a discussion of the declining role of ideology, see Zbigniew Brzezinski, *Between Two Ages: America's Role in the Technetronic Era* (New York: Penguin Books, 1978), pp. 123–95.

55. Kissinger describes convergence in the following manner:

With respect to Communism, the argument is frequently heard that the Soviet Union is in the midst of profound and inevitable transformations. As it produces more consumers' goods, it will become a less ideological and less militant society, increasingly concerned with material comforts. As the standard of living of Soviet citizens improves and they develop a greater stake in their society, so the argument goes, they will exert increasing pressure for the freedom long familiar in the West. Industrialization requires technical skills and education fosters a questioning spirit. The methods appropriate to fostering economic development in a primitive society will no longer work in a highly elaborated one. . . . According to this theory, a key goal of Western policy must be to promote this beneficial evolution. . . . To the degree that we can encourage the Soviet Union to concentrate on the economic development of its vast territory, we will also foster all the elements inconsistent with dictatorial rule and an aggressive foreign policy.

The Necessity for Choice, pp. 287–88. Kissinger's writings on the possibility of negotiations with the Soviets according to this theory are also instructive: "The rationale for the theory of containment was precisely that it would promote the emergence of a more liberal and humane domestic structure within the Soviet Union. The contrary argument, of course, was equally valid. Barring the evolution of the Soviet system negotiations are futile." *The Necessity for Choice*, p. 191.

56. W. W. Rostow, *The Stages of Growth: A Non-Communist Manifesto* (Cambridge: Cambridge University Press, 1960).

57. Ibid., p. 1.

58. Max Millikan and W. W. Rostow, *A Proposal: Key to an Effective Foreign Policy* (New York: Harper & Brothers, 1957).

59. For other works in this genre see: A. F. K. Organiski, *The Stages of Political Development* (New York: Alfred A. Knopf, 1965); Barbara Ward, *The Rich Nations and the Poor Nations* (New York: W. W. Norton, 1962); John H. Kautsky, ed., *Political Change in Underdeveloped Countries: Nationalism and Communism* (New York: John Wiley and Sons, 1962); and Edward A. Shils, *Political Development in the New States* ('s-Gravenhoge, The Netherlands: Morten, 1962).

60. For a full elaboration, see W. W. Rostow, *Politics and the Stages of Growth* (Cambridge: Cambridge University Press, 1971).

61. Rostow, *The Stages of Growth*, p. 162.

62. Ibid., p. 133.

63. Excellent insights into Rostow's thesis are provided in Brzezinski and Huntington, *Political Power: USA/USSR*, p. 12.

64. Kissinger, *The Necessity for Choice*, pp. 288–89.

65. For a discussion of the works of integration theorists such as Amitai Etzioni, Karl Deutsch, and others, see James E. Dougherty and Robert L. Pfaltzgraff, Jr., *Contending Theories of International Relations* (Philadelphia: J. B. Lippincott, 1971), pp. 279–311.

66. See Ernst B. Haas, *Beyond the Nation State* (Stanford: Stanford University Press, 1964), p. 48.

67. David Mitrany, "The Functional Approach to World Organization," *International Affairs* 24 (July 1948): 350–63; see also David Mitrany, *A Working Peace System* (Chicago: Quadrangle Books, 1966).

68. David P. Calleo, *Europe's Future: The Grand Alternatives* (New York: Horizon Press, 1965), p. 55.

69. For a detailed discussion of this point, see Max Beloff, *The United States and the Unity of Europe* (New York: Vintage Books, 1963).

70. Joseph Kraft, *The Grand Design* (New York: Harper & Row, 1962).

71. Kissinger, *The Troubled Partnership*, p. 33.

72. See Calleo, *Europe's Future,* p. 112.
73. Kissinger, *The Troubled Partnership,* p. 36.
74. Kissinger, *The Necessity for Choice,* p. 289.
75. Ibid.
76. Ibid., p. 301.
77. Ibid., pp. 301–2.
78. Ibid., p. 305.
79. Ibid., p. 290.
80. Ibid., p. 296.
81. Ibid., pp. 296–97.
82. Ibid., p. 305.
83. Ibid., p. 300.
84. Ibid.
85. Ibid.
86. Hedrick Smith, *The Russians* (New York: Quadrangle Books, 1976), p. 507. This emphasis on the nonwestern orientation of Russian culture can be found in other recent books about the Soviet Union by distinguished American journalists. See David K. Shipler, *Russia: Broken Idols, Solemn Dreams* (Middlesex, England: Penguin Books, 1983).
87. Kissinger, *The Necessity for Choice,* p. 306.
88. Ibid.
89. Ibid., p. 299.
90. Ibid., p. 310.
91. Ibid., p. 309.
92. Ibid., p. 316.
93. Ibid., p. 315.
94. Ibid., p. 311.
95. Ibid., p. 310.
96. Kissinger, *The Troubled Partnership,* p. 49.
97. Henry Kissinger, "For a New Atlantic Alliance," *The Reporter,* 14 July 1966.
98. Henry Kissinger, "Illusionist: Why We Misread de Gaulle," *Harper's Magazine,* March 1965.
99. Kissinger, *The Troubled Partnership,* p. 49.
100. Ibid.
101. Ibid., p. 61.
102. This is the essence of Kissinger's observation that de Gaulle was an "illusionist." De Gaulle's efforts to personify grandeur conveyed a sense of grandeur to France.
103. Kissinger, "Illusionist," p. 74.
104. Kissinger, "For a New Atlantic Alliance," p. 21. For similar arguments regarding the future of Germany, see Kissinger, "The Search for Stability," *Foreign Affairs* 37 (July 1959): 537–60; and "The Price of German Unity," *The Reporter,* 22 April 1965.
105. Kissinger, *The Troubled Partnership,* p. 9.
106. Ibid.
107. Kissinger, *The Necessity for Choice,* p. 200.
108. Ibid., p. 210.
109. Ibid., p. 308.
110. Ibid., pp. 311–21.
111. Kissinger, *Nuclear Weapons and Foreign Policy,* p. 260.

112. Ibid., p. 223.
113. Similarly, Kissinger opposed the policy of the Kennedy administration, which he said represented a complete aboutface and which fostered neutrality. See "The Cult of Neutralism," *The Reporter,* 24 November 1960.
114. Kissinger, *Nuclear Weapons and Foreign Policy,* pp. 261–63.
115. Ibid., p. 266.
116. Ibid., p. 265.
117. Kissinger, *The Necessity for Choice,* p. 324.
118. Ibid., pp. 324–25.
119. Kissinger, *The Troubled Partnership,* p. 228.
120. Ibid., p. 5.
121. Named for Christian Fouchet, who held several ministerial posts in de Gaulle's government, the Fouchet Plan is synonymous with de Gaulle's confederal structure—Europe of the States, from the Atlantic to the Urals. See David Calleo, *The Atlantic Fantasy: The U.S., NATO, and Europe* (Baltimore: The Johns Hopkins University Press, 1970), p. 66.
122. Kissinger, *The Troubled Partnership,* p. 244.
123. Ibid., p. 245.
124. Ibid., p. 245–46. See also Kissinger, "For an Atlantic Confederacy," *The Reporter,* 2 February 1961.
125. Kissinger, "For an Atlantic Confederacy," p. 20.
126. Kissinger, *The Necessity for Choice,* p. 9.

Chapter 7. The Historian as Statesman: Kissinger's Legacy

1. See Stanley Hoffmann, *Primacy or World Order: American Foreign Policy Since the Cold War* (New York: McGraw-Hill, 1978).
2. Ibid., p. 3.
3. No central focus like that provided by containment or the Nixon-Kissinger approach has characterized American foreign policy since the decline of détente. For an insightful discussion of American policy since the end of the Kissinger years, see Robert Tucker, *The Purposes of American Power* (New York: Praeger, 1981).
4. Hoffmann, *Primacy or World Order,* p. 34.
5. Stephen R. Graubard, *Kissinger: Portrait of a Mind* (New York: W. W. Norton, 1973), pp. xiii–xiv.
6. See G. Warren Nutter, *Kissinger's Grand Design* (Washington, D.C.: American Enterprise Institute for Public Policy Research, 1975).
7. See Pierre Hassner, "The State of Nixon's World (3): Pragmatic Conservatism in the White House," *Foreign Policy* 3 (Summer 1971): 41–61; and Raymond Aron, "Richard Nixon and the Future of American Foreign Policy," *Atlantic Community Quarterly* 10 (Winter 1972): 437–45.
8. See Seymour M. Hersh, *The Price of Power: Kissinger in the Nixon White House* (New York: Simon and Schuster, 1983).
9. Kissinger's negotiations with "revolutionary" powers such as the North Vietnamese are contrasted with his own ideas on diplomatic negotiations expressed in *A World Restored: Metternich, Castlereagh and the Problems of Peace, 1812–1822* (Boston: Houghton Mifflin, 1957), pp. 73–74.
10. The reference is to Daniel Patrick Moynihan's description of Nixon as

following a course similar to that of the nineteenth-century English statesman. Nixon's image as a conservative allowed him to sponsor social reform, such as national welfare legislation. See Rowland Evans, Jr., and Robert D. Novak, *Nixon in the White House: The Frustration of Power* (New York: Vintage Books, 1971), p. 213.

11. This argument has been a mainstay of the criticism by the political right and the neoconservatives. See Norman Podhoretz, *The Present Danger* (New York: Simon and Schuster, 1980); and Richard Pipes, *Survival Is Not Enough* (New York: Simon and Schuster, 1984).

12. Bruce Mazlish, *Kissinger: The European Mind in American Policy* (New York: Basic Books, 1976), p. 188.

13. See Kissinger, *A World Restored,* p. 326.

14. Hans Morgenthau, "The New Diplomacy of Movement," *Encounter* 43 (August 1974): 52–57.

15. Henry Kissinger, "The Process of Détente," Statement delivered to the Senate Foreign Relations Committee, 19 September 1974, in *American Foreign Policy,* 3rd ed. (New York: W. W. Norton, 1977), p. 145.

16. In referring to the Nixon-Kissinger years, I wish to avoid a discussion as to which man was the primary strategist during this period. Both Nixon and Kissinger significantly influenced foreign policy and diplomacy, and both shared responsibility for the major innovations made during these years.

17. Henry Kissinger, Statement to the Senate Foreign Relations Committee, quoted in Nutter, *Kissinger's Grand Design,* p. 88.

18. Hoffmann, *Primacy or World Order,* p. 46.

19. Quoted in Nutter, *Kissinger's Grand Design,* pp. 88–89.

20. This term is frequently used to describe the conceptual framework of American foreign policy during the Nixon-Kissinger years.

21. President Carter himself admitted that the Soviet Union's reaction to his human rights policies surprised his administration. Carter stated that Soviet reaction "constituted a greater obstacle to common goals like SALT than I anticipated." Quoted in Fred Warner Neal, ed., *Détente or Debacle: Common Sense in U.S.–Soviet Relations* (New York: W. W. Norton, 1979), p. 4.

22. Henry Kissinger, "Continuity and Change in American Foreign Policy," The Arthur K. Solomon Lecture, New York University, 19 September 1977, in Henry A. Kissinger, *For the Record: Selected Statements 1977–1980* (Boston: Little, Brown, 1981), p. 89.

23. Ibid., pp. 88–90.

24. Richard M. Nixon, *U.S. Foreign Policy for the 1970's: A New Strategy for Peace* (Washington, D.C.: U.S. Government Printing Office, 1970), p. 2.

25. Richard M. Nixon, *U.S. Foreign Policy for the 1970's: Building for Peace* (Washington, D.C.: U.S. Government Printing Office, 1971), pp. 4–5.

26. Ibid., p. 5.

27. Ibid.

28. Nixon, *A New Strategy for Peace,* p. 7.

29. Ibid., p. 12. Nixon first made this statement in his inaugural address as a signal to the Soviets of the new administration's policies.

30. The Nixon administration quantified the requirements of the balance at the strategic level in the Strategic Arms Limitation Talks. For general purpose forces, the administration stated that the nation required levels capable of supporting a "1½ war" strategy instead of the "2½ war" strategy of the 1960s.

The stated basis of our conventional posture in the 1960s was the so-called "2½ war" principle. According to it, U.S. forces would be maintained for a three month conventional forward defense of NATO, a defense of Korea or Southeast Asia against a full-scale attack, and a minor contingency—all simultaneously. These force levels were never reached. In the effort to harmonize doctrine and capability, we chose what is best described as the "1½ war" strategy. Under it we will maintain in the peacetime general purpose forces adequate for simultaneously meeting a major Communist attack in either Europe or Asia, assisting allies against non-Chinese threats in Asia, and contending with a contingency elsewhere.

The administration redefined the requirements of the global balance in light of the Sino-Soviet hostility. See Nixon, *A New Strategy for Peace*, pp. 128–29.

31. Kissinger, "The Process of Detente," pp. 171–76.

32. See Henry Kissinger, "The White Revolutionary: Reflections on Bismarck," *Daedalus* 97 (Summer 1968): 888–923; see also James Chace, "Bismarck and Kissinger," *Encounter* 42 (June 1974): 44–47.

33. Nixon's policy of an opening to China was foreshadowed in an article that he wrote before he became president. See Richard Nixon, "Asia After Vietnam," *Foreign Affairs* 46 (October 1967): 111–25. This article was widely read in Peking and Moscow. Kissinger referred to triangular diplomacy in foreign policy speeches that he prepared for Nelson Rockefeller during the 1968 presidential primaries.

34. Kissinger presents this portrayal of the communist bloc in *Nuclear Weapons and Foreign Policy* (New York: Harper and Row, 1957); and *The Necessity for Choice: Prospects of American Foreign Policy* (New York: Harper and Row, 1961), as well as in the articles that he wrote in the 1950s and early 1960s.

35. Nixon used the term "sufficiency" to avoid the political fall-out that would result from basing policy on "parity" as well as to suggest that strategic forces would not be based solely on finite deterrence or minimal force levels. See Nixon, *A New Strategy for Peace*, pp. 121–24.

36. For a discussion of this point, see Robert E. Osgood, "The Nixon Doctrine and Strategy," in Osgood et al., *Retreat from Empire: The First Nixon Administration* (Baltimore: The Johns Hopkins University Press, 1973), pp. 3–10.

37. Kissinger, "Central Issues of American Foreign Policy," in *American Foreign Policy*, p. 97.

38. Nixon, *Building for Peace*, p. 171.

39. The "Sonnenfeldt Doctrine" and the opposition it aroused among American conservatives are vividly portrayed in a series of articles by James Burnham, entitled, "The Kissinger-Sonnenfeldt Doctrine," which appeared in the *National Review* from 14 May 1976 to 11 June 1976. Sonnenfeldt, who was State Department counselor during the Kissinger years, provided justifications for détente that angered the American political right. He characterized détente as a process whereby the United States moderated Soviet power, which was now entering its imperial phase. Clearly, the suggestion was that the Soviet Union was the ascending power, America the descending power. See Helmut Sonnenfeldt, "The Meaning of Détente," *Naval War College Review* 28, no. 1 (Summer 1975): 3–8; and idem, "The United States and the Soviet Union in the Nuclear Age," Address at the U.S. Naval Academy, 6 April 1976 (Washington, D.C.: Department of State, Bureau of Public Affairs, 1976).

40. From a speech given in Kansas City, Missouri on 6 July 1971. Quoted in *Department of State Bulletin* no. 65 (26 July 1971), p. 96.

41. From an interview with President Nixon published in *Time*, 3 January 1972.

42. See Lewis Stone Sorley III, "Conventional Arms Transfers and the Nixon Administration," Ph.D. dissertation, The Johns Hopkins University, 1982.

43. Henry Kissinger, "The Permanent Challenge of Peace: U.S. Policy Toward the Soviet Union," Address to the Commonwealth Club and the World Affairs Council of Northern California, San Francisco, 3 February 1976; also published in *American Foreign Policy*, p. 305.

44. John G. Stoessinger, *Henry Kissinger: The Anguish of Power* (New York: W. W. Norton, 1976), p. 81.

45. See Richard A. Falk, *What's Wrong with Henry Kissinger's Foreign Policy*, Policy Memorandum No. 39 (Center of International Studies, Princeton University, July 1974). For an analysis of the Westphalian system and its implications for contemporary international politics, see Lynn H. Miller, *Global Order: Values and Power in International Politics* (Boulder, Colorado: Westview Press, 1985).

46. Falk, *What's Wrong with Henry Kissinger's Foreign Policy*, pp. 34–36.

47. Trilateralism emphasized orienting American policy toward closer relations with the industrial democracies of Western Europe and Japan in contrast to the East-West orientation of the Nixon-Kissinger policies. Most of the prominent foreign policy officials of the Carter administration, including Carter himself, were Trilateralists. For an excellent description of Trilateralism, see Richard H. Ullman, "Trilateralism: 'Partnership' for What?" *Foreign Affairs* 55, no. 1 (October 1976): 1–19.

48. Despite his later criticism of the "undifferentiated globalism" of American foreign policy, Kissinger himself appears to have underestimated the force of nationalism in the Third World. Even in his earlier writings, there is what Stanley Hoffmann terms "a neglect of local conditions." Kissinger at times seems to fall victim to the dilemma of containment. By this I mean the inability to define America's vital foreign policy interests in certain regions, caused by the belief that perceptions are all-important in the East-West rivalry. Hence, the possible perception of weakness leads to American involvement in areas of only marginal geostrategic interest, lest our weakness serve as a pretext for a challenge in an area of true strategic interest.

49. Edward Vose Gulick, *Europe's Classical Balance of Power* (New York: W. W. Norton, 1955), pp. 19–24.

50. Kissinger stated: "In the years ahead, the most profound challenge to American policy will be philosophical: to develop some concept of order in a world which is bipolar militarily but multipolar politically." See Kissinger, "Central Issues of American Foreign Policy," in *American Foreign Policy*, p. 79.

51. Richard Nixon, *Leaders* (New York: Warner Books, 1982), p. 363.

52. For description and analysis of the NSC system under Kissinger, see J. P. Leacacos, "Kissinger's Apparat," *Foreign Policy* 5 (Winter 1971–1972): 3–27; and I. M. Destler, "Can One Man Do?" *Foreign Policy* 5 (Winter 1971–1972): 28–40.

53. Roger Morris, *Uncertain Greatness: Henry Kissinger and American Foreign Policy* (New York: Harper and Row, 1977), p. 91.

54. Ibid.

55. George W. Ball, *Diplomacy for a Crowded World: An American Foreign Policy* (Boston: Little, Brown, 1976), p. 14.

56. Zbigniew Brzezinski characterized Kissinger as an "acrobat" rather than an architect of foreign policy. Brzezinski's criticism is contained in "U.S. Foreign

Policy: The Search for Focus," *Foreign Affairs* 51, no. 4 (July 1973): 708–27 and "America in a Hostile World," *Foreign Policy* 23 (Summer 1976): 65–96.

57. See Richard Rosecrance, *America as an Ordinary Country: U.S. Foreign Policy and the Future* (Ithaca, New York: Cornell University Press, 1976).

58. See Peter W. Dickson, *Kissinger and the Meaning of History* (Cambridge: Cambridge University Press, 1978), pp. 83–116; and Mazlish, *Kissinger: The European Mind in American Policy*, pp. 177–83.

59. Henry Kissinger, "Reflections on a Partnership: British and American Attitudes to Postwar Foreign Policy," in *Observations: Selected Speeches and Essays, 1982–84* (Boston: Little, Brown, 1985), p. 8.

60. Henry Kissinger, "The Meaning of History: Reflections on Spengler, Toynbee, and Kant," unpublished undergraduate honors thesis (Harvard University, 1950), p. 25.

61. Kissinger, "Central Issues of American Foreign Policy," p. 93.

62. See Robert Koehane and Joseph S. Nye, Jr., *Power and Interdependence* (Boston: Little, Brown, 1977).

63. Kissinger, "The Process of Détente," p. 144.

64. Quoted in Nutter, *Kissinger's Grand Design*, p. 22.

65. Henry Kissinger, *The Troubled Partnership: A Re-appraisal of the Atlantic Alliance* (New York: McGraw-Hill, 1965), p. 64.

Bibliography

Works by Henry Kissinger

1985   *Observations: Selected Speeches and Essays, 1982–1984.* Boston: Little, Brown.

1984   Chairman. The Report of the President's National Bipartisan Commission on Central America. New York: Macmillan.

1982   "Britain and the United States: Reflections on a Partnership." *International Affairs* 58, no. 4 (Autumn): 571–87.
     Years of Upheaval. Boston: Little, Brown.

1981   *For the Record: Selected Statements, 1977–1980.* Boston: Little, Brown.

1980   "The Kissinger Doctrine." *Across the Board* 17, no. 7 (July): 9–17.

1979   *White House Years.* Boston: Little, Brown.

1977   *American Foreign Policy.* 3d Ed. New York: W. W. Norton.

1976   "America and the World: Principle and Pragmatism." *Time,* 27 December, pp. 41–43.

1969   *American Foreign Policy: Three Essays.* New York: W. W. Norton.
     "The Viet Nam Negotiations." *Foreign Affairs* 47, no. 2 (January): 211–34.

1968   "The White Revolutionary: Reflections on Bismarck." *Daedalus* 97 (Summer): 888–923.
     "Bureaucracy and Policy Making: The Effects of Insiders and Outsiders on the Policy Process." In *Bureaucracy, Politics and Strategy.* Edited by B. Brodie. Los Angeles: University of California Press.
     "Central Issues of American Foreign Policy." In *Agenda for the Nation.* Edited by K. Gordon. Washington, D.C.: Brookings Institute.

1967   "Fuller Explanation." *The New York Times Book Review,* 12 February, p. 3. This is a review of Raymond Aron's *Peace and War.*

1966   "Domestic Structure and Foreign Policy." *Daedalus* 95 (Spring): 503–27.
     "For a New Atlantic Alliance." *The Reporter* 35, no. 1 (July 14): 18–27.
     "NATO: Evolution or Decline?" *The Texas Quarterly* 9 (Autumn): 110–18.
     "What About the Future?" *The Atlantic Community Quarterly* 14 (Fall): 317–29.
     "Vietnam: What Should We Do Now?" *Look,* 9 August, p. 26.

1965   *The Troubled Partnership: A Re-appraisal of the Atlantic Alliance.* New York: McGraw–Hill.
     Ed. *Problems of National Strategy: A Book of Readings.* New York: Praeger.
     "The Price of German Unity." *The Reporter* 32, no. 8 (April 22): 12–17.
     "Illusionist: Why We Misread de Gaulle." *Harper's Magazine,* March, pp. 69–70.

1964   "Coalition Diplomacy in the Nuclear Age." *Foreign Affairs* 42, no. 4 (July): 524–45.

"Classical Diplomacy: The Congress of Vienna." In *Power and Order: Six Cases in World Politics.* Edited by J. G. Stoessinger and A. F. Westin. New York: Harcourt, Brace and World.

"Goldwater and the Bomb: Wrong Questions, Wrong Answers." *The Reporter* 31 (November): 27–28.

"The Essentials of Solidarity in the Western Alliance." In *The Conservative Papers.* Introduction by Melvin R. Laird. Chicago: Quadrangle Books.

"Reflections on Power." In *The Dimensions of Diplomacy.* Edited by E. A. J. Johnson. Baltimore: The Johns Hopkins University Press.

1963   "NATO's Nuclear Dilemma." *The Reporter* 28, no. 7 (March 28): 22–37.

"The Skybolt Affair." *The Reporter* 28, no. 2 (January 17): 15–19.

"Strains on the Alliance." *Foreign Affairs* 41, no. 2 (January): 261–85.

1962   "Reflections on Cuba." *The Reporter* 27, no. 9 (November 22): 21–23.

"The Unsolved Problems of European Defense." *Foreign Affairs* 40, no. 4 (July): 515–41.

1961   *The Necessity for Choice: Prospects of American Foreign Policy.* New York: Harper and Row.

"For an Atlantic Confederacy." *The Reporter* 24, no. 3 (February 2): 16–20.

1960   "The Next Summit Meeting." *Harper's Magazine,* December, pp. 60–66.

"The Cult of Neutralism." *The Reporter* 23 (November 24): 26–30.

"Arms Control, Inspection, and Surprise Attack." *Foreign Affairs* 38 (July): 557–75.

"Limited War: Nuclear or Conventional?—A Reappraisal." *Daedalus* 89, no. 4 (Fall): 800–17.

1959   "The Khrushchev Visit: Dangers and Hopes." *The New York Times Magazine,* 6 September, p. 5.

"The Search for Stability." *Foreign Affairs* 37 (July): 537–60.

"The Policymaker and the Intellectual." *The Reporter* 20 (March 5): 30–35.

1958   "Nuclear Testing and the Problems of Peace." *Foreign Affairs* 37 (October): 1–8.

"Missiles and the Western Alliance." *Foreign Affairs* 36 (April): 383–400.

Project director. *Prospect for America: The Rockefeller Panel Reports.* Garden City, New York: Doubleday.

1957   *A World Restored: Metternich, Castlereagh and the Problems of Peace, 1812–1822.* Boston: Houghton Mifflin. This book is the published version of Kissinger's doctoral thesis entitled, "Peace, Legitimacy and the Equilibrium: A Study of the Statesmanship of Castlereagh and Metternich," which was submitted to Harvard University in 1954.

Nuclear Weapons and Foreign Policy. New York: Harper and Row.

"Controls, Inspection and Limited War." *The Reporter* 16 (June 13): 14–18.

"Strategy and Organization." *Foreign Affairs* 35, no. 3 (April): 379–94.

1956   "Reflections on American Diplomacy." *Foreign Affairs* 34 (October): 37–56.

"Force and Diplomacy in the Nuclear Age." *Foreign Affairs* 34 (April): 349–66.

"The Congress of Vienna: A Reappraisal." *World Politics* 8 (January): 264–80.

1955   "The Limitations of Diplomacy." *New Republic* 132 (May 9): 7–8.

"Military Policy and Defense of the 'Grey Areas.'" *Foreign Affairs* 33 (April): 416–28.

"American Policy and Preventive War." *Yale Review* 44 (March): 321–39.

1954   "The Conservative Dilemma: Reflections on the Political Thought of Metternich." *American Political Science Review* 48, no. 4 (December): 1017–30.

1950   "The Meaning of History: Reflections on Spengler, Toynbee and Kant." Undergraduate honors thesis, Harvard University.

Works about Henry Kissinger, His Policies and Statecraft

Allison, Graham. "Cold Dawn and the Mind of Kissinger." *Washington Monthly,* March 1974, pp. 39–47.

Alroy, Gil Carl. *The Kissinger Experience: American Policy in the Middle East.* New York: Horizon Books, 1975.

Ball, George W. "Kissinger's Paper Peace: How Not to Handle the Middle East." *The Atlantic Monthly* 237 (February 1976): 41–49.

Bell, Coral. *The Diplomacy of Détente: The Kissinger Era.* New York: St. Martin's Press, 1977.

———. "Kissinger in Retrospect: The Diplomacy of Power-Concert?" *International Affairs* 53 (April 1977): 202–16.

Beloff, Nora. "Professor Kissinger Goes to Washington: Kissinger on the Job." *Atlantic Monthly* 224 (December 1969): 77–89.

Blumenfeld, Ralph, et al. *Henry Kissinger: The Private and Public Story.* New York: New American Library, 1974.

Brenner, Michael J. "The Problem of Innovation and the Nixon-Kissinger Foreign Policy." *International Studies Quarterly* 17 (September 1973): 255–94.

Brodine, Virginia, and Selden, Mark. *Open Secret: The Kissinger-Nixon Doctrine in Asia.* New York: Harper and Row, 1972.

Brown, Seyom. *The Crises of Power: An Interpretation of United States Foreign Policy During the Kissinger Years.* New York: Columbia University Press, 1979.

Buchan, Alastair. "A World Restored?" *Foreign Affairs* 50, no. 4 (July 1972): 644–59.

———. "The Irony of Henry Kissinger." *International Affairs* 50 (July 1974): 367–79.

Caldwell, Dan. *American-Soviet Relations: From 1947 to the Nixon-Kissinger Grand Design.* Westport, Connecticut: Greenwood Press, 1981.

———, ed. *Henry Kissinger: His Personality and Policies.* Durham, North Carolina: Duke University Press, 1983.

Catlin, Sir George E. G. *Kissinger's Atlantic Charter.* Gerrards Cross, England: C. Smythe, 1974.

Chace, James. "Bismarck and Kissinger." *Encounter* 42 (June 1974): 44–47.

———. "The Kissinger Years." *New Republic,* 9 November 1974, pp. 30–33.

Chailand, Gerard. "Kissinger's Diplomacy." *New Outlook* 18, no. 3 (March-April 1975): 11–18.

Davis, Vincent. *Henry Kissinger and Bureaucratic Politics: A Personal Appraisal.* Institute of International Studies Essay Series, The University of South Carolina. Columbia, South Carolina: University of South Carolina Press, 1979.

Destler, I. M. "Can One Man Do?" *Foreign Policy* 5 (Winter 1971–72): 28–40.

Dickson, Peter. *Kissinger and the Meaning of History.* Cambridge: Cambridge University Press, 1978.

Draper, Theodore. "Kissinger's Apologia." *Dissent* 27 (Spring 1980): 233–54.

———. "Detente." *Commentary* 57 (June 1974): 25–47.

El-Khavias, M. A., and Cohen, B., eds. *The Kissinger Study of Southern Africa: National Security Memorandum 39.* Westport, Connecticut: Greenwood Press, 1976.

Falk, Richard A. *What's Wrong with Henry Kissinger's Foreign Policy.* Policy Memorandum No. 39, Center of International Studies, Princeton University, July 1974.

Girling, J. L. S. " 'Kissingerism': The Enduring Problems." *International Affairs* 51 (July 1975): 323–43.

Golan, Matti. *The Secret Conversations of Henry Kissinger: Step-by-Step Diplomacy in the Middle East.* New York: Quadrangle Books, 1976.

Graebner, Norman A. "Henry Kissinger and American Foreign Policy: A Contemporary Appraisal." *The Australian Journal of Politics and History* 22, no. 1 (April 1976): 7–22.

Graubard, Stephen R. *Kissinger: Portrait of a Mind.* New York: W. W. Norton, 1973.

Griffith, Thomas. "Judging Kissinger." *The Atlantic Monthly* 238 (July 1976): 22–23.

Hallett, Douglas. "Kissinger Dolosus: The Domestic Politics of SALT." *The Yale Review* 65 (December 1975): 161–74.

Head, Simon. "The Kissinger Philosophy." *New Statesman,* 2 March 1973, pp. 295–301.

Hersh, Seymour M. *The Price of Power: Kissinger in the Nixon White House.* New York: Summit Books, 1983.

Kalb, Marvin, and Kalb, Bernard. *Kissinger.* Boston: Little, Brown, 1974.

Kraft, Joseph. "In Search of Kissinger." *Harper's Magazine,* January 1971, pp. 54–61.

Lefeber, Walter. "Kissinger and Acheson: The Secretary of State and the Cold War." *Political Science Quarterly* 92 (Summer 1977): 189–97.

Landau, David. *Kissinger: The Uses of Power.* Boston: Houghton Mifflin, 1972.

Laqueur, Walter. "Kissinger and the Politics of Détente." *Commentary* 56 (December 1973): 42–52.

——— and Luttwak, E. N. "Kissinger and the Yom Kippur War." *Commentary* 58 (September 1974): 33–40.

Leacacos, J. P. "Kissinger's Apparat." *Foreign Policy* 5 (Winter 1971–72): 3–27.

Liska, George. *Beyond Kissinger: Ways of Conservative Statecraft.* Baltimore: The Johns Hopkins University Press, 1975.

Mazlish, Bruce. *Kissinger: The European Mind in American Policy.* New York: Basic Books, 1976.

Montgomery, John S. "The Education of Henry Kissinger." *Journal of International Affairs* 9, no. 1 (1975): 49–62.

Morgan, John. "Kissinger and Metternich." *New Statesman,* 23 June 1972, pp. 264–65.

Morgenthau, Hans. "Henry Kissinger, Secretary of State." *Encounter* 43 (November 1974): 57–61.

———. "The New Diplomacy of Movement." *Encounter* 43 (August 1974): 52–57.

Morris, Roger. *Uncertain Greatness: Henry Kissinger and American Foreign Policy.* New York: Harper and Row, 1977.

Neal, Fred Warner, and M. K. Harvey, eds. *Pacem in Terris III: The Nixon-Kissinger Foreign Policy: Opportunities and Contradictions.* Santa Barbara, California: Center for the Study of Democratic Institutions, 1974.

Noer, Thomas J. "Henry Kissinger's Philosophy of History." *Modern Age* 19 (Spring 1975): 180–89.

Nutter, G. Warren. *Kissinger's Grand Design.* Washington, D.C.: American Enterprise Institute for Public Policy Research, 1975.

Perlmutter, Amos. "Crisis Management—Kissinger's Middle East Negotiations (October 1973–June 1974)." *International Studies Quarterly* 19 (September 1975): 316–43.

Podhoretz, Norman. "Kissinger Reconsidered." *Commentary* 73, no. 6 (June 1982): 19–28.

Quandt, William B. "Kissinger and the Arab-Israeli Disengagement Negotiations." *Journal of International Affairs* 29, no. 1 (Spring 1975): 33–48.

Rubin, J. Z. *Dynamics of Third Party Intervention: Kissinger in the Middle East.* New York: Praeger, 1981.

Sewell, James P. "Master Builder or Captain of the Dike? Notes on the Leadership of Kissinger." *International Journal* 31 (Autumn 1976): 648–65.

Shawcross, William. *Sideshow: Kissinger, Nixon and the Destruction of Cambodia.* New York: Simon and Schuster, 1979.

Sheehan, Edward R. F. *The Arabs, Israelis and Kissinger: A Secret History of American Diplomacy in the Middle East.* New York: Readers Digest Press, 1976.

Smart, Ian. "The New Atlantic Charter." *The World Today* 29 (June 1973): 238–43.

Sobel, Lester, ed. *Kissinger and Détente.* New York: Facts on File, 1975.

Starr, Harvey. *Henry Kissinger: Perceptions of International Politics.* Lexington, Kentucky: The University of Kentucky Press, 1984.

Stoessinger, John G. *Henry Kissinger: The Anguish of Power.* New York: W. W. Norton, 1976.

Stone, I. F. "The Flowering of Henry Kissinger." *The New York Review of Books,* 2 November 1972, pp. 21–27.

Thimmesch, Nick. "Dr. Fritz Kraemer: Kissinger's Iron Mentor." *The Washington Post—Potomac Magazine Section,* 2 March 1975, p. 14.

Valeriani, Richard. *Travels with Henry.* Boston: Houghton Mifflin, 1979.

Walker, Stephen G. "The Interface Between Beliefs and Behavior: Henry Kissinger's Operational Code and the Vietnam War." *Journal of Conflict Resolution* 21 (March 1979): 129–68.

Ward, Dana. "Kissinger: A Psychohistory." *History of Childhood Quarterly* 2 (Winter 1975): 287–348.

Watt, D. C. "Henry Kissinger: An Interim Judgment." *The Political Quarterly* 48, no. 1 (January–March 1977): 3–13.

Weber, William T. "Kissinger as Historian: A Historiographical Approach to Statesmanship." *International Affairs* 141, no. 1 (Summer 1978): 40–56.

Windsor, Philip. "Henry Kissinger's Scholarly Contribution." *British Journal of International Studies* 1 (April 1975): 27–37.

Texts and Articles on American Foreign Policy and the Nixon-Kissinger Era

Aron, Raymond. "Richard Nixon and the Future of American Foreign Policy." *Atlantic Community Quarterly* 10 (Winter 1972): 437–45.

Ball, George W. *Diplomacy for a Crowded World: An American Foreign Policy.* Boston: Little, Brown, 1976.

Barber, Stephen. *America in Retreat.* Galeshead, England: Northumberland Press, 1970.

Bell, Daniel. "The End to American Exceptionalism." In *The American Commonwealth—1976.* Edited by Nathan Glazer and Irving Kristol. New York: Basic Books, 1976.

Brandon, Donald. "A New Foreign Policy for America." *World Affairs* 138, no. 2 (Fall 1975): 83–107.

Brandon, Henry. *The Retreat of American Power.* Garden City, New York: Doubleday, 1973.

Brzezinski, Zbigniew. "The State of Nixon's World (1): Half Past Nixon." *Foreign Policy* 3 (Summer 1971): 3–21.

———. "The Balance of Power Delusion." *Foreign Policy* 7 (Summer 1972): 54–59.

———. "How the Cold War Was Played." *Foreign Affairs* 51 (October 1972): 739–66.

———. "U.S. Foreign Policy: The Search for Focus." 51 *Foreign Affairs* (July 1973): 708–27.

———. "The Deceptive Structure of Peace." *Foreign Policy* 14 (Spring 1974): 35–54.

Buchan, Alastair. *Power and Equilibrium in the 1970's.* New York: Praeger, 1973.

———. *The End of the Postwar Era: A New Balance of World Power.* London: Weidenfeld and Nicolson, 1974.

Chace, James. "The Five-Power World of Richard Nixon." *The New York Times Magazine,* February 1972, pp. 14–47.

———. *A World Elsewhere: The New American Foreign Policy.* New York: Charles Scribner's Sons, 1973.

Cox, Arthur Macy. *The Dynamics of Détente.* New York: W. W. Norton, 1976.

Destler, I. M. *Presidents, Bureaucrats and Foreign Policy: The Politics of Organizational Reform.* Princeton: Princeton University Press, 1972.

Dornan, James E., Jr. "The Nixon Doctrine and the Primacy of Détente." *The Intercollegiate Review* 9, no. 2 (Spring 1974): 77–97.

Evans, Rowland, Jr., and Novak, Robert D. *Nixon in the White House: The Frustration of Power.* New York: Random House, 1971.

Ford, Gerald. *A Time to Heal.* New York: Berkeley Books, 1980.

Gardner, Lloyd C. *The Great Nixon Turnaround.* New York: New Viewpoints, 1973.

Garrett, Stephen A. "Nixonian Foreign Policy: A New Balance of Power—or a Revived Concert?" *Polity* 9, no. 3 (Spring 1973): 389–421.

Gilbert, Stephen P. "Implications of the Nixon Doctrine for Military Aid Policy." *Orbis* 16 (Fall 1972): 660–81.

Hahn, Walter F. "The Nixon Doctrine: Design and Dilemmas." *Orbis* 16 (Summer 1972): 361–76.

Hartley, Anthony. *American Foreign Policy in the Nixon Era.* Adelphi Papers 110. London: International Institute for Strategic Studies, 1975.

Hassner, Pierre. "The State of Nixon's World (3): Pragmatic Conservatism in the White House." *Foreign Policy* 3 (Summer 1971): 41–61.

Hoffmann, Stanley. "Will the Balance Balance at Home." *Foreign Policy* 7 (Summer 1972): 60–87.

———. "Weighing the Balance of Power." *Foreign Affairs* 50, no. 4 (July 1972): 618–43.

———. "Notes on the Elusiveness of Modern Power." *International Journal* 30 (Spring 1975): 183–206.

———. "Choices." *Foreign Policy* 12 (Fall 1973): 3–42.

———. "No Choice, No Illusions." *Foreign Policy* 25 (Winter 1976–77): 96–140.

———. "The Uses of American Power." *Foreign Affairs* 56, no. 1 (October 1977): 27–48.

———. *Primacy or World Order: American Foreign Policy Since the Cold War.* New York: McGraw-Hill, 1978.

Jay, Peter. "Regionalism as Geopolitics." *Foreign Affairs* 58 *(America And The World 1979)*: 485–514.

Jones, Alan M., Jr., ed. *U.S. Foreign Policy in a Changing World: The Nixon Administration, 1969–1973.* New York: David McKay, 1973.

Kattenburg, Paul M. "The Nixon 'New Look' in Foreign Policy." *World Affairs* 135 (Fall 1972): 115–27.

Kohl, Wilfred. "The Nixon-Kissinger Foreign Policy System and U.S.-European Relations: Patterns of Policy Making." *World Politics* 27 (October 1975): 1–43.

Kolodziej, Edward A. "Foreign Policy and the Politics of Interdependence: The Nixon Presidency." *Polity* 9, no. 2 (Winter 1976): 121–57.

Laird, Melvin R. *The Nixon Doctrine.* Washington, D.C.: American Enterprise Institute for Public Policy Research, 1972.

Lake, Anthony. *The "Tar Baby" Option: American Policy Toward Southern Rhodesia.* New York: Columbia University Press, 1976.

Lowenthal, Richard. "A World Adrift." *Encounter,* February 1972, pp. 22–29.

Neal, Fred Warner, ed. *Détente or Debacle: Common Sense in U.S.-Soviet Relations.* New York: W. W. Norton, 1979.

Newhouse, John. *Cold Dawn: The Story of SALT.* New York: Holt, Rinehart and Winston, 1973.

Nixon, Richard M. "Asia After Viet Nam." *Foreign Affairs* 46, no. 1 (October 1967): 111–25.

———. *A New Road for America: Major Policy Statements March 1970 to October 1971.* Garden City, New York: Doubleday, 1972.

————. *RN: The Memoirs of Richard Nixon.* New York: Grosset and Dunlap, 1978.

————. *The Real War.* New York: Warner Books, 1980.

————. *Leaders.* New York: Warner Books, 1982.

————. *Real Peace.* Boston: Little, Brown, 1983.

————. *No More Vietnams.* New York: Avon Books, 1985.

Osgood, Robert, ed. *America and the World, Volume II: Retreat from Empire? The First Nixon Administration.* Baltimore: The Johns Hopkins University Press, 1973.

Pierre, Andrew J. "Europe and America in a Pentagonal World." *Survey* 18, no. 1 (Winter 1972): 183–201.

Pranger, Robert J. *Détente and Defense: A Reader.* Washington, D.C.: American Enterprise Institute for Public Policy Research, 1976.

Quandt, William B. *Decade of Decisions: American Policy Toward the Arab-Israeli Conflict, 1967–1976.* Berkeley, California: University of California Press, 1977.

Ravenal, Earl C. "The Nixon Doctrine and Our Asian Commitments." *Foreign Affairs* 49 (January 1971): 201–17.

————. "The State of Nixon's World (2): The Political-Military Gap." *Foreign Policy* 3 (Summer 1971): 22–40.

Rosecrance, Richard. "Détente or Entente?" *Foreign Affairs* 53, no. 3 (April 1975): 464–81.

————, ed. *America as an Ordinary Country: U.S. Foreign Policy and the Future.* Ithaca, New York: Cornell University Press, 1976.

Safire, William. *Before the Fall: An Inside View of the Pre-Watergate White House.* Garden City, New York: Doubleday, 1975.

Schell, Jonathan. *Time of Illusion.* New York: Alfred A. Knopf, 1976.

Shulman, Marshall. "What Does Security Mean Today." *Foreign Affairs* 49, no. 4 (July 1971): 607–18.

Smith, Gerard. *Doubletalk: The Story of the First Strategic Arms Limitation Talks.* Garden City, New York: Doubleday, 1980.

Snepp, Frank. *Decent Interval.* New York: Random House, 1977.

Sonnenfeldt, Helmut. "The Meaning of Détente." *Naval War College Review* 28, no. 1 (Summer 1975): 3–8.

————. "The United States and the Soviet Union in the Nuclear Age." Address to the U.S. Naval Academy, 6 April 1976. Washington, D.C.: Department of State, Bureau of Public Affairs, 1976.

————. "Russia, America and Detente." *Foreign Affairs* 56, no. 2 (January 1978): 275–94.

Spanier, John W. *American Foreign Policy Since World War II.* 4th edition. New York: Praeger, 1972.

Steibel, Gerald. *Détente: Promises and Pitfalls.* New York: Crane, Russak, 1975.

Stoessinger, John G. *Crusaders and Pragmatists: Movers of Modern American Foreign Policy.* New York: W. W. Norton, 1979.

Szulc, Tad. "Lisbon and Washington: Behind Portugal's Revolution." *Foreign Policy* 21 (Winter 1975–76): 3–62.

————. *The Illusion of Peace: Foreign Policy in the Nixon Years.* New York: Viking Press, 1978.

Wood, Robert Jefferson. "Military Assistance and the Nixon Doctrine." *Orbis* 15 (Spring 1971): 247–74.

American Foreign Policy

Acheson, Dean. *Power and Diplomacy.* New York: Atheneum, 1966.

————. *Present at the Creation.* New York: W. W. Norton, 1969.

Adler, Selig. *The Isolationist Impulse: The Twentieth Century Reaction.* New York: Collier Books, 1961.

Allison, Graham T. *Essence of Decision: Explaining the Cuban Missile Crisis.* Boston: Little, Brown, 1971.

Almond, Gabriel A. *The American People and Foreign Policy.* New York: Praeger, 1965.

Aron, Raymond. *On War.* New York: Doubleday, 1957.

————. *The Great Debate: Theories of Nuclear Strategy.* New York: Doubleday, 1965.

Barghoorn, Fredrick C. *Politics in the USSR.* Boston: Little, Brown, 1972.

Beloff, Max. *The United States and the Unity of Europe.* New York: Vintage Books, 1963.

Black, C. E. *The Dynamics of Modernization: A Study in Comparative History.* New York: Harper and Row, 1975.

Bloomfield, Lincoln P. *The Foreign Policy Process: A Modern Primer.* Englewood Cliffs, New Jersey: Prentice-Hall, 1982.

Bohlen, Charles E. *The Transformation of American Power.* New York: W. W. Norton, 1969.

Brodie, Bernard. *Strategy In the Missile Age.* Princeton: Princeton University Press, 1959.

Brogan, D. W. *The American Character.* New York: Alfred A. Knopf, 1944.

Brzezinski, Zbigniew, and Huntington, Samuel P. *Political Power: USA/USSR.* New York: Viking Press, 1963.

Brzezinski, Zbigniew. *Between Two Ages: America's Role in the Technetronic Era.* Middlesex, England: Penguin Books, 1971.

————. "America in a Hostile World." *Foreign Policy* 23 (Summer 1976): 65–96.

————. *Power and Principle: Memoirs of the National Security Adviser, 1977–1981.* New York: Farrar, Straus, Giroux, 1983.

Bull, Hedley. *The Anarchical Society: A Study of Order in World Politics.* New York: Columbia University Press, 1977.

Calleo, David P. *Europe's Future: The Grand Alternatives.* New York: Horizon Press, 1965.

————. *The Atlantic Fantasy: The U.S., NATO and Europe.* Baltimore: The Johns Hopkins University Press, 1970.

Calvocoressi, Peter. *International Politics Since 1945.* New York: Praeger, 1968.

Campbell, John Franklin. *The Foreign Affairs Fudge Factory.* New York: Basic Books, 1971.

Charlesworth, James C., ed. *Contemporary Political Analysis.* New York: The Free Press, 1967.

de Tocqueville, Alexis. *Democracy in America.* New York: The New American Library, 1956. First published in 1835 and 1840.

Donovan, John C. *The Cold Warriors: A Policy-Making Elite.* Lexington, Kentucky: University of Kentucky Press, 1974.

Dougherty, James E., and Pfaltzgraff, Robert L., Jr. *Contending Theories of International Relations.* Philadelphia: J. B. Lippincott, 1971.

Gaddis, John Lewis. *Strategies of Containment: A Critical Appraisal of Postwar American National Security Policy.* New York: Oxford University Press, 1982.

Galbraith, John Kenneth. *The New Industrial State.* 4th ed. Boston: Houghton Mifflin, 1985.

Gati, Charles, ed. *Caging the Bear: Containment and the Cold War.* Indianapolis: Bobbs-Merrill, 1974.

Gellman, Barton. *Contending with Kennan: Toward a Philosophy of American Power.* New York: Praeger, 1984.

Glazer, Nathan, and Kristol, Irving, eds. *The American Commonwealth.* New York: Basic Books, 1976.

Goldman, Eric F. *The Crucial Decade and After: America, 1945–1960.* New York: Vintage Books, 1960.

Graebner, Norman. *The New Isolationism: A Study in Politics and Foreign Policy Since 1950.* New York: Ronald Press, 1956.

Haig, Alexander, M. *Caveat: Realism, Reagan, and Foreign Policy.* New York: Macmillan, 1984.

Haile, Pennington. *The Eagle and the Bear: The Philosophical Roots of Democracy and Communism.* New York: David McKay Company, 1965.

Halberstam, David. *The Best and the Brightest.* Greenwich, Connecticut: Fawcett, 1973.

Halperin, Morton. *Limited War: An Essay on the Development of the Theory and an Annotated Bibliography.* Cambridge: Harvard University Center for International Affairs, 1962.

———. *Limited War in the Nuclear Age.* New York: John Wiley, 1963.

———. *Bureaucratic Politics and Foreign Policy.* Washington, D.C.: Brookings Institute, 1974.

Herz, John H. *International Politics in the Atomic Age.* New York: Columbia University Press, 1959.

Hilsman, Roger. *The Politics of Policy Making in Defense and Foreign Affairs.* New York: Harper and Row, 1971.

Hoffmann, Stanley. *The State of War: Essays in the Theory and Practice of International Politics.* New York: Praeger, 1965.

———. *Gulliver's Troubles, or The Setting of American Foreign Policy.* New York: McGraw-Hill, 1968.

Hoopes, Townsend. *The Devil and John Foster Dulles.* Boston: Little, Brown, 1973.

Huntington, Samuel P. *The Common Defense: Strategic Problems in National Politics.* New York: Columbia University Press, 1961.

Irish, Marion D. "The Organization Man in the Presidency." *Journal of Politics* 20 (May 1958): 259–77.

Kaufmann, William W. *The McNamara Strategy.* New York: Harper and Row, 1964.

Kautsky, John H., ed. *Political Change in Underdeveloped Countries: Nationalism and Communism.* New York: John Wiley and Sons, 1962.

Kennan, George F. "America's Administrative Response to Its World Problems." *Daedalus* 87 (Spring 1958): 5–24.

——. *Realities of American Foreign Policy.* New York: W. W. Norton, 1966.

——. *The Cloud of Danger: Current Realities of American Foreign Policy.* Boston: Little, Brown, 1977.

Kinnard, Douglas. *President Eisenhower and Strategy Management: A Study in Defense Politics.* Lexington, Kentucky: University of Kentucky Press, 1977.

Kraft, Joseph. *The Grand Design.* New York: Harper and Row, 1962.

Levine, Robert A. *The Arms Debate.* Cambridge: Harvard University Press, 1963.

Lippmann, Walter. *The Cold War: A Study in U.S. Foreign Policy.* New York: Harper and Brothers, 1947.

——. *U.S. Foreign Policy: Shield of the Republic.* New York: Pocket Books, 1943.

——. *The Public Philosophy.* New York: New American Library, 1955.

McFadden, Charles J. *The Philosophy of Communism.* New York: Benziger Brothers, 1963.

Mendel, Arthur P., ed. *The Essential Works of Marxism.* New York: Bantam Books, 1961.

Millikan, Max, and Rostow, W. W. *A Proposal: Key to an Effective Foreign Policy.* New York: Harper and Brothers, 1957.

Morgenthau, Hans J. *In Defense of the National Interest: A Critical Examination of American Foreign Policy.* New York: Alfred A. Knopf, 1951.

——. "Can We Entrust Defense to a Committee?" *New York Times Magazine,* 7 June 1959.

——. *Politics Among Nations.* 5th ed. New York: Alfred A. Knopf, 1973.

Nathan, James A., and Oliver, James K. *United States Foreign Policy and World Order.* Boston: Little, Brown, 1981.

Neibuhr, Reinhold. *The Irony of American History.* New York: Scribner's, 1952.

Neustadt, Richard E. *Presidential Power: The Politics of Leadership.* New York: John Wiley, 1960.

——. *Alliance Politics.* New York: Columbia University Press, 1970.

Organiski, A. F. K. *The Stages of Political Development.* New York: Alfred A. Knopf, 1965.

Osgood, Robert E. *Limited War: The Challenge to American Security.* Chicago: University of Chicago Press, 1957.

——. *Ideals and Self-Interest in America's Foreign Relations.* 5th ed. Chicago: University of Chicago Press, 1965.

——. *Alliances and American Foreign Policy.* Baltimore: The Johns Hopkins University Press, 1971.

——. *Limited War Revisited.* Boulder, Colorado: Westview Press, 1979.

Pipes, Richard. *Survival Is Not Enough: Soviet Realities and America's Future.* New York: Simon and Schuster, 1984.

Potter, David M. *People of Plenty: Economic Abundance and the American Character.* Chicago: University of Chicago Press, 1954.

Rostow, W. W. *The Stages of Economic Growth: A Non-Communist Manifesto.* Cambridge: Cambridge University Press, 1960.

——. *The Dynamics of Soviet Society.* New York: W. W. Norton, 1967.

——. *Politics and the Stages of Growth.* Cambridge: Cambridge University Press, 1971.

Salmon, Jeffrey; O'Leary, James P.; and Schultz, Richard, eds. *Power, Principles & Interests: A Reader for World Politics.* Boston: Ginn Press, 1985.

Schaetzel, Robert J. *The Unhinged Alliance: America and the European Community.* New York: Harper and Row, 1975.

Snyder, Glenn H. *Deterrence and Defense: Toward a Theory of National Security.* Princeton: Princeton University Press, 1961.

Spanier, John. *World Politics in an Age of Revolution.* New York: Praeger, 1967.

———. *Games Nations Play: Analyzing International Politics.* New York: Praeger, 1972.

Steel, Ronald. *Pax Americana.* New York: Viking Press, 1967.

Stone, I. F. *The Haunted Fifties.* New York: Random House, 1963.

Strausz-Hupe, Robert; Kinter, William R.; and Possony, Stefan T. *A Forward Strategy for America.* New York: Harper and Brothers, 1961.

Taylor, Maxwell D. *The Uncertain Trumpet.* New York: Harper and Brothers, 1959.

Toynbee, Arnold J. *America and the World Revolution.* New York: Oxford University Press, 1962.

Tucker, Robert W. *The Inequality of Nations.* New York: Basic Books, 1977.

Ulam, Adam. *The Rivals: America and Russia Since World War II.* New York: Viking Press, 1971.

Ungar, Sanford J., ed. *Estrangement: America and the World.* New York: Oxford University Press, 1985.

Vance, Cyrus. *Hard Choices: Critical Years in America's Foreign Policy.* New York: Simon and Schuster, 1983.

Waltz, Kenneth N. *Man, the State, and War.* New York: Columbia University Press, 1959.

Ward, Barbara. *The Rich Nations and the Poor Nations.* New York: W. W. Norton, 1962.

Wolfers, Arnold. *Discord and Collaboration: Essays on International Politics.* Baltimore: The Johns Hopkins University Press, 1965.

Public Documents

U.S. President. *U.S. Foreign Policy for the 1970's: A New Strategy for Peace.* A Report to the Congress by Richard M. Nixon, President of the United States, 18 February 1970. Washington, D.C.: U.S. Government Printing Office, 1970.

U.S. President, *U.S. Foreign Policy for the 1970's: Building for Peace.* A Report to the Congress by Richard M. Nixon, President of the United States, 25 February 1971. Washington, D.C.: U.S. Government Printing Office, 1971.

U.S. President. *U.S. Foreign Policy for the 1970's: The Emerging Structure of Peace.* A Report to the Congress by Richard M. Nixon, President of the United States, 9 February 1972. Washington, D.C.: U.S. Government Printing Office, 1972.

U.S. President, *U.S. Foreign Policy for the 1970's: Shaping a Durable Peace.* A Report to the Congress by Richard M. Nixon, President of the United States, 3 May 1973. Washington, D.C.: U.S. Government Printing Office, 1973.

Kissinger Interviews

Fallaci, Oriana. "Henry Kissinger." *Interview with History.* Boston: Houghton Mifflin, 1976, pp. 17–45.

Reston, James. "Partial Transcript of an Interview with Kissinger on the State of the Western World." *New York Times,* 13 October 1974.

———. "Excerpts from an Interview with Kissinger: Eight Years in Washington Evaluated." *New York Times,* 20 January 1977.

Dissertations and Theses Concerning Kissinger and the Nixon-Kissinger Foreign Policy Approach

Bendel, Jeffry R. "Scholar Versus Statesman: The Record of Henry Kissinger. The United States and Western Europe." Ph.D. dissertation, University of Massachusetts, 1982.

Caldwell, Dan Edward. "American-Soviet Détente and the Nixon-Kissinger Grand Design and Grand Strategy." Ph.D. dissertation, Stanford University, 1978.

Ghanayem, Ishaq Isa. "The Nixon-Kissinger Middle East Strategy, 1969–1974." Ph.D. dissertation, University of California, Santa Barbara, 1980.

Lee, Jung Ha. "The Impact of the Nixon Doctrine on South Korea: A Critical Analysis of U.S.–South Korean Relations, 1969–1976." Ph.D. dissertation, The Catholic University of America, 1980.

Richardson, Mary Theresa. "Henry Kissinger: A Leadership Analysis Using Erik Erikson's Model of Identity Growth." Ph.D. dissertation, University of Michigan, 1980.

Roncelli, Janet Maria. "A Symbolic Analysis of Henry Kissinger's Public Image in the Print Media, 1969–1976." Ph.D. dissertation, Wayne State University, 1978.

Rosenberger, Leif Roderic. "The Evolution of the Nixon-Kissinger Policy Toward the Soviet Union: An Analysis of the Cold War Legacy and the Ambivalent Pursuit of Détente." Ph.D. dissertation, Claremont Graduate School, 1979.

Smith, Michael Joseph. "Realism as an Approach to International Relations: A Critical Analysis." Ph.D. dissertation, Harvard University, 1982.

Sorley, Lewis Stone, III. "Conventional Arms Transfers and the Nixon Administration." Ph.D. dissertation, The Johns Hopkins University, 1979.

Sullivan, Denis Joseph. "A Comparative Analysis of John Foster Dulles and Henry A. Kissinger and the Impact of Their Personalities on the Formulation of American Foreign Policy." Master's thesis, Western Michigan University, 1981.

Texts and Articles Concerning the Continental Tradition

Acton, Lord. *Historical Essays and Studies.* London: Macmillan, 1926.

Antoni, Carlo. *From History to Sociology: The Transition in German Historical Thinking.* Detroit: Wayne State University Press, 1959.

Bagley, Philip. *Culture and History: Prolegomena to the Comparative Study of Civilizations.* Berkeley and Los Angeles: University of California Press, 1959.

Barber, John. *The Superhistorians: Makers of Our Past.* New York: Charles Scribner's Sons, 1982.

Barnard, F. M., ed. *J. G. Herder on Social and Political Culture.* Cambridge: Cambridge University Press, 1969.

Barrett, William. *The Illusion of Technique.* Garden City, New York: Anchor Press/Doubleday, 1978.

Beck, Louis White, ed. *Kant on History.* Indianapolis: Bobbs-Merrill, 1968.

Beck, Robert N., and Lee, Dwight E. "The Meaning of Historicism." *The American Historical Review* 59, no. 3 (April 1954): 468–77.

Becker, Carl. *The Heavenly City of the Eighteenth-Century Philosophers.* New Haven and London: Yale University Press, 1975.

Bergson, Henri. *The Creative Mind: An Introduction to Metaphysics.* New York: Philosophical Library, 1946.

Berlin, Isaiah, ed. *The Age of Enlightenment.* New York: New American Library, 1956.

———. "The Concept of Scientific History." *History and Theory* (1960): 1–31.

———. *Vico and Herder.* New York: Viking Press, 1976.

Bredvold, Louis. *The Brave New World of the Enlightenment.* Ann Arbor, Michigan: University of Michigan Press, 1961.

Brinton, Crane. *The Shaping of Modern Thought.* Englewood Cliffs, New Jersey: Prentice-Hall, 1950.

Broad, C. D. *Leibniz: An Introduction.* Cambridge: Cambridge University Press, 1975.

Carr, Edward Hallett. *The Twenty Years' Crisis, 1919–1939: An Introduction to the Study of International Relations.* New York: Harper and Row, 1964.

———. *What Is History?* New York: Vintage Books, 1967.

Carr, Herbert Weldon. *Leibniz.* New York: Dover, 1960.

Cassirer, Ernst. *The Philosophy of the Enlightenment.* Boston: Beacon Press, 1955.

Coker, F. W. *Organismic Theories of the State.* New York: Longmens, Green, 1910.

Colinger, Ronald; Marchend, James W.; and Risse, Guenter B. *The Influence of Early Enlightenment Thought Upon German Classical Sciences and Letters.* New York: Science History Publications, 1972.

Collingwood, R. G. "Oswald Spengler and the Theory of Historical Cycles." *Antiquity* 1 (September 1927): 311–25.

———. *Idea of History.* New York: Oxford University Press, 1956.

Craig, Gordon A. *From Bismarck to Adenauer: Aspects of German Statecraft.* Rev. ed. New York: Harper and Row, 1965.

Crankshaw, Edward. *Bismarck.* New York: Viking Press, 1981.

D'Arcy, M. C. S. J. *The Sense of History Secular and Sacred.* London: Faber and Faber, 1959.

Davis, H. W. C. *The Political Thought of Heinrich von Treitschke.* New York: Charles Scribner's Sons, 1915.

Dehio, Ludwig. *The Precarious Balance: Four Centuries of the European Power Struggle.* New York: Vintage Books, 1965.

DeMadriaga, Salvador. *Englishmen, Frenchmen, Spaniards.* New York: Hill and Wang, 1969.

Dewey, John. *German Philosophy and Politics*. New York: Henry Holt, 1915.

Dickens, A. G. *Reformation and Society in Sixteenth Century Europe*. London: Themes and Hudson, 1966.

Dray, William. "Toynbee's Search for Historical Laws." *History and Theory* 1 (1960): 32–54.

Elliott, William Y. *The Pragmatic Revolt in Politics: Syndicalism, Fascism and the Constitutional State*. New York: Macmillan, 1928.

————, and McDonald, Neil A. *Western Political Heritage*. New York: Prentice-Hall, 1949.

Engel-Janosi, Friedrich. *The Growth of German Historicism*. Baltimore: The Johns Hopkins University Press, 1944.

Fennelly, John F. *Twilight of the Evening Lands: Oswald Spengler—A Half Century Later*. New York: Brookdale Press, 1972.

Flint, Robert. *The Philosophy of History in France and Germany*. Geneva: Slatkine Reprints, 1971.

Frankfurt, Harry G. *Leibniz: A Collection of Critical Essays*. Garden City, New York: Doubleday, 1972.

Friedrich, Carl J., ed. *The Philosophy of Kant*. New York: Modern Library, 1949.

————, ed. *The Philosophy of Hegel*. New York: Modern Library, 1953.

————. *Constitutional Reason of State: The Survival of the Constitutional Order*. Providence, Rhode Island: Brown University Press, 1957.

————. *An Introduction to Political Theory*. New York: Harper and Row, 1967.

Gardiner, Patrick, ed. *Theories of History*. New York: Free Press, 1959.

Gargan, Edward T., ed. *The Intent of Toynbee's History*. Chicago: Loyola University Press, 1961.

Geyl, Pieter; Toynbee, Arnold J.; and Sorokin, Pitrim A. *The Pattern of The Past: Can We Determine It?* Boston: Beacon Press, 1949.

Gilliam, Harriet. "The Dialectics of Realism and Idealism in Modern Historiographic Theory." *History and Theory* 15, no. 3 (1976): 231–56.

Goddard, E. H., and Gibbons, P. A. *Civilisation or Civilisations: An Essay on the Spenglerian Philosophy of History*. New York: Boni and Liveright, 1926.

Gooch, G. P. *History and Historians in the Nineteenth Century*. Boston: Beacon Hill Press, 1959.

Guilland, Antoine. *Modern Germany and Her Historians*. Westport, Connecticut: Greenwood Press, 1970.

Hale, William Harlan. *Challenge to Defeat: Modern Man in Goethe's World and Spengler's Century*. New York: Harcourt, Brace, 1932.

Hampson, Norman. *The Enlightenment*. Middlesex, England: Penguin Books, 1968.

Hegel, Georg Wilhelm Friedrich. *The Philosophy of History*. New York: Dover, 1956.

Hinsley, F. H. *Power and the Pursuit of Peace: Theory and Practice in the History of Relations Between States*. Cambridge: Cambridge University Press, 1967.

Hobhouse, L. T. *The Metaphysical Theory of the State*. 6th ed. London: Georg Allen and Unwin, 1960.

Hocking, Ernest William. *Types of Philosophy*. 3d ed. New York: Charles Scribner's Sons, 1959.

Hoernle, R. F. Alfred. *Idealism as a Philosophy.* New York: George H. Doran, 1927.

Holborn, Hajo. *Germany and Europe.* Garden City, New York: Doubleday, 1979.

Hook, Sidney. *The Hero in History: A Study in Limitation and Possibility.* Boston: Beacon Press, 1955.

Hughes, H. Stuart. *Oswald Spengler: A Critical Estimate.* New York: Charles Scribners, 1952.

————. *History as Art and as Science.* New York: Harper and Row, 1964.

Iggers, Georg G. *The German Conception of History: The National Tradition of Historical Thought from Herder to the Present.* Middletown, Connecticut: Wesleyan University Press, 1968.

————. "The Image of Ranke in American and German Historical Thought." *History and Theory* 2, no. 1 (1962): 17–40.

Jaspers, Karl. *Kant.* New York: Harcourt, Brace and World, 1962.

Kelly, George Armstrong. *Idealism, Politics and History: Sources of Hegelian Thought.* Cambridge: Cambridge University Press, 1969.

Kennedy, Gail, ed. *Pragmatism and American Culture.* Boston: D. C. Heath, 1950.

Kohn, Hans. *The Mind of Germany.* New York: Charles Scribner's Sons, 1960.

Krieger, Leonard. *The German Idea of Freedom: History of a Political Tradition.* Chicago and London: University of Chicago Press, 1957.

————. *Ranke: The Meaning of History.* Chicago: University of Chicago Press, 1977.

Kuypers, Mary Shaw. *Studies in the Eighteenth-Century Background of Hume's Empiricism.* New York: Russell and Russell, 1966.

Liebel, Helen P. "Philosophical Idealism in the Historische Zeitschrift, 1859–1914." *History and Theory* 3, no. 3 (1963): 316–30.

Lindsay, A. D. *The Philosophy of Bergson.* Port Washington, New York: Kenniket Press, 1968.

Ludwig, Emil. *Bismarck.* New York: Cornwall Press, 1930.

May, Arthur. *The Age of Metternich, 1814–1848.* New York: Henry Holt, 1933.

Meinecke, Friedrich. *The German Catastrophe.* Boston: Beacon Press, 1950.

————. *Machiavellism: The Doctrine of Raison d'Etat and Its Place in Modern History.* New York: Praeger, 1957.

————. *Cosmopolitanism and the Nation State.* Princeton: Princeton University Press, 1970.

————. *Historism: The Rise of a New Historical Outlook.* New York: Herder and Herder, 1972.

————. *The Age of German Liberation, 1795–1815.* Berkeley and Los Angeles: University of California Press, 1977.

Montagu, M. F. Ashley, ed. *Toynbee and History: Critical Essays and Reviews.* Boston: P. Sargent, 1956.

Morgenthau, Hans J. *Scientific Man Versus Power Politics.* Chicago: University of Chicago Press, 1946.

Nicolson, Harold. *The Congress of Vienna: A Study in Allied Unity: 1812–1822.* New York: Viking Press, 1969.

Northrop, F. S. C. *The Meeting of East and West.* New York: Macmillan, 1953.

O'Brien, George Dennis. "Does Hegel Have a Philosophy of History?" *History and Theory* 10, no. 3 (1971): 293–317.

Pinson, Koppel A. *Pietism as a Factor in the Rise of German Nationalism.* New York: Octagon Books, 1968.

Pois, Robert A. *Friedrich Meinecke and German Politics in the Twentieth Century.* Berkeley and Los Angeles: University of California Press, 1972.

Prawer, Siegebert, ed. *The Romantic Period in Germany.* New York: Schocken Books, 1970.

Reill, Peter Hans. *The German Enlightenment and the Rise of Historicism.* Berkeley and Los Angeles: University of California Press, 1975.

Reiss, H. S., ed. *The Political Thoughts of the German Romantics, 1793–1815.* Oxford: Basil Blackwell, 1955.

Rescher, Nicholas. *Leibniz: An Introduction to the Philosophy.* Totawa, New Jersey: Powman and Littlefield, 1979.

Rickman, H. P., ed. *Meaning in History: W. Dilthey's Thoughts on History and Society.* London: Georg Allen & Unwin, 1961.

Sandeman, G. A. C. *Metternich.* New York: Brentano's, 1911.

Santayana, George. *The German Mind: A Philosophical Diagnosis.* New York: Thomas Y. Crowell, 1968.

Saw, Lydia Ruth. *Leibniz.* Harmendsworth, Middlesex: Penguin Books, 1954.

Schevill, Ferdinand. *Six Historians.* Chicago: University of Chicago Press, 1956.

Schlereth, Thomas J. *The Cosmopolitan Ideal in Enlightenment Thought: Its Form and Function in the Ideas of Franklin, Hume, and Voltaire 1694–1790.* South Bend, Indiana: University of Notre Dame Press, 1977.

Schweitzer, Albert. *The Philosophy of Civilization.* New York: Macmillan, 1950.

Scruton, Roger. *Kant.* Oxford: Oxford University Press, 1982.

Seaman, L. C. B. *From Vienna to Versailles.* New York: Harper and Row, 1963.

Singer, C. Gregg. *Toynbee.* Grand Rapids, Michigan: Baker Book House, 1965.

Singer, Peter. *Hegel.* Oxford: Oxford University Press, 1983.

Sorokin, Pitrim A. *Social Philosophies of an Age of Crisis.* Boston: Beacon Press, 1950.

Spengler, Oswald. *The Decline of the West.* Abridged edition by Helmut Werner and Arthur Helps. New York: Alfred A. Knopf, 1962.

———. *Man and Technics: A Contribution to a Philosophy of Life.* New York: Alfred A. Knopf, 1963.

———. *Selected Essays.* Chicago: Henry Regnery, 1967.

Sterling, Richard W. *Ethics in a World of Power: The Political Ideas of Friedrich Meinecke.* Princeton: Princeton University Press, 1958.

Stromberg, Roland N. *European Intellectual History Since 1789.* 2d ed. Englewood Cliffs, New Jersey: Prentice-Hall, 1975.

Sullivan, John Edward. *Prophets of the West: An Introduction to the Philosophy of History.* New York: Holt, Rinehart and Winston, 1970.

Sutton, Claud. *The German Tradition in Philosophy.* London: Weidenfeld and Nicolson, 1974.

Sweet, Paul R. "The Historical Writing of Heinrich von Srbik." *History and Theory* 9, no. 1 (1970): 37–58.

Talman, J. L. *Romanticism and Revolt: Europe 1815–1848.* New York: Harcourt, Brace and World, 1967.

Tawney, R. H. "Dr. Toynbee's Study of History." *International Affairs* 13, no. 6 (November–December 1939): 798–806.

Taylor, A. J. P. *Bismarck: The Man and the Statesman.* New York: Vintage Books, 1967.

Thakurdes, Frank. *German Political Idealism.* Atlantic Highlands, New Jersey: Humanities Press, 1980.

Tholfsen, Trygve. *Historical Thinking.* New York: Harper and Row, 1967.

Thompson, Kenneth W. "Toynbee's Approach to History Reviewed." *Ethics* 65, no. 4 (July 1955): 287–303.

Toynbee, Arnold J. *Civilization on Trial.* New York: Oxford University Press, 1948.

———. *The World and the West.* London and New York: Oxford University Press, 1953.

———. *Change and Habit: The Challenge of Our Time.* London and New York: Oxford University Press, 1960.

———. *A Study of History.* 2 Vol. Abridgement by D. C. Somervell. New York: Dell Books, 1965.

Walsh, W. H. *An Introduction to Philosophy of History.* 3d ed. Westport, Connecticut: Greenwood Press, 1967.

Weigert, Hans W. "Oswald Spengler, Twenty-Five Years After." *Foreign Affairs* 21, no. 1 (October 1942): 120–31.

White, Martin. *Pragmatism and the American Mind.* New York: Oxford University Press, 1973.

Wild, John. "What Is Realism?" *The Journal of Philosophy* 44, no. 6 (March 1947): 148–57.

Wilkens, Burleigh Taylor. "Teleology in Kant's Philosophy of History." *History and Theory* 5, no. 2 (1966): 172–85.

———. *Hegel's Philosophy of History.* Ithaca and London: Cornell University Press, 1974.

Wolfers, Arnold, and Martin, Lawrence W., eds. *The Anglo-American Tradition in Foreign Affairs.* New Haven: Yale University Press, 1956.

Index